Learning AWK Programming

A fast, and simple cutting-edge utility for text-processing on the Unix-like environment

Shiwang Kalkhanda

BIRMINGHAM - MUMBAI

Learning AWK Programming

Commissioning Editor: Sunith Shetty
Acquisition Editor: Viraj Madhav
Content Development Editor: Cheryl Dsa
Technical Editor: Suwarna Patil
Copy Editors: Vikrant Phadkay, Safis Editing
Project Coordinator: Nidhi Joshi
Proofreader: Safis Editing
Indexer: Rekha Nair
Graphics: Tania Dutta
Production Coordinator: Shantanu Zagade

First published: March 2018

Production reference: 1210318

Published by Packt Publishing Ltd.
Livery Place
35 Livery Street
Birmingham
B3 2PB, UK.

ISBN 978-1-78839-103-0

www.packtpub.com

To my father, the late Ranvir Singh

`mapt.io`

Mapt is an online digital library that gives you full access to over 5,000 books and videos, as well as industry leading tools to help you plan your personal development and advance your career. For more information, please visit our website.

Why subscribe?

- Spend less time learning and more time coding with practical eBooks and Videos from over 4,000 industry professionals

- Improve your learning with Skill Plans built especially for you

- Get a free eBook or video every month

- Mapt is fully searchable

- Copy and paste, print, and bookmark content

PacktPub.com

Did you know that Packt offers eBook versions of every book published, with PDF and ePub files available? You can upgrade to the eBook version at `www.PacktPub.com` and as a print book customer, you are entitled to a discount on the eBook copy. Get in touch with us at `service@packtpub.com` for more details.

At `www.PacktPub.com`, you can also read a collection of free technical articles, sign up for a range of free newsletters, and receive exclusive discounts and offers on Packt books and eBooks.

Contributors

About the author

Shiwang Kalkhanda (RHCA, RHCSS, MCSE) is a Linux geek and consultant with expertise in the automation of infrastructure deployment and management. He has more than 10 years of experience in security, system, and network administration and training on open source tech. For most of his automation work, he uses shell scripting, Python & Go. He holds a master's and bachelor's degree in computer application. He enjoys traveling and spending time with his kids.

I thank my parents, the late Ranvir Singh and Vijay Lata, for their unconditional love and support throughout my life. To my beautiful wife, Reetu, for making me complete and understanding me better than myself. To my son, Ranvijay, whose precious time as a father I stole to complete this book. To my brother, Pranjal, and my friends Sanjay Bandyopadhyay, Tej Pratap Singh, Rajneesh Pandey for their constant support.

About the reviewers

John C Kennedy has worked with UNIX and Linux since 1998. He has worked with Nagios as a monitoring tool for much of the past 5 years.

He has been reviewing and tech-editing books in his spare time since 2001 and has about 20 open source books to his credit. He believes the best part of reviewing is that he learns something from every book he works on.

He was born in the USA and grew up in Northern Virginia, USA. He spent some time in the US Air Force and has lived in Germany and the UK. He has been married to Michele since 1994 and has two children, Denise and Kieran. He lives in Virginia.

> *I would like to thank my family, including my nephews, Aiden and Mason, and my niece, Harriet, for supporting all the silly things I do and for giving me the time to work on this.*

Marco Ippolito is an Italian software engineer working as director of software development for Imagining IT. Marco completed his postgraduate in software engineering in Oxford and has worked for large corporations such as Google, Oracle, Intel, HP, and Dell, as well as for start-ups such as Platform.sh. He can be reached at marco.ippolito@imaginingit.com and has experience working in teams speaking Italian, English, Spanish, Brazilian Portuguese, German, and French, remotely or on-site.

Doug Ortiz is an experienced enterprise cloud, big data, data analytics, and solutions architect who has designed, developed, re-engineered, and integrated enterprise solutions. His other expertise is in Amazon Web Services, Azure, Google Cloud, business intelligence, Hadoop, Spark, NoSQL databases, and SharePoint, to mention a few.

He is the founder of Illustris, LLC and is reachable at dougortiz@illustris.org.

> *Huge thanks to my wonderful wife, Milla, as well as Maria, Nikolay, and our children for all their support.*

Packt is searching for authors like you

If you're interested in becoming an author for Packt, please visit `authors.packtpub.com` and apply today. We have worked with thousands of developers and tech professionals, just like you, to help them share their insight with the global tech community. You can make a general application, apply for a specific hot topic that we are recruiting an author for, or submit your own idea.

Table of Contents

Preface

This book is for anyone who is inclined to learn text processing and data extraction in a Unix-like environment. Readers will gain sufficient practical knowledge to write AWK one-liners for extracting data and write clean and small AWK programs to solve complex problems. You will be able to automate the process of cleaning any raw data, remove any extra unnecessary stuff, and create a desired reportable output. Examples given in the book are easily reproducible and will help you better understand AWK.

Text processing is used in data mining, data cleaning of CSV, and other similar-format database files. System administrators use it in their shell scripts to automate tasks and filter out command output. It is used extensively with `grep`, `egrep`, `fgrep`, and regular expressions for parsing text files. Its use cases vary from industry to industry, such as telecom enterprises and business process organizations that deal with large CSV files for storing logs and other user information. They use AWK for cleaning and transforming the structure of data from one form to another.

AWK one of the oldest and most powerful utilities that exists in all and Linux distributions. It is used as a command-line utility for performing basic text processing operations and as a programming language when dealing with complex text processing. The best thing about AWK is that it is a data-driven language: you describe the data you wish to work with, and the set of actions you want to perform in the case of a pattern match. This book will provide you with a rundown, explaining the concepts to help you get started with AWK. We will cover every element of functions, variables, and more.

This book will enable the user to perform text filtering, text cleaning, and parsing of input in user-defined formats to create elegant reports. Our main focus throughout the book is on learning AWK with examples and small scripts to quickly solve user problems. The mission of this book is to make the reader comfortable and friendly with AWK.

Who this book is for

The book is written from the beginners' point of view. It covers the basic to intermediate skills that are essential for text processing in a simple and effective manner. But at the same time, there is good amount of stuff that a seasoned AWK user shall find interesting. It covers a wide range of audience and shall be useful to the following people:

- Data scientists who need to extract and clean data for analysis
- Developers who perform parsing of flat text files, HTML files, XML files, or CSV files
- System administrators who parse log files for analysis
- Any GNU/Linux hobbyist or enthusiast who likes to play with GNU/Linux filters for data manipulation

It is written in such a manner that any user with a basic familiarity with the GNU/Linux command line can start using it. The only requisite for it is to have a GNU/Linux box for practicing the stuff covered. This book begins with the essentials of text processing, that is, regular expressions (followed by the structure of the AWK program), variables, constants, functions, arrays, printing options, control flow of the program, and use of different operators to carry out various text processing and mining tasks.

For advanced users, Chapter 9, *GNU's Implementation of AWK – GAWK (GNU AWK)*, covers GAWK implementation in networking, inter-process communication, and debugging. It is followed by practical examples for text processing and pattern matching. For system administrators, we have covered quick one liners that they will find useful in their daily operations. This book has got something for every learner who is working on GNU/Linux.

What this book covers

Chapter 1, *Getting Started with AWK Programming*, introduces AWK's essentials. In this chapter, you will learn how to set up an AWK environment on a Linux machine. You will run AWK programs in different ways with basic examples. This chapters lays the foundation for other chapters.

Chapter 2, *Working with Regular Expressions*, introduces regular expressions and explains how they are handled with AWK. You will get to know regular expressions with suitable examples.

`Chapter 3`, *AWK Variables and Constants*, focuses on the usage of AWK variables. You will understand how to use built-in and user-defined variables while writing AWK programs and command lines. You will also learn how string and numeric constants can be used to process different fields in data files.

`Chapter 4`, *Working with Arrays in AWK*, focuses on associative arrays in AWK. You will understand various features of associative arrays, such as these: indexes do not need to be in order, one can use either a string or a number as an array index, and array size can expand/shrink at runtime and is not statically defined.

`Chapter 5`, *Printing Output in AWK*, focuses on the `print` and `printf` functions and how they can be used efficiently to produce formatted reports. You will also learn how to use redirections in an AWK program.

`Chapter 6`, *AWK Expressions*, describes the expressions that build the core logic of a program in any programming language. The reader will learn how to create and use different types of expression in AWK language.

`Chapter 7`, *AWK Control Flow Statements*, covers the usage of different conditional statements to control the flow of AWK programs, with examples.

`Chapter 8`, *AWK Functions*, covers the different types of built-in functions available in AWK. In addition, you will learn the usage of user-defined functions to perform repetitive tasks in AWK.

`Chapter 9`, *GNU's Implementation of AWK – GAWK (GNU AWK)*, covers the advanced features of GNU AWK, such as network communication, debugging, and inter-process communication in GAWK. These are not present in AWK.

`Chapter 10`, *Practical Implementation of AWK*, illustrates various use cases of text processing. You will learn how a system administrator can use the AWK command line and scripts to automate repetitive tasks. Programmers and data scientists dealing with raw data in text files will learn how to clean raw data and produce formatted reports.

To get the most out of this book

We have put our best efforts in to making this book's code and content relevant for the larger audience working on GNU/Linux. All the examples covered in the book are based on openSUSE Leap 42.3 Linux distribution with GAWK version 4.1.3 installed. You can use any Linux distribution having GAWK version 4.1.3 or above installed to practice the examples. GAWK is GNU's open source implementation of AT&T's original AWK.

Only requirement for this book is the GAWK utility. Users can install the Windows variant of GAWK on their system if they want to practice the examples, but we strongly recommend using any Linux distribution for this purpose. For Windows and OS X, those who would like to practice it on a virtual environment can use VMware of Virtualbox to set up their favorite Linux distribution and then use AWK to execute the examples. For beginners, we have covered the installation of AWK programs on popular GNU/Linux distributions using package management and source code.

A basic understanding of GNU/Linux operating systems and familiarity with any text editor such as emacs, vi or nano are required. An understanding of shell scripting will be an added advantage to the reader.

Download the example code files

You can download the example code files for this book from your account at `www.packtpub.com`. If you purchased this book elsewhere, you can visit `www.packtpub.com/support` and register to have the files emailed directly to you.

You can download the code files by following these steps:

1. Log in or register at `www.packtpub.com`.
2. Select the **SUPPORT** tab.
3. Click on **Code Downloads & Errata**.
4. Enter the name of the book in the **Search** box and follow the onscreen instructions.

Once the file is downloaded, please make sure that you unzip or extract the folder using the latest version of:

- WinRAR/7-Zip for Windows
- Zipeg/iZip/UnRarX for Mac
- 7-Zip/PeaZip for Linux

The code bundle for the book is also hosted on GitHub at `https://github.com/PacktPublishing/Learning-AWK-Programming`. In case there's an update to the code, it will be updated on the existing GitHub repository.

We also have other code bundles from our rich catalog of books and videos available at `https://github.com/PacktPublishing/`. Check them out!

Conventions used

There are a number of text conventions used throughout this book.

`CodeInText`: Indicates code words in text, database table names, folder names, filenames, file extensions, path names, dummy URLs, user input, and Twitter handles. Here is an example: "We can check that using the `which` command, which will return the absolute path of AWK on our system."

Any command-line input or output is written as follows:

```
[ shiwang@linux ~ ] $ sudo apt-get update -y
[ shiwang@linux ~ ] $ sudo apt-get install gawk -y
```

Bold: Indicates a new term, an important word, or words that you see onscreen. For example, words in menus or dialog boxes appear in the text like this. Here is an example: "It was updated and replaced in the mid-1980s with an enhanced version called **New AWK (NAWK)**."

Warnings or important notes appear like this.

Tips and tricks appear like this.

Get in touch

Feedback from our readers is always welcome.

General feedback: Email `feedback@packtpub.com` and mention the book title in the subject of your message. If you have questions about any aspect of this book, please email us at `questions@packtpub.com`.

Errata: Although we have taken every care to ensure the accuracy of our content, mistakes do happen. If you have found a mistake in this book, we would be grateful if you would report this to us. Please visit www.packtpub.com/submit-errata, selecting your book, clicking on the Errata Submission Form link, and entering the details.

Piracy: If you come across any illegal copies of our works in any form on the Internet, we would be grateful if you would provide us with the location address or website name. Please contact us at copyright@packtpub.com with a link to the material.

If you are interested in becoming an author: If there is a topic that you have expertise in and you are interested in either writing or contributing to a book, please visit authors.packtpub.com.

Reviews

Please leave a review. Once you have read and used this book, why not leave a review on the site that you purchased it from? Potential readers can then see and use your unbiased opinion to make purchase decisions, we at Packt can understand what you think about our products, and our authors can see your feedback on their book. Thank you!

For more information about Packt, please visit packtpub.com.

1
Getting Started with AWK Programming

Welcome to your journey with AWK programming. We all interact with data in our daily life in one way or another. Retrieving the desired, useful information from this data can seem like a difficult task, however, if we have the correct tools and proper knowledge of how to handle them, it's really not that difficult. This book will teach you how to efficiently handle one of the best of these tools, known as AWK. It is a standard feature of a Unix-like operating system to retrieve information from raw data. It will help you to understand trivial data-processing concepts in a user-friendly way.

This chapter is designed to give you a kickstart for writing your own simple AWK programs. Throughout the book, we will explain AWK, and work with useful and interesting examples to develop your problem-solving skills in AWK.

In this chapter, we will cover the following:

- An overview of the AWK programming language
- Different installation methods of AWK on the Linux environment
- Understanding the AWK workflow
- Learning how to create and run basic AWK programs in multiple ways
- Working with sample data files with a simple usage of AWK
- Understanding different AWK options

AWK programming language overview

In this section, we will explore the AWK philosophy and different types of AWK that exist today, starting from its original implementation in 1977 at AT&T's Laboratories, Inc. We will also look at the various implementation areas of AWK in data science today.

What is AWK?

AWK is an interpreted programming language designed for text processing and report generation. It is typically used for data manipulation, such as searching for items within data, performing arithmetic operations, and restructuring raw data for generating reports in most Unix-like operating systems. Using AWK programs, one can handle repetitive text-editing problems with very simple and short programs. AWK is a pattern-action language; it searches for patterns in a given input and, when a match is found, it performs the corresponding action. The pattern can be made of strings, regular expressions, comparison operations on numbers, fields, variables, and so on. AWK reads the input files and splits each input line of the file into fields automatically.

AWK has most of the well-designed features that every programming language should contain. Its syntax particularly resembles that of the C programming language. It is named after its original three authors:

- Alfred V. Aho
- Peter J. Weinberger
- Brian W. Kernighan

AWK is a very powerful, elegant, and simple tool that every person dealing with text processing should be familiar with.

Types of AWK

The AWK language was originally implemented as an AWK utility on Unix. Today, most Linux distributions provide **GNU implementation of AWK** (**GAWK**), and a symlink for AWK is created from the original GAWK binary. The AWK utility can be categorized into the following three types, depending upon the type of interpreter it uses for executing AWK programs:

- **AWK**: This is the original AWK interpreter available from AT&T Laboratories. However, it is not used much nowadays and hence it might not be well-maintained. Its limitation is that it splits a line into a maximum 99 fields. It was updated and replaced in the mid-1980s with an enhanced version called **New AWK (NAWK)**.

- **NAWK**: This is AT&T's latest development on the AWK interpreter. It is well-maintained by one of the original authors of AWK - Dr. Brian W. Kernighan.

- **GAWK**: This is the GNU project's implementation of the AWK programming language. All GNU/Linux distributions are shipped with GAWK by default and hence it is the most popular version of AWK. GAWK interpreter is fully compatible with AWK and NAWK.

Beyond these, we also have other, less popular, AWK interpreters and translators, mentioned as follows. These variants are useful in operations when you want to translate your AWK program to C, C++, or Perl:

  - **MAWK**: Michael Brennan interpreter for AWK.
  - **TAWK**: Thompson Automation interpreter/compiler/Microsoft Windows DLL for AWK.
  - **MKSAWK**: Mortice Kern Systems interpreter/compiler/for AWK.
  - **AWKCC**: An AWK translator to C (might not be well-maintained).
  - **AWKC++**: Brian Kernighan's AWK translator to C++ (experimental). It can be downloaded from: `https://9p.io/cm/cs/who/bwk/awkc++.ps`.
  - **AWK2C**: An AWK translator to C. It uses GNU AWK libraries extensively.
  - **A2P**: An AWK translator to Perl. It comes with Perl.
  - **AWKA**: Yet another AWK translator to C (comes with the library), based on MAWK. It can be downloaded from: `http://awka.sourceforge.net/download.html`.

When and where to use AWK

AWK is simpler than any other utility for text processing and is available as the default on Unix-like operating systems. However, some people might say Perl is a superior choice for text processing, as AWK is functionally a subset of Perl, but the learning curve for Perl is steeper than that of AWK; AWK is simpler than Perl. AWK programs are smaller and hence quicker to execute. Anybody who knows the Linux command line can start writing AWK programs in no time. Here are a few use cases of AWK:

- Text processing
- Producing formatted text reports/labels
- Performing arithmetic operations on fields of a file
- Performing string operations on different fields of a file

Programs written in AWK are smaller than they would be in other higher-level languages for similar text processing operations. AWK programs are interpreted on a GNU/Linux Terminal and thus avoid the compiling, debugging phase of software development in other languages.

Getting started with AWK

This section describes how to set up the AWK environment on your GNU/Linux system, and we'll also discuss the workflow of AWK. Then, we'll look at different methods for executing AWK programs.

Installation on Linux

All the examples in this book are covered using Linux distribution (openSUSE Leap 42.3). In order to practice examples discussed in this book, you need GNU AWK version 4.1.3 or above to be installed on your systems. Although there won't be drastic changes if you use earlier versions, we still recommend you use the same version to get along.

Generally, AWK is installed by default on most GNU/Linux distributions. Using the `which` command, you can check whether it is installed on your system or not. In case AWK is not installed on your system, you can do so in one of two ways:

- Using the package manager of the corresponding GNU/Linux system
- Compiling from the source code

Let's take a look at each method in detail in the following sections.

Using the package manager

Different flavors of GNU/Linux distribution have different package-management utilities. If you are using a Debian-based GNU/Linux distribution, such as Ubuntu, Mint, or Debian, then you can install it using the **Advance Package Tool** (**APT**) package manager, as follows:

```
[ shiwang@linux ~ ] $ sudo apt-get update -y
[ shiwang@linux ~ ] $ sudo apt-get install gawk -y
```

Similarly, to install AWK on an RPM-based GNU/Linux distribution, such as Fedora, CentOS, or RHEL, you can use the **Yellowdog Updator Modified** (**YUM**) package manager, as follows:

```
[ root@linux ~ ] # yum update -y
[ root@linux ~ ] # yum install gawk -y
```

For installation of AWK on openSUSE, you can use the `zypper` (`zypper` command line) package-management utility, as follows:

```
[ root@linux ~ ] # zypper update -y
[ root@linux ~ ] # zypper install gawk -y
```

Once installation is finished, make sure AWK is accessible through the command line. We can check that using the `which` command, which will return the absolute path of AWK on our system:

```
[ root@linux ~ ] # which awk
/usr/bin/awk
```

You can also use `awk --version` to find the AWK version on our system:

```
[ root@linux ~ ] # awk --version
```

```
GNU Awk 4.1.3, API: 1.1 (GNU MPFR 3.1.4, GNU MP 6.1.0)
Copyright (C) 1989, 1991-2015 Free Software Foundation.

This program is free software; you can redistribute it and/or modify
it under the terms of the GNU General Public License as published by
the Free Software Foundation; either version 3 of the License, or
(at your option) any later version.

This program is distributed in the hope that it will be useful,
but WITHOUT ANY WARRANTY; without even the implied warranty of
MERCHANTABILITY or FITNESS FOR A PARTICULAR PURPOSE.  See the
GNU General Public License for more details.

You should have received a copy of the GNU General Public License
along with this program. If not, see http://www.gnu.org/licenses/.
```

Compiling from the source code

Like every other open source utility, the GNU AWK source code is freely available for download as part of the GNU project. Previously, you saw how to install AWK using the package manager; now, you will see how to install AWK by compiling from its source code on the GNU/Linux distribution. The following steps are applicable to most of the GNU/Linux software for installation:

1. Download the source code from a GNU project ftp site. Here, we will use the `wget` command line utility to download it, however you are free to choose any other program, such as `curl`, you feel comfortable with:

   ```
   [ shiwang@linux ~ ] $ wget
   http://ftp.gnu.org/gnu/gawk/gawk-4.1.3.tar.xz
   ```

2. Extract the downloaded source code:

   ```
   [ shiwang@linux ~ ] $ tar xvf gawk-4.1.3.tar.xz
   ```

3. Change your working directory and execute the `configure` file to configure the GAWK as per the working environment of your system:

```
[ shiwang@linux ~ ] $ cd gawk-4.1.3  &&  ./configure
```

4. Once the `configure` command completes its execution successfully, it will generate the `make` file. Now, compile the source code by executing the `make` command:

```
[ shiwang@linux ~ ] $ make
```

5. Type `make install` to install the programs and any data files and documentation. When installing into a prefix owned by root, it is recommended that the package be configured and built as a regular user, and only the `make install` phase is executed with root privileges:

```
[ shiwang@linux ~ ] $ sudo make install
```

6. Upon successful execution of these five steps, you have compiled and installed AWK on your GNU/Linux distribution. You can verify this by executing the `which awk` command in the Terminal or `awk --version`:

```
[ root@linux ~ ] # which awk
/usr/bin/awk
```

Now you have a working AWK/GAWK installation and we are ready to begin AWK programming, but before that, our next section describes the workflow of the AWK interpreter.

 If you are running on macOS X, AWK, and not GAWK, would be installed as a default on it. For GAWK installation on macOS X, please refer to MacPorts for GAWK.

Workflow of AWK

Having a basic knowledge of the AWK interpreter workflow will help you to better understand AWK and will result in more efficient AWK program development. Hence, before getting your hands dirty with AWK programming, you need to understand its internals. The AWK workflow can be summarized as shown in the following figure:

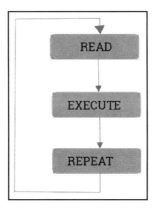

Figure 1.1: AWK workflow

Let's take a look at each operation:

- **READ OPERATION**: AWK reads a line from the input stream (file, pipe, or stdin) and stores it in memory. It works on text input, which can be a file, the standard input stream, or from a pipe, which it further splits into records and fields:
  - **Records**: An AWK record is a single, continuous data input that AWK works on. Records are bounded by a record separator, whose value is stored in the RS variable. The default value of **RS** is set to a newline character. So, the lines of input are considered records for the AWK interpreter. Records are read continuously until the end of the input is reached. *Figure 1.2* shows how input data is broken into records and then goes further into how it is split into fields:

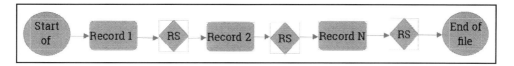

Figure 1.2: AWK input data is split into records with the record separator

- **Fields**: Each record can further be broken down into individual chunks called fields. Like records, fields are bounded. The default field separator is any amount of whitespace, including tab and space characters. So by default, lines of input are further broken down into individual words separated by whitespace. You can refer to the fields of a record by a field number, beginning with 1. The last field in each record can be accessed by its number or with the NF special variable, which contains the number of fields in the current record, as shown in *Figure 1.3*:

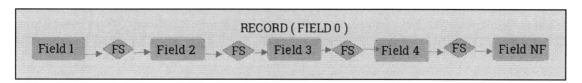

Figure 1.3: Records are split into fields by a field separator

- **EXECUTE OPERATION**: All AWK commands are applied sequentially on the input (records and fields). By default, AWK executes commands on each record/line. This behavior of AWK can be restricted by the use of patterns.
- **REPEAT OPERATION**: The process of read and execute is repeated until the end of the file is reached.

The following flowchart depicts the workflow of the AWK interpreter:

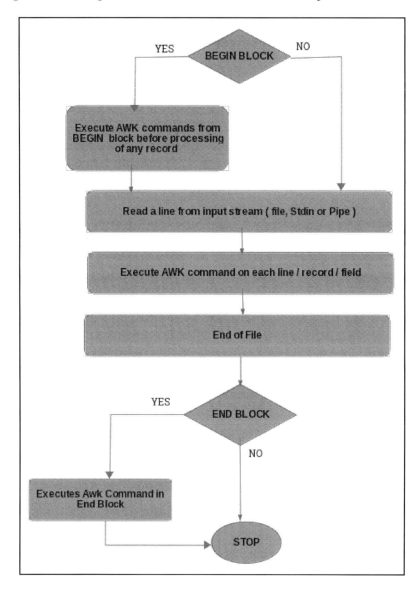

Figure 1.4: Workflow of the AWK interpreter

Action and pattern structure of AWK

AWK programs are sequences of one or more patterns followed by action statements. These action-pattern statements are separated by newlines. Both actions (AWK commands) and patterns (search patterns) are optional, hence we use { } to distinguish them:

/ search pattern / { action / awk-commands }/ search pattern / { action / awk-commands }

AWK reads each input line one after the other, and searches for matches of the given pattern. If the current input line matches the given pattern, a corresponding action is taken. Then, the next input line is read and the matching of patterns starts again. This process continues until all input is read.

Throughout this book, we will be using the terms patterns or search patterns and actions or AWK commands interchangeably.

In AWK syntax, we can omit either patterns or actions (but not both) in a single pattern-action statement. Where a search pattern has no action statement (AWK command), each line for which a pattern matches is printed to the output.

Each action statement can be single or multiple AWK commands. Multiple AWK commands on a single line are seperated by a semicolon (;).

A semicolon can be put at the end of any statement.

Example data file

Before proceeding, let's create a `empinfo.txt` file for practice. Each line in the file contains the name of the employee, their phone number, email address, job profile, salary in USD, and working days in a week:

```
Jack 9857532312 jack@gmail.com hr 2000 5
Jane 9837432312 jane@gmail.com hr 1800 5
Eva 8827232115 eva@gmail.com lgs 2100 6
amit 9911887766 amit@yahoo.com lgs 2350 6
Julie 8826234556 julie@yahoo.com hr 2500 5
```

Pattern-only statements

The syntax of the `awk` command with a pattern only is as follows:

awk '/ pattern /' inputfilename

In the given example, all lines of the `empinfo.txt` file are processed, and those that contain the `Jane` pattern are printed:

```
$ awk '/Jane/' empinfo.txt
Jane 9837432312 jane@gmail.com hr 1800 5
```

Action-only statements

The syntax of the `awk` command with an action only is as follows:

awk '{ action statements / awk-commands }' inputfilenames

If you omit the pattern and give the action statement (AWK commands), then the given action is performed on all input lines, for example:

```
$ awk '{ print $1 }' empinfo.txt
Jack
Jane
Eva
amit
Julie
```

In the given example, all employee names are printed on the screen as `$1`, representing the first field of each input line.

 An empty pattern, that is / /, matches the null character and is equivalent to giving no pattern at all. If we specify an empty pattern, it will print each input record of the input file. An empty action, that is { }, specifies that doing nothing will not print any input record of the input file.

Printing each input line/record

We can print each input record of the input file in multiple ways, as shown in the following example. All the given examples will produce the same result by printing all the input records of the input file.

In our first example, we specify the empty pattern without any action statement to print each input record of the input file, as follows:

```
$ awk '//' empinfo.txt
```

In this example, we specify the print action statement only, without giving any pattern for matching, and print each input record of the input file, as follows:

```
$ awk '{ print }' empinfo.txt
```

In this example, we specify the $0 default variable, along with the print action statement, to print each input record of the input file, as follows:

```
$ awk '{ print $0 }' empinfo.txt
```

In this example, we specify the empty expression along with the print action statement to print each input record of the input file, as follows:

```
$ awk '//{ print }' empinfo.txt
```

All of the given examples perform the basic printing operation using AWK. On execution of any of the preceding examples, we will get the following output:

```
Jack 9857532312 jack@gmail.com hr 2000 5
Jane 9837432312 jane@gmail.com hr 1800 5
Eva 8827232115 eva@gmail.com lgs 2100 6
amit 9911887766 amit@yahoo.com lgs 2350 6
Julie 8826234556 julie@yahoo.com hr 2500 5
```

Using the BEGIN and END blocks construct

AWK contains two special keywords, BEGIN and END, for patterns where an action is required. Both of them are optional and are used without slashes. They don't match any input lines.

The BEGIN block

The BEGIN block is executed in the beginning, before the first input line of the first input file is read. This block is executed once only when the AWK program is started. It is frequently used to initialize the variables or to change the value of the AWK built-in variables, such as FS. The syntax of the BEGIN block is as follows:

BEGIN { action / awk-commands }

The body block

It is the same pattern-action block that we discussed at the beginning of the chapter. The syntax of the body block is as follows:

/ search pattern / { action / awk-commands }

In the body block, AWK commands are applied by default on each input line, however, we can restrict this behavior with the help of patterns. There are no keywords for the body block.

The END block

The END block is executed after the last input line of the last input file is read. This block is executed at the end and is generally used for rendering totals, averages, and for processing data and figures that were read in the various input records. The syntax of the END block is as follows:

END { action / awk-commands }

We can have multiple BEGIN or END blocks in a program. The action in that block will get executed as per the appearance of the block in that program. It is not mandatory to have BEGIN first and END last. The BEGIN and END blocks do not contain patterns, they contain action statements only.

Here is an example of the usage of the BEGIN and END blocks:

```
$ awk  'BEGIN { print "==Employee Info==" }        # begin block
{ print }                                          # body block
END { print "==ends here==" }'  empinfo.txt        # end block
```

On executing the code, we get the following result:

```
==Employee Info==
Jack 9857532312 jack@gmail.com hr 2000 5
Jane 9837432312 jane@gmail.com hr 1800 5
Eva 8827232115 eva@gmail.com lgs 2100 6
amit 9911887766 amit@yahoo.com lgs 2350 6
Julie 8826234556 julie@yahoo.com hr 2500 5
===ends here==
```

Patterns

In pattern-action statements, the pattern is something that determines when an action is to be executed. We can summarize the usage of patterns as follows:

- **BEGIN { statements }**: The statements are executed once before any input has been read.
- **END { statements }**: The statements are executed once after all input has been read.
- **expression { statements }**: The statements are executed at each input line where the expression is true, that is, non-zero or non-null.
- **/ regular expression / { statements }**: The statements are executed at each input line that contains a string matched by the regular expression.
- **compound pattern { statements }**: A compound pattern combines expressions with && (AND), || (OR), ! (NOT), and parentheses; the statements are executed at each input line where the compound pattern is true.
- **pattern 1, pattern 2 { statements }**: A range pattern matches each input line from a line matched by pattern 1 to the next line matched by pattern 2, inclusive; the statements are executed at each matching line. Here, the pattern range could be of regular expressions or addresses.

BEGIN and END do not combine with other patterns. A range pattern cannot be part of any other pattern. BEGIN and END are the only patterns that require an action.

Actions

In pattern-action statements, actions are single or multiple statements that are separated by a newline or semicolon. The statements in actions can include the following:

- **Expression statements**: These are made up of constants, variables, operators, and function calls. For example, $x = x + 2$ is an assignment expression.
- **Printing statements**: These are print statements made with either `print` or `printf`. For example, `print "Welcome to awk programming "`.
- **Control-flow statements**: These consist of various decision-making statements made with `if...else` and looping statements made with the `while`, `for`, and `do` constructs. Apart from these, `break`, `continue`, `next`, and `exit` are used for controlling the loop iterations. These are similar to C programming control-flow constructs.
- **{ statements }**: This format is used for grouping a block of different statements.

We will study these different types of action and pattern statements in detail in future chapters.

Running AWK programs

There are different ways to run an AWK program. For a short program, we can directly execute AWK commands on the Terminal, and for long AWK programs, we generally create an AWK program script or source file. In this section, we will discuss different methods of executing AWK programs.

AWK as a Unix command line

This is the most-used method of running AWK programs. In this method program, AWK commands are given in single quotes as the first argument of the AWK command line, as follows:

```
$ awk  'program' input file1 file2 file3 .......fileN
```

Here, `program` refers to the sequence of pattern-action statements discussed earlier. In this format, the AWK interpreter is invoked from the shell or Terminal to process the input line of files. The quotes around `program` instruct the shell not to interpret the AWK character as a special shell character and treat the entire argument as singular, for the AWK program not for the shell. It also enables the program to continue on more than one line.

The format used to call the AWK program from inside of a shell script is the same one we used on the Unix/Linux command line. For example:

```
$ awk  '{ print }' empinfo.txt /etc/passwd
```

The preceding command will print every line of the empinfo.txt file, followed by the lines of the /etc/passwd file on your system, as follows:

```
Jack 9857532312 jack@gmail.com hr 2000 5
Jane 9837432312 jane@gmail.com hr 1800 5
Eva 8827232115 eva@gmail.com lgs 2100 6
amit 9911887766 amit@yahoo.com lgs 2350 6
Julie 8826234556 julie@yahoo.com hr 2500 5
at:x:25:25:Batch jobs daemon:/var/spool/atjobs:/bin/bash
avahi:x:481:480:User for Avahi:/run/avahi-daemon:/bin/false
avahi-autoipd:x:493:493:User for Avahi IPv4LL:/var/lib/avahi-
autoipd:/bin/false
bin:x:1:1:bin:/bin:/bin/bash
daemon:x:2:2:Daemon:/sbin:/bin/bash
games:x:12:100:Games account:/var/games:/bin/bash
man:x:13:62:Manual pages viewer:/var/cache/man:/bin/bash
messagebus:x:499:499:User for D-Bus:/run/dbus:/bin/false
.....................
..................... till last line in /etc/passwd
```

AWK as a filter (reading input from the Terminal)

Filter commands can take their input from stdin instead of reading it from the file. We can omit giving input filenames at the command line while executing the awk program, and simply call it from the Terminal as:

```
$ awk  'program'
```

In the previous example, AWK applies the program to whatever you type on the standard input, that is, the Terminal, until you type end-of-file by pressing *Ctrl + D*, for example:

```
$ awk  '$2==50{ print }'
apple 50
apple 50
banana 60
litchi 50
litchi 50
mango 55
grapes 40
pineapple 60
........
```

The line that contains 50 in the second field is printed, hence it's repeated twice on the Terminal. This functionality of AWK can be used to experiment with AWK; all you need is to type your AWK commands first, then type data, and see what happens next. The only thing you have to take care of here is to enclose your AWK commands in single quotes on the command line. This prevents the shell expansion of special characters, such as $, and also allows your program to be longer than one line.

Here is one more example in which we take input from the pipe and process it with the AWK command:

```
$ echo -e "jack \nsam \ntarly \njerry" | awk '/sam/{ print }'
```

On executing this code, you get the following result:

```
sam
```

We will be using examples of executing the AWK command line on the Terminal throughout the book for explaining various topics. This type of operation is performed when the program (AWK commands) is short (up to a few lines).

Running AWK programs from the source file

When AWK programs are long, it is more convenient to put them in a separate file. Putting AWK programs in a file reduces errors and retyping. Its syntax is as follows:

```
$ awk -f source_file inputfile1 inputfile2 ...........inputfileN
```

The -f option tells the AWK utility to read the AWK commands from source_file. Any filename can be used in place of source_file. For example, we can create a cmd.awk text file containing the AWK commands, as follows:

```
$ vi cmd.awk
BEGIN { print "***Emp Info***" }
{ print }
```

Now, we instruct AWK to read the commands from the cmd.awk file and perform the given actions:

```
$ awk -f cmd.awk empinfo.txt
```

On executing the preceding command, we get the following result:

```
***Emp Info***
Jack 9857532312 jack@gmail.com hr 2000 5
Jane 9837432312 jane@gmail.com hr 1800 5
```

```
Eva 8827232115 eva@gmail.com lgs 2100 6
amit 9911887766 amit@yahoo.com lgs 2350 6
Julie 8826234556 julie@yahoo.com hr 2500 5
```

It does the same thing as this:

```
$ awk 'BEGIN { print "***Emp Info***" } { print }' empinfo.txt
```

We don't usually need to put the filename specified with `-f` in single quotes, because filenames generally don't contain any shell special characters. In the `cmd.awk` source file, we didn't put the AWK commands in single quotes. The quotes are only needed when we execute the AWK command from the command line. We added the `.awk` extension in the filename to clearly identify the AWK program file; it doesn't affect the execution of the AWK program and hence is not mandatory.

AWK programs as executable script files

We can write self-contained AWK scripts to execute AWK commands, like we have with shell scripts to execute shell commands. We create the AWK script by using `#!`, followed by the absolute path of the AWK interpreter and the `-f` optional argument. The line beginning with `#!` tells the operating system to run the immediately-followed interpreter with the given argument and the full argument list of the executed program. For example, we can update the `cmd.awk` file to `emp.awk`, as follows:

```
$ vi emp.awk
#!/usr/bin/awk -f
BEGIN { print "***Emp Info***" }
{ print }
```

Give this file executable permissions (with the `chmod` utility), then simply run `./emp.awk empinfo.txt` at the shell and the system will run AWK as if you had typed `awk -f cmd.awk empinfo.txt`:

```
$ chmod +x emp.awk
$ ./emp.awk empinfo.txt
***Emp Info***
Jack 9857532312 jack@gmail.com hr 2000 5
Jane 9837432312 jane@gmail.com hr 1800 5
Eva 8827232115 eva@gmail.com lgs 2100 6
amit 9911887766 amit@yahoo.com lgs 2350 6
Julie 8826234556 julie@yahoo.com hr 2500 5
```

Self-contained executable AWK scripts are useful when you want to write AWK programs that users can invoke without having to know it was written in AWK.

Extending the AWK command line on multiple lines

For short AWK programs, it is most convenient to execute them on the command line. This is done by enclosing AWK commands in single quotes. Yet at times, the AWK commands that you want to execute on the command line are longer than one line. In these situations, you can extend the AWK commands to multiple lines using \ as the last element on each line. It is also mandatory at that time to enclose AWK commands in single quotes. For example:

```
$ awk   'BEGIN { print "***Emp Info***" } \
> { print } \
> END { print "***Ends Here***" } '    empinfo.txt
```

It is the same as if we have executed the AWK command on a single line, as follows:

```
$ awk 'BEGIN { print "***Emp Info***" } { print } END{ print "***Ends
Here***" }' empinfo.txt
```

The output of the previous executed AWK command is:

```
***Emp Info***
Jack 9857532312 jack@gmail.com hr 2000 5
Jane 9837432312 jane@gmail.com hr 1800 5
Eva 8827232115 eva@gmail.com lgs 2100 6
amit 9911887766 amit@yahoo.com lgs 2350 6
Julie 8826234556 julie@yahoo.com hr 2500 5
***Ends Here***
```

Comments in AWK

A comment is some text that is included in a program for documentation or human information. It is not an executable part of the program. It explains what a program does and how it does it. Almost every programming language has comments, as they make the program construct understandable.

In the AWK programming language, a comment begins with the hash symbol (#) and continues till the end of the line. It is not mandatory to have # as the first character on the line to mark it as a comment. Anything written after # is ignored by the AWK commands. For example, we can put the following in emp.awk and update it as emp_comment.awk:

```
$ vi emp_comment.awk
#!/usr/bin/awk -f

# Info        : This program displays the employees information
# Date        : 09 Sept 2017
# Version     : 1.0
# Author      : Shiwang

# Header part is defined in BEGIN block to display Company information

BEGIN { print "****Employee Information of HMT Corp.****" }
# Body Block comment
{ print }
# End Block comment
END { print "***Information Database ends here****" }
```

Now, give this program executable permission (using chmod) and execute it as follows:

```
$ ./emp_comment.awk empinfo.txt
```

Here is the output:

```
****Employee Information of HMT Corp.****
Jack 9857532312 jack@gmail.com hr 2000 5
Jane 9837432312 jane@gmail.com hr 1800 5
Eva 8827232115 eva@gmail.com lgs 2100 6
amit 9911887766 amit@yahoo.com lgs 2350 6
Julie 8826234556 julie@yahoo.com hr 2500 5
***Information Database ends here****
```

Shell quotes with AWK

As you have seen, we will be using the command line for most of our short AWK programs. The best way to use it is by enclosing the entire program in single quotes, as follows:

```
$ awk '/ search pattern / { awk commands }' inputfile1 inputfile2
```

When you are working on a shell, it is good to have a basic understanding of shell quoting rules. The following rules apply only to the POSIX-compliant, GNU Bourne Again Shell:

- Quoted and non-quoted items can be concatenated together. The same is true for quoted and non-quoted item concatenation. For example:

```
$ echo "Welcome to " Learning "awk"
>>>
Welcome to Learning awk
```

- If you precede any character with a backslash (\) in double quotes, the shell removes the backslash on execution and treats subsequent characters as literal without having any special meaning:

```
$ echo  "Apple are \$10 a dozen"
>>>
Apple are $10 a dozen
```

- Single quotes prevent shell expansions of the command and variable. Anything between the opening and closing quotes is not interpreted by the shell, it is passed as such to the command with which it is used:

```
$ echo 'Apple are $10 a dozen'
>>>
Apple are $10 a dozen
```

 It is impossible to embed a single quote inside single-quoted text.

- Double quotes allow variable and command substitution. The $, ` , \, and " characters have special meanings on the shell, and must be preceded by a backslash within double quotes if they are to be passed on as literal to the program:

```
$ echo  "Hi, \" Jack \" "
>>>
Hi, "Jack"
```

- Here is an AWK example with single and double quotes:

```
$ awk  'BEGIN { print "Hello world" }'
```

It can be performed as follows:

```
$ awk  "BEGIN { print \"Hello world \" }"
```

- Both give the same output:

```
Hello world
```

Sometimes, dealing with single quotes or double quotes becomes confusing. In these instances, you can use octal escape sequences. For example:

- Printing single quotes within double quotes:

```
$ awk "BEGIN { print \"single quote' \" }"
```

- Printing single quotes within single quotes:

```
$ awk 'BEGIN { print "single quote'\'' " }'
```

- Printing single quotes within single quotes using the octal escape sequence:

```
$ awk 'BEGIN { print "single quote\47" }'
```

- Printing single quotes using the command-line variable assignment:

```
$ awk -v q="'" 'BEGIN { print "single quote"q }'
```

- All of the preceding AWK program executions give the following output:

```
single quote'
```

Data files used as examples in this book

Throughout the book, most of our examples will be taking their input from two sample data files. The first one is emp.dat, which represents the sample employee information database. It consists of the following columns from left to right, each separated by a single tab:

- Employee's first name
- Last name
- Phone number

- Email address
- Gender
- Department
- Salary in USD

```
Jack     Singh    9857532312   jack@gmail.com      M   hr    2000
Jane     Kaur     9837432312   jane@gmail.com      F   hr    1800
Eva      Chabra   8827232115   eva@gmail.com       F   lgs   2100
Amit     Sharma   9911887766   amit@yahoo.com      M   lgs   2350
Julie    Kapur    8826234556   julie@yahoo.com     F   Ops   2500
Ana      Khanna   9856422312   anak@hotmail.com    F   Ops   2700
Hari     Singh    8827255666   hari@yahoo.com      M   Ops   2350
Victor   Sharma   8826567898   vics@hotmail.com    M   Ops   2500
John     Kapur    9911556789   john@gmail.com      M   hr    2200
Billy    Chabra   9911664321   bily@yahoo.com      M   lgs   1900
Sam      khanna   8856345512   sam@hotmail.com     F   lgs   2300
Ginny    Singh    9857123466   ginny@yahoo.com     F   hr    2250
Emily    Kaur     8826175812   emily@gmail.com     F   Ops   2100
Amy      Sharma   9857536898   amys@hotmail.com    F   Ops   2500
Vina     Singh    8811776612   vina@yahoo.com      F   lgs   2300
```

The second file used is `cars.dat`, which represents the sample car dealer database. It consists of the following columns from left to right, each separated by a single tab.

- Car's make
- Model
- Year of manufacture
- Mileage in kilometers
- Price in lakhs

The data from the file is illustrated as follows:

```
maruti      swift      2007    50000       5
honda       city       2005    60000       3
maruti      dezire     2009    3100        6
chevy       beat       2005    33000       2
honda       city       2010    33000       6
chevy       tavera     1999    10000       4
toyota      corolla    1995    95000       2
maruti      swift      2009    4100        5
maruti      esteem     1997    98000       1
ford        ikon       1995    80000       1
honda       accord     2000    60000       2
fiat        punto      2007    45000       3
```

Any other sample file, if used, will be shared in the corresponding chapter before using it in any example. Our next section demonstrates AWK command usages with examples.

Some simple examples with default usage

This section describes various useful AWK commands and their usage. We will be using the two sample files, `cars.dat` and `emp.dat`, for illustrating various useful AWK examples to kick-start your journey with AWK. Most of these examples will be short one-liners that you can include in your daily task automation. You will get the most out of this section if you practice the examples with us in your system while going through them.

Printing without pattern: The simplest AWK program can be as basic as the following:

awk { print } filename

This program consists of only one line, which is an action. In the absence of a pattern, all input lines are printed on the `stdout`. Also, if you don't specify any field with the `print` statement, it takes `$0`, so `print $0` will do the same thing, as `$0` represents the entire input line:

```
$ awk  '{ print }'   cars.dat
```

This can also be performed as follows:

```
$ awk  '{ print $0 }' cars.dat
```

This program is equivalent of the `cat` command implemented on Linux as `cat cars.dat`. The output on execution of this code is as follows:

```
maruti      swift       2007      50000      5
honda       city        2005      60000      3
maruti      dezire      2009      3100       6
chevy       beat        2005      33000      2
honda       city        2010      33000      6
chevy       tavera      1999      10000      4
toyota      corolla     1995      95000      2
maruti      swift       2009      4100       5
maruti      esteem      1997      98000      1
ford        ikon        1995      80000      1
honda       accord      2000      60000      2
fiat        punto       2007      45000      3
```

Printing without action statements: In this example, the program has a pattern, but we don't specify any action statements. The pattern is given between forward slashes, which indicates that it is a regular expression:

```
$ awk '/honda/' cars.dat
```

The output on execution of this code is as follows:

```
honda           city        2005        60000       3
honda           city        2010        33000       6
honda           accord      2000        60000       2
```

In this case, AWK selects only those input lines that contain the `honda` pattern/string in them. When we don't specify any action, AWK assumes the action is to print the whole line.

Printing columns or fields: In this section, we will print fields without patterns, with patterns, in a different printing order, and with regular expression patterns:

- **Printing fields without specifying any pattern**: In this example, we will not include any pattern. The given AWK command prints the first field (`$1`) and third field (`$3`) of each input line that is separated by a space (the output field separator, indicated by a comma):

  ```
  $ awk '{ print $1, $3 }' cars.dat
  ```

  The output on execution of this code is as follows:

  ```
  maruti 2007
  honda 2005
  maruti 2009
  chevy 2005
  honda 2010
  chevy 1999
  toyota 1995
  maruti 2009
  maruti 1997
  ford 1995
  honda 2000
  fiat 2007
  ```

- **Printing fields with matching patterns**: In this example, we will include both actions and patterns. The given AWK command prints the first field ($1) separated by tab (specifying \t as the output separator) with the third field ($3) of input lines, which contain the maruti string in them:

```
$ awk '/maruti/{ print $1 "\t" $3 }' cars.dat
```

The output on execution of this code is as follows:

```
maruti   2007
maruti   2009
maruti   2009
maruti   1997
```

- **Printing fields for matching regular expressions**: In this example, AWK selects the lines containing matches for the ith regular expression in them and prints the first ($1), second ($2), and third ($3) field, separated by tab:

```
$ awk '/i/{ print $1 "\t" $2 "\t" $3 }'  cars.dat
```

The output on execution of this code is as follows:

```
maruti   swift    2007
honda    city     2005
maruti   dezire   2009
honda    city     2010
maruti   swift    2009
maruti   esteem   1997
ford     ikon     1995
fiat     punto    2007
```

- **Printing fields in any order with custom text**: In this example, we will print fields in different orders. Here, in the action statement, we put the "Mileage in kms is : " text before the $4 field and the " for car model -> " text before the $1 field in the output:

```
$ awk '{ print "Mileage in kms is : " $4 ", for car model -> "
$1,$2 }'  cars.dat
```

The output on execution of this code is as follows:

```
Mileage in kms is : 50000, for car model -> maruti swift
Mileage in kms is : 60000, for car model -> honda city
Mileage in kms is : 3100, for car model -> maruti dezire
Mileage in kms is : 33000, for car model -> chevy beat
Mileage in kms is : 33000, for car model -> honda city
Mileage in kms is : 10000, for car model -> chevy tavera
Mileage in kms is : 95000, for car model -> toyota corolla
Mileage in kms is : 4100, for car model -> maruti swift
Mileage in kms is : 98000, for car model -> maruti esteem
Mileage in kms is : 80000, for car model -> ford ikon
Mileage in kms is : 60000, for car model -> honda accord
Mileage in kms is : 45000, for car model -> fiat punto
```

Printing the number of fields in a line: You can print any number of fields, such as $1 and $2. In fact, you can use any expression after $ and the numeric outcome of the expression will print the corresponding field. AWK has built-in variables to count and store the number of fields in the current input line, for example, NF. So, in the given example, we will print the number of the field for each input line, followed by the first field and the last field (accessed using NF):

```
$ awk '{ print NF, $1, $NF }' cars.dat
```

The output on execution of this code is as follows:

```
5 maruti 5
5 honda 3
5 maruti 6
5 chevy 2
5 honda 6
5 chevy 4
5 toyota 2
5 maruti 5
5 maruti 1
5 ford 1
5 honda 2
5 fiat 3
```

Deleting empty lines using NF: We can print all the lines with at least 1 field using NF > 0. This is the easiest method to remove empty lines from the file using AWK:

```
$ awk 'NF > 0 { print }' /etc/hosts
```

On execution of the preceding command, only non-empty lines from the `/etc/hosts` file will be displayed on the Terminal as output:

```
#
# hosts          This file describes a number of hostname-to-address
#                mappings for the TCP/IP subsystem.  It is mostly
#                used at boot time, when no name servers are running.
#                On small systems, this file can be used instead of a
#                "named" name server.
# Syntax:
#
# IP-Address  Full-Qualified-Hostname  Short-Hostname
#
127.0.0.1      localhost
# special IPv6 addresses
::1            localhost ipv6-localhost ipv6-loopback
fe00::0        ipv6-localnet
ff00::0        ipv6-mcastprefix
ff02::1        ipv6-allnodes
ff02::2        ipv6-allrouters
ff02::3        ipv6-allhosts
```

Printing line numbers in the output: AWK has a built-in variable known as NR. It counts the number of input lines read so far. We can use NR to prefix $0 in the print statement to display the line numbers of each line that has been processed:

```
$ awk '{ print NR, $0 }' cars.dat
```

The output on execution of this code is as follows:

```
1 maruti      swift      2007      50000      5
2 honda       city       2005      60000      3
3 maruti      dezire     2009      3100       6
4 chevy       beat       2005      33000      2
5 honda       city       2010      33000      6
6 chevy       tavera     1999      10000      4
7 toyota      corolla    1995      95000      2
8 maruti      swift      2009      4100       5
9 maruti      esteem     1997      98000      1
10 ford        ikon       1995      80000      1
11 honda       accord     2000      60000      2
12 fiat        punto      2007      45000      3
```

Count the numbers of lines in a file using NR: In our next example, we will count the number of lines in a file using NR. As NR stores the current input line number, we need to process all the lines in a file, so we will not specify any pattern. We also don't want to print the line numbers for each line, as our requirement is to just fetch the total lines in a file. Since the END block is executed after processing the input line is done, we will print NR in the END block to print the total number of lines in the file:

```
$ awk ' END { print "The total number of lines in file are : " NR } '
cars.dat
>>>
The total number of lines in file are : 12
```

Printing numbered lines exclusively from the file: We know NR contains the line number of the current input line. You can easily print any line selectively, by matching the line number with the current input line number stored in NR, as follows:

```
$ awk   'NR==2 { print NR, $0 }'  cars.dat
>>>
2 honda          city        2005        60000        3
```

Printing the even-numbered lines in a file: Using NR, we can easily print even-numbered files by specifying expressions (divide each line number by 2 and find the remainder) in pattern space, as shown in the following example:

```
$ awk 'NR % 2 == 0 { print NR, $0 }'  cars.dat
```

The output on execution of this code is as follows:

```
2 honda        city      2005      60000      3
4 chevy        beat      2005      33000      2
6 chevy        tavera    1999      10000      4
8 maruti       swift     2009      4100       5
10 ford         ikon      1995      80000      1
12 fiat         punto     2007      45000      3
```

Printing odd-numbered lines in a file: Similarly, we can print odd-numbered lines in a file using NR, by performing basic arithmetic operations in the pattern space:

```
$ awk ' NR % 2 == 1 { print NR, $0 } ' cars.dat
```

The output on execution of this code is as follows:

```
 1 maruti         swift        2007      50000     5
 3 maruti         dezire       2009       3100     6
 5 honda          city         2010      33000     6
 7 toyota         corolla      1995      95000     2
 9 maruti         esteem       1997      98000     1
11 honda          accord       2000      60000     2
```

Printing a group of lines using the range operator (,) and NR: We can combine the range operator (,) and NR to print a group of lines from a file based on their line numbers. The next example displays the lines 4 to 6 from the `cars.dat` file:

```
$ awk ' NR==4, NR==6 { print NR, $0 }' cars.dat
```

The output on execution of this code is as follows :

```
4 chevy          beat         2005      33000     2
5 honda          city         2010      33000     6
6 chevy          tavera       1999      10000     4
```

Printing a group of lines using the range operator and patterns: We can also combine the range operator (,) and string in pattern space to print a group of lines in a file starting from the first pattern, up to the second pattern. The following example displays the line starting from the first appearance of the `/ford/` pattern to the occurrence of the second `/fiat/` pattern in the `cars.dat` file:

```
$ awk ' /ford/,/fiat/ { print NR, $0 }' cars.dat
```

The output on execution of this code is as follows:

```
10 ford          ikon         1995      80000     1
11 honda          accord       2000      60000     2
12 fiat           punto        2007      45000     3
```

Printing by selection: AWK patterns allows the selection of desired input lines for further processing. As patterns without actions print all the matching lines, on most occasions, AWK programs consist of a single pattern. The following are a few examples of useful patterns:

- **Selection using the match operator (~)**: The match operator (~) is used for matching a pattern in a specified field in the input line of a file. In the next example, we will select and print all lines containing `'c'` in the second field of the input line, as follows:

  ```
  $ awk  ' $2 ~ /c/ { print NR, $0 } ' cars.dat
  ```

The output on execution of this code is as follows:

```
2  honda        city        2005        60000        3
5  honda        city        2010        33000        6
7  toyota       corolla     1995        95000        2
11 honda        accord      2000        60000        2
```

- **Selection using the match operator (~) and anchor (^)**: The caret (^) in regular expressions (also known as `anchor`) is used to match at the beginning of a line. In the next example, we combine it with the match operator (~) to print all the lines in which the second field begins with the `'c'` character, as follows:

```
$ awk  ' $2 ~ /^c/ { print NR, $0 } '  cars.dat
```

The output on execution of this code is as follows:

```
2  honda        city        2005        60000        3
5  honda        city        2010        33000        6
7  toyota       corolla     1995        95000        2
```

- **Selection using the match operator (~) and character classes ([ ])**: The character classes, [ ], in regular expressions are used to match a single character out of those specified within square brackets. Here, we combine the match operator (~) with character classes (/^[cp]/) to print all the lines in which the second field begins with the `'c'` or `'p'` character, as follows:

```
$ awk  ' $2 ~ /^[cp]/ { print NR, $0 } '  cars.dat
```

The output on execution of this code is as follows:

```
2  honda        city        2005        60000        3
5  honda        city        2010        33000        6
7  toyota       corolla     1995        95000        2
12 fiat         punto       2007        45000        3
```

- **Selection using the match operator (~) and anchor ($)**: The dollar sign ($) in regular expression (also known as anchor) is used to match at the end of a line. In the next example, we combine it with the match operator (~) to print all the lines in the second field end with the `'a'` character, as follows:

```
$ awk  ' $2 ~ /a$/ { print NR, $0 } '  cars.dat
```

The output on execution of this code is as follows:

```
6 chevy         tavera        1999      10000       4
7 toyota        corolla       1995      95000       2
```

- **Selection by numeric comparison**: You can use relation operators (==, =>, <=, >, <, !=) for performing numeric comparison. Here, we perform a numeric match (==) to print the lines that have the 2005 value in the third field, as follows:

```
$ awk   ' $3 == 2005 { print NR, $0 } '  cars.dat
```

The output on execution of this code is as follows:

```
2 honda         city          2005      60000       3
4 chevy         beat          2005      33000       2
```

- **Selection by text content/string matching in a field**: Besides numeric matches, we can use string matches to find the lines containing a particular string in a field. String content for matches should be given in double quotes as a string. In our next example, we print all the lines that contain "swift" in the second field ($2), as follows:

```
$ awk   ' $2 == "swift" { print NR, $0 } '  cars.dat
```

The output on execution of this code is as follows:

```
1 maruti        swift         2007      50000       5
8 maruti        swift         2009      4100        5
```

- **Selection by combining patterns**: You can combine patterns with parentheses and logical operators, &&, ||, and !, which stand for AND, OR, and NOT. Here, we print the lines containing a value greater than or equal to 2005 in the third field and a value less than or equal to 2010 in the third field. This will print the cars that were manufactured between 2005 and 2010 from the cars.dat file:

```
$ awk   ' $3 >= 2005 && $3 <= 2010 { print NR, $0 } '  cars.dat
```

The output on execution of this code is as follows:

```
1 maruti        swift         2007      50000       5
2 honda         city          2005      60000       3
3 maruti        dezire        2009      3100        6
4 chevy         beat          2005      33000       2
5 honda         city          2010      33000       6
8 maruti        swift         2009      4100        5
12 fiat         punto         2007      45000       3
```

Data validation: Human error is difficult to eliminate from gathered data. In this situation, AWK is a reliable tool for checking that data has reasonable values and is in the right format. This process is generally known as data validation. Data validation is the reverse process of printing the lines that have undesirable properties. In data validation, we print the lines with errors or those that we suspect to have errors.

In the following example, we use the validation method while printing the selected records. First, we check whether any of the records in the input file don't have 5 fields, that is, a record with incomplete information, by using the AWK NF built-in variable. Then, we find the cars whose manufacture year is older than 2000 and suffix these rows with the `car fitness expired` text. Next, we print those records where the car's manufacture year is newer than 2009, and suffix these rows with the `Better car for resale` text, shown as follows :

```
$ vi validate.awk
NF !=5 { print $0, "number of fields is not equal to 5" }
$3 < 2000 { print $0, "car fitness expired" }
$3 > 2009 { print $0, "Better car for resale" }

$ awk -f validate.awk cars.dat
```

The output on execution of this code is as follows :

```
honda        city       2010     33000      6 Better car for resale
chevy        tavera     1999     10000      4 car fitness expired
toyota       corolla    1995     95000      2 car fitness expired
maruti       esteem     1997     98000      1 car fitness expired
ford         ikon       1995     80000      1 car fitness expired
```

BEGIN and END pattern examples: BEGIN is a special pattern in which actions are performed before the processing of the first line of the first input file. END is a pattern in which actions are performed after the last line of the last file has been processed.

Using BEGIN to print headings: The BEGIN block can be used for printing headings, initializing variables, performing calculations, or any other task that you want to be executed before AWK starts processing the lines in the input file.

In the following AWK program, `BEGIN` is used to print a heading for each column for the `cars.dat` input file. Here, the first column contains the make of each car followed by the model, year of manufacture, mileage in kilometers, and price. So, we print the heading for the first field as `Make`, for the second field as `Model`, for the third field as `Year`, for the fourth field as `Kms`, and for the fifth field as `Price`. The heading is separated from the body by a blank line. The second action statement, `{ print }`, has no pattern and displays all lines from the input as follows:

```
$ vi header.awk
BEGIN { print "Make Model Year Kms Price" ; print "" }
{ print }

$ awk -f header.awk cars.dat
```

The output on execution of this code is as follows:

Make	Model	Year	Kms	Price
maruti	swift	2007	50000	5
honda	city	2005	60000	3
maruti	dezire	2009	3100	6
chevy	beat	2005	33000	2
honda	city	2010	33000	6
chevy	tavera	1999	10000	4
toyota	corolla	1995	95000	2
maruti	swift	2009	4100	5
maruti	esteem	1997	98000	1
ford	ikon	1995	80000	1
honda	accord	2000	60000	2
fiat	punto	2007	45000	3

In the preceding example, we have given multiple action statements on a single line by separating them with a semicolon. The print " " prints a blank line; it is different from plain print, which prints the current input line.

Using END to print the last input line: The `END` block is executed after the processing of the last line of the last file is completed, and `$0` stores the value of each input line processed, but its value is not retained in the `END` block. The following is one way to print the last input line:

```
$ awk '{ last = $0 } END { print last }' cars.dat
```

The output on execution of this code is as follows:

```
fiat            punto       2007        45000       3
```

And to print the total number of lines in a file we use NR, because it retains its value in the END block, as follows:

```
$ awk 'END { print "Total no of lines in file : ", NR }' cars.dat
```

The output on execution of this code is as follows:

```
Total no of lines in file : 12
```

Length function: By default, the `length` function stores the count of the number of characters in the input line. In the next example, we will prefix each line with the number of characters in it using the `length` function, as follows:

```
$ awk '{ print length, $0 }'    /etc/passwd
```

The output on execution of this code is as follows:

```
56 at:x:25:25:Batch jobs daemon:/var/spool/atjobs:/bin/bash
59 avahi:x:481:480:User for Avahi:/run/avahi-daemon:/bin/false
79 avahi-autoipd:x:493:493:User for Avahi IPv4LL:/var/lib/avahi-
autoipd:/bin/false
28 bin:x:1:1:bin:/bin:/bin/false
35 daemon:x:2:2:Daemon:/sbin:/bin/fale
53 dnsmasq:x:486:65534:dnsmasq:/var/lib/empty:/bin/false
42 ftp:x:40:49:FTP account:/srv/ftp:/bin/false
49 games:x:12:100:Games account:/var/games:/bin/false
49 lp:x:4:7:Printing daemon:/var/spool/lpd:/bin/false
60 mail:x:8:12:Mailer daemon:/var/spool/clientmqueue:/bin/false
56 man:x:13:62:Manual pages viewer:/var/cache/man:/bin/false
56 messagebus:x:499:499:User for D-Bus:/run/dbus:/bin/false
...................................
...................................
```

Changing the field separator using FS: The fields in the examples we have discussed so far have been separated by space characters. The default behavior of FS is any number of space or tab characters; we can change it to regular expressions or any single or multiple characters using the FS variable or the -F option. The value of the field separator is contained in the FS variable and it can be changed multiple times in an AWK program. Generally, it is good to redefine FS in a BEGIN statement.

In the following example, we demonstrate the use of `FS`. In this, we use the `/etc/passwd` file of Linux, which delimits fields with colons (`:`). So, we change the input of `FS` to a colon before reading any data from the file, and print the list of usernames, which is stored in the first field of the file, as follows:

```
$ awk 'BEGIN { FS = ":"} { print $1 }'    /etc/passwd
```

Alternatively, we could use the `-F` option:

```
$ awk -F: '{ print $1 }'    /etc/passwd
```

The output on execution of the code is as follows:

```
at
avahi
avahi-autoipd
bin
daemon
dnsmasq</strong>
ftp
.........
.........
```

Control structures: AWK supports control (flow) statements, which can be used to change the order of the execution of commands within an AWK program. Different constructs, such as the `if...else`, `while`, and `for` control structures are supported by AWK. In addition, the `break` and `continue` statements work in combination with the control structures to modify the order of execution of commands. We will look at these in detail in future chapters.

Let's try a basic example of a `while` loop to print a list of numbers under `10`:

```
$ awk   'BEGIN{ n=1; while (n < 10 ){ print n; n++; } }'
```

Alternatively, we can create a script, such as the following:

```
$ vi while1.awk
BEGIN { n=1
while ( n < 10)
    {
        print n;
        n++;
    }
}

$ awk -f while1.awk
```

The output on execution of both of these commands is as follows:

```
1
2
3
4
5
6
7
8
9
```

Multiple rules with AWK

AWK can have multiple pattern-action statements. They are executed in the order in which they appear in the AWK program. If one pattern-action rule matches the same line that was matched with the previous rule, then it is printed twice. This continues until the program reaches the end of the file. In the next example, we have an AWK program with two rules:

```
$ awk '/maruti/ { print NR, $0 }
/2007/ { print NR, $0 }' cars.dat
```

The output on execution of this code is as follows:

```
1 maruti        swift        2007        50000        5
1 maruti        swift        2007        50000        5
3 maruti        dezire       2009        3100         6
8 maruti        swift        2009        4100         5
9 maruti        esteem       1997        98000        1
12 fiat         punto        2007        45000        3
```

The record number 1 is printed twice because it matches both `rule1` and `rule2`.

Using standard input with names in AWK

Sometimes, we may need to read input from standard input and from the pipe. The way to name the standard input, with all versions of AWK, is by using a single minus or dash sign, `-`. For example:

```
$ cat cars.dat | awk '{ print }' -
```

This can also be performed as follows:

```
$ cat cars.dat | awk  '{ print }'  /dev/stdin ( used with gawk only )
```

The output on execution of this code is as follows:

```
maruti          swift       2007        50000       5
honda           city        2005        60000       3
maruti          dezire      2009        3100        6
chevy           beat        2005        33000       2
honda           city        2010        33000       6
chevy           tavera      1999        10000       4
toyota          corolla     1995        95000       2
maruti          swift       2009        4100        5
maruti          esteem      1997        98000       1
ford            ikon        1995        80000       1
honda           accord      2000        60000       2
fiat            punto       2007        45000       3
```

We can also first read the input from one file, then read the standard input coming from the pipe, and then read another file again. In that case, the first file's data, the data from the pipe, and the other file's data, all become a single input. All of that data is read consecutively. In the following example, the input from `cars.dat` is read first, then the `echo` statement is taken as input, followed by the `emp.dat` file. Any pattern you apply in this AWK program will be applied on the whole input and not each file, as follows:

```
$ echo "=====================================================" | \
awk '{ print NR , $0 }' cars.dat - emp.dat
```

The output on execution of this code is as follows:

```
1 maruti          swift       2007        50000       5
2 honda           city        2005        60000       3
3 maruti          dezire      2009        3100        6
4 chevy           beat        2005        33000       2
5 honda           city        2010        33000       6
6 chevy           tavera      1999        10000       4
7 toyota          corolla     1995        95000       2
8 maruti          swift       2009        4100        5
9 maruti          esteem      1997        98000       1
10 ford            ikon       1995        80000       1
11 honda           accord     2000        60000       2
12 fiat            punto      2007        45000       3
13 =====================================================
14 Jack   Singh   9857532312  jack@gmail.com      M   hr    2000
15 Jane   Kaur    9837432312  jane@gmail.com      F   hr    1800
16 Eva    Chabra  8827232115  eva@gmail.com       F   lgs   2100
```

```
17 Amit     Sharma    9911887766    amit@yahoo.com       M    lgs    2350
18 Julie    Kapur     8826234556    julie@yahoo.com      F    Ops    2500
19 Ana      Khanna    9856422312    anak@hotmail.com     F    Ops    2700
20 Hari     Singh     8827255666    hari@yahoo.com       M    Ops    2350
21 Victor   Sharma    8826567898    vics@hotmail.com     M    Ops    2500
22 John     Kapur     9911556789    john@gmail.com       M    hr     2200
23 Billy    Chabra    9911664321    bily@yahoo.com       M    lgs    1900
24 Sam      khanna    8856345512    sam@hotmail.com      F    lgs    2300
25 Ginny    Singh     9857123466    ginny@yahoo.com      F    hr     2250
26 Emily    Kaur      8826175812    emily@gmail.com      F    Ops    2100
27 Amy      Sharma    9857536898    amys@hotmail.com     F    Ops    2500
28 Vina     Singh     8811776612    vina@yahoo.com       F    lgs    2300
```

Using command-line arguments: The AWK command line can have different forms, as follows:

awk 'program' file1 file2, file3 ....

awk -f source_file file1 file2, file3 ....

awk -Fsep 'program' file1 file2, file3 ....

awk -Fsep -f source_file file1 file2, file3 ....

In the given command lines, `file1`, `file2`, `file3`, and so on are command-line arguments that generally represent filenames. The command-line arguments are accessed in the AWK program with a built-in array called `ARGV`. The number of arguments in the AWK program is stored in the `ARGC` built-in variable, its value is one more than the actual number of arguments in the command line. For example:

```
$ awk -f source_file a b c
```

Here, `ARGV` is AWKs' built-in array variable that stores the value of command-line arguments. We access the value stored in the `ARGV` array by suffixing it with an array index in square brackets, as follows:

- `ARGV [ 0 ]` contains `awk`
- `ARGV [ 1 ]` contains `a`
- `ARGV [ 2 ]` contains `b`
- `ARGV [ 3 ]` contains `c`

ARGC has the value of four, ARGC is one more than the number of arguments because in AWK the name of the command is counted as argument zero, similar to C programs.

For example, the following program displays the number of arguments given to the AWK command and displays their value:

```
$ vi displayargs.awk
# echo - print command-line arguments
BEGIN {
     printf  "No. of command line args is : %d\n", ARGC-1;
     for  ( i = 1; i < ARGC; i++)
     printf "ARG [ %d ] is : %s \n", i, ARGV[ i ]
}
```

Now, we call this AWK program with the hello how are you command line argument. Here, hello is the first command line argument, how is the second, are is the third, and you is the fourth:

```
$ awk -f displayargs.awk hello how are you
```

The output on execution of the preceding code is as follows:

```
No. of command line args is : 4
ARG[1] is : hello
ARG[2] is : how
ARG[3] is : are
ARG[4] is : you
```

The AWK commands, source filename, or other options, such as -f or -F followed by field separator, are not treated as arguments. Let's try another useful example of a command-line argument. In this program, we use command-line arguments to generate sequences of integers, as follows:

```
$ vi seq.awk

# Program to print sequences of integers
BEGIN {

# If only one argument is given start from number 1
if  ( ARGC == 2 )
    for ( i = 1; i <= ARGV[1]; i++ )
    print i

# If 2 arguments are given start from first number upto second number
else if (  ARGC == 3  )
    for ( i = ARGV[1]; i <= ARGV[2]; i++ )
    print i
```

```
# If 3 arguments are given start from first number through second with a
stepping of third number
else if (  ARGC == 4  )
    for ( i = ARGV[1]; i <= ARGV[2]; i += ARGV[3] )
    print i
}
```

Now, let's execute the preceding script with three different parameters:

```
$ awk -f seq.awk 10
$ awk -f seq.awk 1 10
$ awk -f seq.awk 1 10 1
```

All the given commands will generate the integers one through ten. Without the second argument, it begins printing the numbers from 1 to the first argument. If two arguments are given, then it prints the number starting from the first argument to the second argument. In the third case, if you specify three arguments, then it prints the numbers between the first and second argument, leaving out the third argument. The output on execution of any of these commands is as follows:

```
1
2
3
4
5
6
7
8
9
10
```

AWK standard options

In this section, we discuss the three standard options that are available with all versions of AWK and other GAWK-supported options or GNU extensions. Each option in AWK begins with a dash and consists of a single character. GNU-style long options are also supported, which consist of two dashes (- -) followed by a keyword, which is the full form of an abbreviated option to uniquely identify it. If the option takes an argument, it is either immediately followed by the = sign and an argument value or a keyword, and the argument's value separated by whitespace. If an option with a value is given more than once, its last value is used.

Standard command-line options

AWK supports the following standard options, which can be provided in a long or short form interchangeably from the command line.

The -F option – field separator

By default, fields in the input record are separated by any number of spaces or tabs. This behavior can be altered by using the -F option or the FS variable. The value of the field separator can be either a single character or a regular expression. It controls the way AWK splits an input record into fields:

-Ffs

--field-separator

In the next example, we illustrate the use of the -F option. Here we used the -F to print the list of usernames that has been assigned to the bash shell from the /etc/passwd file. This file contains userdetails separated by a colon (:):

```
$ awk -F: '/bash/ { print $1 }' /etc/passwd
```

This can also be performed as follows:

```
$ awk --field-separator=: '/bash/ { print $1 }' /etc/passwd
```

The output on execution of this code is as follows:

```
at
bin
daemon
ftp
games
lp
man
news
nobody
. . . . . . . . . . . . . . . . . .
. . . . . . . . . . . . . . . . . .
```

The -f option (read source file)

This option is used to read the program source from the source file instead of in the first non-option argument. If this option is given multiple times, the program consists of the concatenation of the contents of each specified source file:

-f source-file

--file=source-file

First, we will create 2 programs to print line number 2 and line number 4, respectively. Then, we will use the -f option to source those files for execution with the interpreter, as follows:

```
$ vi f1.awk
NR==2 { print NR, $0 }
$ vi f2.
NR==4 { print NR, $0 }
```

Now, first use only f1. for sourcing:

```
$ awk -f f1.awk  cars.dat
```

This can also be performed as follows:

```
awk --file=f1.awk cars.dat
```

The output on execution of this code is as follows:

```
2 honda          city       2005        60000       3
```

Now, we will source both the files together. AWK will concatenate the contents of the two sourced files and execute them on the cars.dat filename, as follows:

```
$ awk -f f1.awk -f f2.awk cars.dat
```

This can also be performed as follows:

```
$ awk --file=f1.awk --file=f2.awk  cars.dat
```

The output on execution of this code is as follows:

```
2 honda          city        2005        60000       3
4 chevy          beat        2005        33000       2
```

The -v option (assigning variables)

This option assigns a value to a variable before the program executes. Such variable values are available inside the BEGIN block. The -v option can only set one variable at a time, but it can be used more than once, setting another variable each time:

-v var=val

--assign var=val

The following example describes the usage of the -v option:

```
$ awk -v name=Jagmohon 'BEGIN{ printf "Name = %s\n", name }'
```

This can also be performed as follows:

```
$ awk --assign=Jagmohan 'BEGIN{ printf "Name = %s\n", name }'
```

The output on execution of this code is as follows:

```
Name = Jagmohan
```

Here is a multiple-value assignment example:

```
$ awk -v name=Jagmohon -v age=42 'BEGIN{ printf "Name = %s\nAge = %s\n",
name, age }'
```

The output on execution of this code is:

```
Name = Jagmohan
Age = 42
```

GAWK-only options

Till now, we have discussed standard POSIX options. In the following section, we will discuss some important GNU extension options of GAWK.

The --dump-variables option (AWK global variables)

This option is used to print a sorted list of global variables, their types, and final values to file. By default, it prints this list to a file named `awkvars.out` in the current directory. It is good to have a list of all global variables to avoid errors that are created by using the same name function in your programs. The following is the command to print the list in the default file:

-d[file]
--dump-variables[=file]

```
$ awk --dump-variables ' '
```

This can also be performed as follows:

```
$ awk   -d   ' '
```

On execution of this command, we will have a file with the name `awkvars.out` in our current working directory, which has the following contents:

```
$ cat awkvars.out
ARGC: 1
ARGIND: 0
ARGV: array, 1 elements
BINMODE: 0
CONVFMT: "%.6g"
ENVIRON: array, 99 elements
ERRNO: ""
FIELDWIDTHS: ""
FILENAME: ""
FNR: 0
FPAT: "[^[:space:]]+"
FS: " "
IGNORECASE: 0
LINT: 0
NF: 0
NR: 0
OFMT: "%.6g"
OFS: " "
ORS: "\n"
PREC: 53
PROCINFO: array, 15 elements
RLENGTH: 0
ROUNDMODE: "N"
RS: "\n"
RSTART: 0
```

```
RT: ""
SUBSEP: "\034"
TEXTDOMAIN: "messages"
```

The --profile option (profiling)

This option enables the profiling of AWK programs, that is, it generates a pretty-printed version of the program in a file. By default, the profile is created in a file named `awkprof.out`. The optional file argument allows you to specify a different filename for the profile file. No space is allowed between `-p` and the filename, if a filename is supplied:

-p[file]
--profile[=file]

The profile file created contains execution counts for each statement in the program in the left margin, and function call counts for each function. In the next example, we will create a file with a name sample and redirect the output of the AWK command to `/dev/null`:

```
$ awk --profile=sample \
'BEGIN { print "**header**" }
{ print }
END{ print "**footer**" }' cars.dat > /dev/null
```

This same action can also be performed as follows:

```
$ awk -psample \
'BEGIN { print "**header**" }
{ print }
END{ print "**footer**" }' cars.dat > /dev/null
```

To view the content of `profile`, we execute the `cat` command, as follows:

```
$ cat sample
        # gawk profile, created Thu Sep 14 17:20:27 2017

        # BEGIN rule(s)

        BEGIN {
    1           print "**header**"
        }

        # Rule(s)

   12   {
```

```
12          print $0
      }

   # END rule(s)

   END {
1          print "**footer**"
      }
```

The –pretty-print option: It is the same profiling option discussed in the preceding section:

> *-o[file]*
> *--pretty-print[=file]*

The --sandbox option

This option disables the execution of the `system()` function, which can execute shell commands supplied as an expression to AWK. It also disables the input redirections with `getline`, output redirections with `print` and `printf`, and dynamic extensions. This is very useful when you want to run AWK scripts from questionable/untrusted sources and need to make sure the scripts can't access your system (other than the specified input data file):

> *-S*
>
> *--sandbox*

In the following example, we first execute the `echo` command within the `system` function without the `--sandbox` option, and then again with the `--sandbox` option to see the difference:

```
$ awk 'BEGIN { system("echo hello") }'
```

The preceding AWK command executes the `echo hello` command using the `system` function and returns a 0 value to the system upon successful execution. The output on execution of the preceding command is:

```
hello
```

Now, we use the `--sandbox` option with the AWK command to disable the execution of the `echo hello` shell command using the system function of AWK. In the next example, the system function will not execute as we have used the `--sandbox` option while executing it:

```
$ awk --sandbox 'BEGIN{ system("echo hello")}'
```

The output on execution of the preceding command is:

```
awk: cmd. line:1: fatal: 'system' function not allowed in sandbox mode
```

The -i option (including other files in your program)

This option is equivalent to the `@include` directive, which is used to source a file in the current AWK program. However, it is different from the `-f` option in two aspects. First, when we use the `-i` option, the program sourced is not loaded if it has been previously loaded, whereas `-f` always loads a file. The second difference is this after processing an `-i` argument, GAWK still expects to find the main source code via the `-f` option or on the command line:

-i source-file
--include source-file

In the next example, we will use the `f1.awk` and `f2.awk` files we created earlier to describe how the `-i` option works:

```
$ awk  -i  f1.awk  'NR==5 { print NR,  $0 }'  cars.dat
```

The output on execution of the given code is:

```
2 honda            city        2005        60000        3
5 honda            city        2010        33000        6
```

Now, we are using the `-i` option to include the `f1.awk` file inside the `-f` option to execute `f2.awk`, as follows:

```
$ awk  -i  f1.awk   -f  f2.awk    cars.dat
```

The output on execution of the preceding code is:

```
2 honda            city        2005        60000        3
4 chevy            beat        2005        33000        2
```

The next example shows it is mandatory to specify the AWK command or main source file using the -f option for executing a program with the -i option:

```
$ awk  -i  f1.awk cars.dat
```

The output on execution of the code is:

```
awk: cmd. line:1: cars.dat
awk: cmd. line:1:      ^ syntax error
```

Include other files in the GAWK program (using @include)

This is a feature that is specific to GAWK. The @include keyword can be used to read external AWK source files and load in your running program before execution. Using this feature, we can split large AWK source files into smaller programs and also reuse common AWK code from various AWK scripts. It is useful for grouping together various AWK functions in a file and creating function libraries, using the @include keyword and including it in your program. It is similar to the -i option, which we discussed earlier.

 It is important to note that the filename needs to be a literal string constant in double quotes.

The following example illustrates this. We'll create two AWK scripts, inc1 and inc2. Here is the inc1 script:

```
$ vi inc1
BEGIN { print "This is inc1." }
```

And now we create inc2, which includes inc1, using the @include keyword:

```
$ vi inc2
@include "inc1"
BEGIN { print "This is inc2." }

$ gawk -f  inc2
```

On executing GAWK with inc2, we get the following output:

```
This is inc1.
This is inc2.
```

So, to include external AWK source files, we just use `@include` followed by the name of the file to be included, enclosed in double quotes. The files to be included may be nested. For example, create a third script, `inc3`, that will include `inc2`:

```
$ vi inc3
@include "inc2"
BEGIN {  print "This is inc3." }

$ gawk -f inc3
```

On execution of GAWK with the `inc3` script, we get the following results:

```
This is inc1.
This is inc2.
This is inc3.
```

The filename can be a relative path or an absolute path. For example:

```
@include "/home/usr/scripts/inc1"
```

This can also be performed as follows:

```
@include "../inc1"
```

Since AWK has the ability to specify multiple `-f` options on the command line, the `@include` mechanism is not strictly necessary. However, the `@include` keyword can help you in constructing self-contained GAWK programs, and eliminates the need to write complex command lines repetitively.

The -V option

This option displays the version information for a running copy of GAWK as well as license info. This allows you to determine whether your copy of GAWK is up to date with respect to whatever the **Free Software Foundation** (**FSF**) is currently distributing. This can be done as shown in the following code block:

```
$ awk -V
```

It can also be performed as follows:

```
$ awk --version
```

The output on execution of the preceding code is:

```
shiwang@debian:~$ awk --version
GNU Awk 4.1.4, API: 1.1 (GNU MPFR 3.1.5, GNU MP 6.1.2)
Copyright (C) 1989, 1991-2016 Free Software Foundation.

This program is free software; you can redistribute it and/or modify
it under the terms of the GNU General Public License as published by
the Free Software Foundation; either version 3 of the License, or
(at your option) any later version.

This program is distributed in the hope that it will be useful,
but WITHOUT ANY WARRANTY; without even the implied warranty of
MERCHANTABILITY or FITNESS FOR A PARTICULAR PURPOSE.  See the
GNU General Public License for more details.

You should have received a copy of the GNU General Public License
along with this program. If not, see http://www.gnu.org/licenses/.
```

Summary

In this chapter, we learned that the basic construct of the AWK program is pattern-action pairs. We saw how it can be installed on the Linux system using different package managers or by compiling from the source code. We learned AWK basic usage, such as how to run AWK programs in different ways, as per the requirement. We looked at how to use comments and quotes with AWK. We also learned the usage of the backslash for extending our program across multiple lines. Finally, we covered three standard options for all versions of AWK, which are -f, -F, and -v, as well as other GNU extensions of AWK (GAWK) options, such as profiling, dumping variables, and including other files in your program.

In next chapter, we will learn about regular expressions and how they are handled with AWK.

2
Working with Regular Expressions

AWK is a pattern-matching language. It searches for a pattern in a file and, upon finding the corresponding match, it performs the file's action on the input line. This pattern could consist of fixed strings or a pattern of text. This variable content or pattern is generally searched for with the help of regular expressions. Hence, regular expressions form a very important part of AWK programming language. In this chapter, we will look at regular expressions and how they are handled with AWK.

In this chapter, we will cover the following:

- Regular expressions and their usage in AWK
- The basic regular expression construct
- Understanding the metacharacters of regular expression
- The precedence of regular expressions
- GAWK-specific regular expressions
- Case-sensitive matching
- Escape sequences

Introduction to regular expressions

In this section, you will learn about regular expressions and why we use them. Then we will discuss the usage of regular expressions in AWK.

What is a regular expression?

A **regular expression**, or **regexpr**, is a set of characters used to describe a pattern. A regular expression is generally used to match lines in a file that contain a particular pattern. Many Unix utilities operate on plain text files line by line, such as `grep`, `sed`, and `awk`. Regular expressions search for a pattern on a single line in a file.

 A regular expression doesn't search for a pattern that begins on one line and ends on another. Other programming languages may support this, notably Perl.

Why use regular expressions?

Generally, all editors have the ability to perform search-and-replace operations. Some editors can only search for patterns, others can also replace them, and others can also print the line containing that pattern. A regular expression goes many steps beyond this simple search, replace, and printing functionality, and hence it is more powerful and flexible. We can search for a word of a certain size, such as a word that has four characters or numbers. We can search for a word that ends with a particular character, let's say `e`. You can search for phone numbers, email IDs, and so on, and can also perform validation using regular expressions. They simplify complex pattern-matching tasks, and hence form an important part of AWK programming. Other regular expression variations also exist, notably those for Perl.

Using regular expressions with AWK

There are mainly two types of regular expressions in Linux:

- Basic regular expressions that are used by `vi`, `sed`, `grep`, and so on
- Extended regular expressions that are used by `awk`, `nawk`, `gawk`, and `egrep`

Here, we will refer to extended regular expressions as regular expressions in the context of AWK.

In AWK, regular expressions are enclosed in forward slashes, `'/'`, (forming the AWK pattern) and match every input record whose text belongs to that set.

The simplest regular expression is a string of letters, numbers, or both that matches itself. For example, here we use the `ly` regular expression string to print all lines that contain the `ly` pattern in them. We just need to enclose the regular expression in forward slashes in AWK:

```
$ awk '/ly/' emp.dat
```

The output on execution of this code is as follows:

```
Billy    Chabra   9911664321   bily@yahoo.com       M   lgs   1900
Emily    Kaur     8826175812   emily@gmail.com      F   Ops   2100
```

In this example, the `/ly/` pattern matches when the current input line contains the `ly` sub-string, either as `ly` itself or as some part of a bigger word, such as `Billy` or `Emily`, and prints the corresponding line.

Regular expressions as string-matching patterns with AWK

Regular expressions are used as string-matching patterns with AWK in the following three ways. We use the `'~'` and `'! ~'` match operators to perform regular expression comparisons:

- **/regexpr/**: This matches when the current input line contains a sub-string matched by regexpr. It is the most basic regular expression, which matches itself as a string or sub-string. For example, `/mail/` matches only when the current input line contains the `mail` string as a string, a sub-string, or both. So, we will get lines with Gmail as well as Hotmail in the email ID field of the employee database as follows:

  ```
  $ awk '/mail/' emp.dat
  ```

  The output on execution of this code is as follows:

  ```
  Jack     Singh    9857532312   jack@gmail.com       M   hr    2000
  Jane     Kaur     9837432312   jane@gmail.com       F   hr    1800
  Eva      Chabra   8827232115   eva@gmail.com        F   lgs   2100
  Ana      Khanna   9856422312   anak@hotmail.com     F   Ops   2700
  Victor   Sharma   8826567898   vics@hotmail.com     M   Ops   2500
  John     Kapur    9911556789   john@gmail.com       M   hr    2200
  Sam      khanna   8856345512   sam@hotmail.com      F   lgs   2300
  Emily    Kaur     8826175812   emily@gmail.com      F   Ops   2100
  Amy      Sharma   9857536898   amys@hotmail.com     F   Ops   2500
  ```

In this example, we do not specify any expression, hence it automatically matches a whole line, as follows:

```
$ awk '$0 ~ /mail/' emp.dat
```

The output on execution of this code is as follows:

```
Jack      Singh     9857532312    jack@gmail.com       M    hr     2000
Jane      Kaur      9837432312    jane@gmail.com       F    hr     1800
Eva       Chabra    8827232115    eva@gmail.com        F    lgs    2100
Ana       Khanna    9856422312    anak@hotmail.com     F    Ops    2700
Victor    Sharma    8826567898    vics@hotmail.com     M    Ops    2500
John      Kapur     9911556789    john@gmail.com       M    hr     2200
Sam       khanna    8856345512    sam@hotmail.com      F    lgs    2300
Emily     Kaur      8826175812    emily@gmail.com      F    Ops    2100
Amy       Sharma    9857536898    amys@hotmail.com     F    Ops    2500
```

- **expression ~ /regexpr /**: This matches if the string value of the expression contains a sub-string matched by regexpr. Generally, this left-hand operand of the matching operator is a field. For example, in the following command, we print all the lines in which the value in the second field contains a /Singh/ string:

```
$ awk '$2 ~ /Singh/{ print }' emp.dat
```

We can also use the expression as follows:

```
$ awk '{ if($2 ~ /Singh/) print}' emp.dat
```

The output on execution of the preceding code is as follows:

```
Jack      Singh     9857532312    jack@gmail.com       M    hr     2000
Hari      Singh     8827255666    hari@yahoo.com       M    Ops    2350
Ginny     Singh     9857123466    ginny@yahoo.com      F    hr     2250
Vina      Singh     8811776612    vina@yahoo.com       F    lgs    2300
```

- **expression !~ /regexpr /**: This matches if the string value of the expression does not contain a sub-string matched by regexpr. Generally, this expression is also a field variable. For example, in the following example, we print all the lines that don't contain the Singh sub-string in the second field, as follows:

```
$ awk '$2 !~ /Singh/{ print }' emp.dat
```

The output on execution of the preceding code is as follows:

```
Jane     Kaur      9837432312   jane@gmail.com      F   hr    1800
Eva      Chabra    8827232115   eva@gmail.com       F   lgs   2100
Amit     Sharma    9911887766   amit@yahoo.com      M   lgs   2350
Julie    Kapur     8826234556   julie@yahoo.com     F   Ops   2500
Ana      Khanna    9856422312   anak@hotmail.com    F   Ops   2700
Victor   Sharma    8826567898   vics@hotmail.com    M   Ops   2500
John     Kapur     9911556789   john@gmail.com      M   hr    2200
Billy    Chabra    9911664321   bily@yahoo.com      M   lgs   1900
Sam      khanna    8856345512   sam@hotmail.com     F   lgs   2300
Emily    Kaur      8826175812   emily@gmail.com     F   Ops   2100
Amy      Sharma    9857536898   amys@hotmail.com    F   Ops   2500
```

Any expression may be used in place of /regexpr/ in the context of ~; and !~. The expression here could also be `if`, `while`, `for`, and `do` statements.

Basic regular expression construct

Regular expressions are made up of two types of characters: normal text characters, called **literals**, and special characters, such as the asterisk (*, +, ?, .), called **metacharacters**. There are times when you want to match a metacharacter as a literal character. In such cases, we prefix that metacharacter with a backslash (\), which is called an **escape sequence**.

The basic regular expression construct can be summarized as follows:

Here is the list of metacharacters, also known as **special characters**, that are used in building regular expressions:

$$\backslash \quad \wedge \quad \$ \quad . \quad [\quad] \quad | \quad (\quad) \quad * \quad + \quad ?$$

The following table lists the remaining elements that are used in building a basic regular expression, apart from the metacharacters mentioned before:

Literal	A literal character (non-metacharacter), such as A, that matches itself.
Escape sequence	An escape sequence that matches a special symbol: for example \t matches tab.
Quoted metacharacter (\)	In quoted metacharacters, we prefix metacharacter with a backslash, such as \$ that matches the metacharacter literally.

Anchor (^)	Matches the beginning of a string.
Anchor ($)	Matches the end of a string.
Dot (.)	Matches any single character.
Character classes (. . .)	A character class [ABC] matches any one of the A, B, or C characters. Character classes may include abbreviations, such as [A-Za-z]. They match any single letter.
Complemented character classes	Complemented character classes [^0-9] match any character except a digit.

These operators combine regular expressions into larger ones:

Alternation (|)	A|B matches A or B.
Concatenation	AB matches A immediately followed by B.
Closure (*)	A* matches zero or more As.
Positive closure (+)	A+ matches one or more As.
Zero or one (?)	A? matches the null string or A.
Parentheses ()	Used for grouping regular expressions and back-referencing. Like regular expressions, (r) can be accessed using \n digit in future.

In the next section, we will look at regular expression metacharacters and their examples in AWK in more depth.

Understanding regular expression metacharacters

When we use special characters in regular expressions, they are called metacharacters because they have a special meaning. They enhance the flexibility, power, and usage of regular expressions. Now, we will discuss the list of metacharacters in regular expressions. All characters, that are not either metacharacters or escape sequences, match themselves in regular expressions. Let's understand each of them in detail.

Quoted metacharacter

A regular expression consisting of a literal or character (letter or digit) is a basic regular expression that matches itself. Sometimes, if we need to use the literal meaning of a metacharacter in a regular expression, we precede it with a backslash. If a character is preceded by a single backslash, \, we say the character is quoted. Quoting suppresses the special meaning of a character when matching. For example, if we want to match the dollar sign, $, in a string, we need to quote it as follows:

```
$ echo -e "500$\n500INR" | awk '/\$/{ print }'
```

The output on execution of the preceding code is as follows:

```
500$
```

Anchors

Anchors do not match the characters at all. Anchors are used to match the characters at certain positions, such as at the beginning or end of a line. If the anchors are not used in the proper position, either at the beginning or end of a regular expression, they do not act as anchors. The ^ and $ are two metacharacters that are known as anchors in regular expressions.

Matching at the beginning of a string

The unquoted caret ^ matches the string at the beginning of line. The ^ is only the anchor if it is the first character in the regular expression. For example, we use the /^J/ regular expression to match all the lines that begin with J. It will print the employee information of those whose first name begins with the J character in the employee database:

```
$ awk '/^J/{ print }' emp.dat
```

The output on execution of the preceding code is as follows:

```
Jack    Singh   9857532312   jack@gmail.com     M   hr    2000
Jane    Kaur    9837432312   jane@gmail.com     F   hr    1800
Julie   Kapur   8826234556   julie@yahoo.com    F   Ops   2500
John    Kapur   9911556789   john@gmail.com     M   hr    2200
```

We can also use the anchor, ^ (caret), with the string match operator (~) to match the field beginning with a specified character. In the following example, we print all the lines whose second field begins with S. It will print employee information for those employees whose last name begins with the S character, as follows:

```
$ awk '$2 ~ /^S/{ print }' emp.dat
```

The output on execution of the preceding code is as follows:

```
Jack     Singh    9857532312    jack@gmail.com      M    hr     2000
Amit     Sharma   9911887766    amit@yahoo.com      M    lgs    2350
Hari     Singh    8827255666    hari@yahoo.com      M    Ops    2350
Victor   Sharma   8826567898    vics@hotmail.com    M    Ops    2500
Ginny    Singh    9857123466    ginny@yahoo.com     F    hr     2250
Amy      Sharma   9857536898    amys@hotmail.com    F    Ops    2500
Vina     Singh    8811776612    vina@yahoo.com      F    lgs    2300
```

Matching at the end of a string

The unquoted dollar, $, matches the string at the end of the line. The '$' is only the anchor if it is the last character in the regular expression. For example, '0$' matches all the lines that end with 0. It will print employee details of those whose salary ends with the '0' character in the employee database:

```
$ awk '/0$/{ print }' emp.dat
```

The output on execution of this code is as follows:

```
Jack     Singh    9857532312    jack@gmail.com      M    hr     2000
Jane     Kaur     9837432312    jane@gmail.com      F    hr     1800
Eva      Chabra   8827232115    eva@gmail.com       F    lgs    2100
Amit     Sharma   9911887766    amit@yahoo.com      M    lgs    2350
Julie    Kapur    8826234556    julie@yahoo.com     F    Ops    2500
Ana      Khanna   9856422312    anak@hotmail.com    F    Ops    2700
Hari     Singh    8827255666    hari@yahoo.com      M    Ops    2350
Victor   Sharma   8826567898    vics@hotmail.com    M    Ops    2500
John     Kapur    9911556789    john@gmail.com      M    hr     2200
Billy    Chabra   9911664321    bily@yahoo.com      M    lgs    1900
Sam      khanna   8856345512    sam@hotmail.com     F    lgs    2300
Ginny    Singh    9857123466    ginny@yahoo.com     F    hr     2250
Emily    Kaur     8826175812    emily@gmail.com     F    Ops    2100
Amy      Sharma   9857536898    amys@hotmail.com    F    Ops    2500
Vina     Singh    8811776612    vina@yahoo.com      F    lgs    2300
```

Like ^, we can also use anchor, $ (dollar), with the string match operator (~) to match the field ending with a specific character. In the following example, we print all the lines whose second field ends with the 'a' letter, as follows:

```
$ awk '$2 ~ /a$/{ print }' emp.dat
```

The output on execution of this code is as follows:

```
Eva       Chabra    8827232115    eva@gmail.com      F    lgs    2100
Amit      Sharma    9911887766    amit@yahoo.com     M    lgs    2350
Ana       Khanna    9856422312    anak@hotmail.com   F    Ops    2700
Victor    Sharma    8826567898    vics@hotmail.com   M    Ops    2500
Billy     Chabra    9911664321    bily@yahoo.com     M    lgs    1900
Sam       khanna    8856345512    sam@hotmail.com    F    lgs    2300
Amy       Sharma    9857536898    amys@hotmail.com   F    Ops    2500
```

A summary of the anchors is as follows:

Pattern	Matches
^C	Matches "C" at the beginning of a line
C$	Matches "C" at the end of a line
C^	Matches "C^" anywhere on a line
$C	Matches "$C" anywhere on a line
^C$	Matches the string consisting of a single "C" character
^^	Matches "^" at the beginning of a line
$$	Matches "$" at the end of a line
^$	Matches an empty line (which begins and ends immediately)

Dot

The " . " character is one of those special metacharacters that matches any character, except the end-of-line character. In the following example, we match a sequence of three characters that begin with C and end with T, as follows:

```
$ echo -e "C1T\nCaT\nC@T\ncAT" | awk '/C.T/ { print }'
```

The output on execution of the preceding program is as follows:

```
C1T
CaT
C@T
```

Let's create one file for practicing dot regular expressions:

```
$ vi dot_regex.txt
Lets go for a walk
Singing is good hobby
We will talk on this matter
Ping me when you are free
(that is cool)
My son birthday is on 24/04/14
I will be going to Singapore on 24-04-14
(this)
```

Now, let's execute some regular expressions on the dot_regex.txt file:

1. Match all strings with any character preceded by 'ing', as follows:

   ```
   $ awk '/.ing/{ print }' dot_regex.txt
   ```

   The output on execution of this code is:

   ```
   Singing is good hobby
   Ping me when you are free
   I will be going to Singapore on  24-04-14
   ```

2. Match all strings that contain a space, followed by a character, and further followed by 'alk':

   ```
   $ awk '/ .alk/{ print }' dot_regex.txt
   ```

The output on execution of the preceding code is as follows:

```
Lets go for a walk
We will talk on this matter
```

3. Match the date with any separator, as follows:

```
$ awk '/24.04.14/{ print }' dot_regex.txt
```

The output on execution of the given code is as follows:

```
My son birthday is on 24/04/14
I will be going to Singapore on  24-04-14
```

A summary of dot/period is as follows:

Pattern	Matches
.	Matches any single character anywhere
.C	Matches any single character followed by "C" anywhere on the line
A.C	Matches a sequence of three characters that begin with A and end with C anywhere on the line
^.$	Matches any string containing exactly one character
...	Matches any three consecutive characters anywhere on the line
\.$	Matches a period at the end of the line

Brackets expressions

If we want to match a specific character in a line, we enclose it in square brackets, such regular expressions are generally called a **bracket expression**. It matches any one of the characters that is within the square brackets. The order of the characters does not matter. For example, '[APz]' will match any one of the 'A', 'P', or 'z' characters in a string.

Character classes

Character classes, also known as a character set, is a regular expression consisting of a group of characters enclosed in brackets. It matches any one of the enclosed characters, irrespective of the order of occurrence of that character in the bracket. For example, [abcdefgh] matches any of the a, b, c, d, e, f, g, or h characters.

In the following example, we print the employee information for those whose names begin with any of the characters enclosed within brackets:

```
$ awk '/^[ ABCDEFGHIJ ]/{ print }' emp.dat
```

The output on execution of the given code is as follows:

```
Jack    Singh    9857532312    jack@gmail.com      M    hr     2000
Jane    Kaur     9837432312    jane@gmail.com      F    hr     1800
Eva     Chabra   8827232115    eva@gmail.com       F    lgs    2100
Amit    Sharma   9911887766    amit@yahoo.com      M    lgs    2350
Julie   Kapur    8826234556    julie@yahoo.com     F    Ops    2500
Ana     Khanna   9856422312    anak@hotmail.com    F    Ops    2700
Hari    Singh    8827255666    hari@yahoo.com      M    Ops    2350
John    Kapur    9911556789    john@gmail.com      M    hr     2200
Billy   Chabra   9911664321    bily@yahoo.com      M    lgs    1900
Ginny   Singh    9857123466    ginny@yahoo.com     F    hr     2250
Emily   Kaur     8826175812    emily@gmail.com     F    Ops    2100
Amy     Sharma   9857536898    amys@hotmail.com    F    Ops    2500
```

We can specify ranges of characters in abbreviated form by using a hyphen. The character immediately to the left of the hyphen defines the beginning of the range and the character immediately to the right defines the end. Thus, the preceding example can be rewritten using a hyphen as follows:

```
$ awk '/^[ A-J ]/{ print }' emp.dat
```

The output on execution of the preceding code is as follows:

```
Jack    Singh    9857532312    jack@gmail.com      M    hr     2000
Jane    Kaur     9837432312    jane@gmail.com      F    hr     1800
Eva     Chabra   8827232115    eva@gmail.com       F    lgs    2100
Amit    Sharma   9911887766    amit@yahoo.com      M    lgs    2350
Julie   Kapur    8826234556    julie@yahoo.com     F    Ops    2500
Ana     Khanna   9856422312    anak@hotmail.com    F    Ops    2700
Hari    Singh    8827255666    hari@yahoo.com      M    Ops    2350
John    Kapur    9911556789    john@gmail.com      M    hr     2200
Billy   Chabra   9911664321    bily@yahoo.com      M    lgs    1900
```

```
Ginny    Singh    9857123466   ginny@yahoo.com     F   hr    2250
Emily    Kaur     8826175812   emily@gmail.com     F   Ops   2100
Amy      Sharma   9857536898   amys@hotmail.com    F   Ops   2500
```

We can print the info of employees whose names begin with 'Ja' and are followed by any two characters, as follows:

```
$ awk '/Ja[a-z][a-z]/{ print }' emp.dat
```

The output on execution of this code is as follows:

```
Jack    Singh    9857532312   jack@gmail.com      M   hr    2000
Jane    Kaur     9837432312   jane@gmail.com      F   hr    1800
```

Similarly, you can print the info of employees whose salary is either 2300 or 2500, as follows:

```
$ awk '/2[35]00/{ print }' emp.dat
```

The output on execution of the preceding code is as follows:

```
Julie    Kapur    8826234556   julie@yahoo.com     F   Ops   2500
Victor   Sharma   8826567898   vics@hotmail.com    M   Ops   2500
Sam      khanna   8856345512   sam@hotmail.com     F   lgs   2300
Amy      Sharma   9857536898   amys@hotmail.com    F   Ops   2500
Vina     Singh    8811776612   vina@yahoo.com      F   lgs   2300
```

Without both left- and right-range characters, a hyphen in a character class denotes itself, hence the [-] character classes match –:

```
$ echo -e "-\n
+\n
a\n
b"  | awk '/[-]/'
```

The output on execution of this code is as follows:

```
-
```

We can also put a hyphen at the beginning or end of a range-specified character class to match the hyphen itself, as shown here:

```
$  echo -e "-\n
+\n
a\n
b"  | awk '/[a-z-]/'
```

This can also be performed as follows:

```
$ echo -e "-\n
+\n
a\n
b" | awk '/[-a-z ]/'
```

The output on execution of the preceding code is as follows:

```
-
a
b
```

The only metacharacters valid inside the bracket expression are '\', ']', '-', or '^'. We have to put a '\' in front of them to use them inside character classes.

As in the case of anchors, if they are not placed at the appropriate position in regular expressions they lose their meaning, the same is true for the hyphen, '-', and also ']'. For example:

```
$ echo -e "-\n
+\n
a\n
b\n
]\n
\\" | awk '/[\^ab\-\]\\]/'
```

The output on execution of this code is as follows:

```
-
a
b
]
\
```

A summary of the character classes is as follows:

Pattern	Matches
[f-k]	Matches any single character between [fghijk]
[0-9]	Matches any single digit between [0123456789]
[-]	Matches a hyphen
[0-9-]	Matches any number or a hyphen
[-0-9]	Matches any number or a hyphen

`[]0-9]`	Matches any number or a]
`[0-9]]`	Matches any number followed by]
`[0-9\-\]]`	Matches any number, a hyphen, or]
`[0-9\\]`	Matches any number or backslash, `"\"`
`[\^0-9]`	Matches any number or caret, `"^"`
`[a-z]`	Matches any small letter
`[A-Z]`	Matches any capital letter
`[a-zA-Z]`	Matches any alphabet
`[a-zA-Z0-9]`	Matches any alphanumeric character
`[5-9G-Lr-z]`	Matches any single character among `[56789GHIJKLrstuvwxyz]`
`[a-zA-Z][0-9]`	Matches a letter followed by a digit
`[a-zA-Z-]+`	Matches a letter that includes a hyphen

Named character classes (POSIX standard)

Named character classes is a feature introduced in the POSIX standard. A named character class is a special notation that describes the lists of characters that have a specific attribute, but the actual characters can vary from country to country or from one character set to another. For example, the alphabetic character set can differ between India and China.

A named character class is valid in a regexp, when it is given inside the brackets of a bracket expression. The named character class is enclosed between ' `[:` ' and ' `:]` '.

For example, if you want to search for lines having alphabets (uppercase and lowercase both), we can write it as follows:

```
$ awk '/[[:alpha:]]/'   dot_regex.txt
```

The output on execution of the preceding code is as follows:

```
Let's go for a walk
Singing is a good hobby
We will talk on this matter
Ping me when you are free
(that is cool)
My son's birthday is on 24/04/14
I will be going to Singapore on  24-04-14
(this)
```

The preceding regex prints all the lines of the file because each line contains alphabets.

Now, let's use the `[:digit:]` named character class to print the lines with digits in them:

```
$ awk '/[[:digit:]]/'  dot_regex.txt
```

The output on execution of the given code is as follows:

```
My son birthday is on 24/04/14
I will be going to Singapore on  24-04-14
```

A summary of the character classes defined by the POSIX standard is as follows:

Class	Meaning
`[:digit:]`	Numeric characters
`[:alpha:]`	Alphabetic characters
`[:alnum:]`	Alphanumeric characters
`[:lower:]`	Lowercase alphabetic characters
`[:upper:]`	Uppercase alphabetic characters
`[:blank:]`	Blank characters space and tab
`[:space:]`	Space characters tab, newline, vertical tab, form feed, carriage return, and space
`[:cntrl:]`	Control characters have octal codes 000 to 037 and 177
`[:xdigit:]`	Characters that are hexadecimal digits
`[:graph:]`	Characters that are both printable and visible, `'[:alnum:]'` and `'[:punct:]'` (a space is printable but not visible, whereas an `'a'` is both)
`[:print:]`	Printable characters (characters that are not control characters)

	Punctuation characters (characters that are not letters, digits, control characters, or space characters),
[:punct:]	! " # $ % & ' ( ) * + , - . / : ; < = > ? @ [\ ] ^ _ ` { | } ~

Here is a summary table for named character classes and equivalent character classes:

Named character class	Character classes
[:digit:]	[0-9]
[:alpha:]	[a-zA-Z]
[:alnum:]	[a-zA-Z0-9]
[:lower:]	[a-z]
[:upper:]	[A-Z]
[:blank:]	Blank characters are space and tab
[:space:]	Space characters are tab, newline, vertical tab, form feed, carriage return, and space
[:cntrl:]	Control characters: have octal codes 000 to 037 and 177
[:xdigit:]	Hexadecimal digits are 0 1 2 3 4 5 6 7 8 9 A B C D E F a b c d e f
[:graph:]	Characters that are both printable and visible: '[:alnum:]' and '[:punct:]' (a space is printable but not visible, whereas an 'a' is both)
[:print:]	Printable characters (characters that are not control characters)
[:punct:]	Punctuation characters (characters that are not letters, digits, control characters, or space characters), ! " # $ % & ' ( ) * + , - . / : ; < = > ? @ [\ ] ^ _ ` { | } ~

Complemented bracket expressions

A complemented bracket expression is one in which the first character after the `[` must be caret, `^`. This character class matches any character except those in the square brackets. For example, `[^abc]` will match any character but not `'a'`, `'b'`, or `'c'`. Similarly, `[^0-9]` matches any character except a digit.

Complemented character classes

In a complementary character set, the first character after `[` is caret, `^`, and it negates the set of characters in the square brackets. For example, to match any character except a vowel, we can use the following regular expression:

```
$ echo -e "a\nb\nc\nd\ne" | awk '/[^aeiou]/{ print }'
```

The output on execution of the preceding code is as follows:

```
b
c
d
```

Similarly, in the employee database (`emp.dat`), if we want to print information for all those employees whose email ID doesn't begin with either `'j'` or `'v'`, that is, `[^jv]`, we can use the following expression:

```
$ awk '$4 ~ /^[^jv]/{ print $4 }' emp.dat
```

The output on execution of the given code is as follows:

```
eva@gmail.com
amit@yahoo.com
anak@hotmail.com
hari@yahoo.com
bily@yahoo.com
sam@hotmail.com
ginny@yahoo.com
emily@gmail.com
amys@hotmail.com
```

Some examples of complemented character classes are given as follows:

Named character class	Matches
`[^a-z]`	Matches any character except a lowercase letter
`[^A-Z]`	Matches any character except an uppercase letter
`[^a-zA-Z]`	Matches any character except an alphabet character
`[^a-zA-Z0-9]`	Matches any character except an alphanumeric character
`[^5-9G-Lr-z]`	Matches any single character except among `[56789GHIJKLrstuvwxyz]`
`[^0-9]`	Matches any character except any digit
`^[^ABC]`	Matches any character at the beginning of a string except ABC
`^[ABC]`	Matches ABC at the beginning of a string
`^[^a-z]$`	Matches any single-character except a lowercase letter
`^[^^]`	Matches any character except ^ at the beginning

Complemented named character classes

In complemented named character classes, the first character after `[` is caret, `^`, and it is followed by the named character class, which is enclosed in `'[:'` and `':]'`. For example, if you want to search for a line without letters (lowercase), we can write it as follows:

```
$ echo -e "a
\nb
\nc
\n1
\n2
\nd
\n3" | awk '/[^[:lower:]]/'
```

The output on execution of the preceding code is as follows:

```
1
2
3
```

We can mix the old and new POSIX styles, for example, to any number between 1–5 or any lowercase letter. For this, we can use the following:

```
$ echo -e "a\n1\ne\n5\nz\n8" | awk '/[1-5[:lower:]]/'
```

The output on execution of the preceding code is as follows:

```
a
1
e
5
z
```

Alternation operator

The alternation operator is used to specify alternatives. The alternation operator is a vertical bar or pipe symbol, it matches one regular expression out of several regular expressions. The ' | ' alternation operator has the lowest precedence among all the regular expression operators. For example, in the employee database, if we want to print the lines that have first name of the employee as Emily, Jack, or Ana, we can write the following regular expression:

```
$ awk '/Emily|Jack|Ana/' emp.dat
```

In AWK, it is generally used with the ( ) grouping operator, as follows:

```
$ awk '/(Emily|Jack|Ana)/' emp.dat
```

The output on execution of the given code is as follows:

```
Jack    Singh    9857532312    jack@gmail.com      M    hr     2000
Ana     Khanna   9856422312    anak@hotmail.com    F    Ops    2700
Emily   Kaur     8826175812    emily@gmail.com     F    Ops    2100
```

With the alternation operator, we can combine multiple regular expressions together, as follows:

```
$ awk '/^J|^V/' emp.dat
```

The output on execution of the preceding code is as follows:

```
Jack      Singh     9857532312    jack@gmail.com      M    hr     2000
Jane      Kaur      9837432312    jane@gmail.com      F    hr     1800
Julie     Kapur     8826234556    julie@yahoo.com     F    Ops    2500
Victor    Sharma    8826567898    vics@hotmail.com    M    Ops    2500
John      Kapur     9911556789    john@gmail.com      M    hr     2200
Vina      Singh     8811776612    vina@yahoo.com      F    lgs    2300
```

So, in the previous example, we could print the employee details for those whose first name begins with J or V.

The alternation applies to the largest possible regular expressions on either side. For example, if we want to print the lines that begin with either J or V, or the email ID of users beginning with v, as follows:

```
$ awk '/(^J|^V)|($4 ~ ^v)/' emp.dat
```

The output on execution of the preceding code is as follows:

```
Jack      Singh     9857532312    jack@gmail.com      M    hr     2000
Jane      Kaur      9837432312    jane@gmail.com      F    hr     1800
Julie     Kapur     8826234556    julie@yahoo.com     F    Ops    2500
Victor    Sharma    8826567898    vics@hotmail.com    M    Ops    2500
John      Kapur     9911556789    john@gmail.com      M    hr     2200
Vina      Singh     8811776612    vina@yahoo.com      F    lgs    2300
```

Unary operator for repetition

The *, +, and ? symbols are known as unary operators, which are used to specify repetitions in regular expressions. They are also known as modifiers. For example, we can use the unary operator for repeating character classes. However, the important thing is it repeats entire character class and not just the character it matched. The [0-9]+ regular expression can match one or more digits; it can be 987654321, or 222, or 333, and so on.

Closure

The closure, or asterisk or star, means that the item immediately preceded by * is matched zero or more times. For example, in the given expression, we match a letter, immediately followed by a lowercase letter or digit. The first character class matches a letter. The second character class matches a letter or digit. The star repeats the second character class:

```
$ echo -e "ca\n
c\n
c1\n
1\n
;\n
c;\n
cc" | awk '/[a-z][a-z0-9]*/'
```

The output on execution of this code is as follows:

```
ca
c
c1
c;
cc
```

Let's have another example to explain it. In this example, we print all the lines that contain the ca string and it is followed by zero or more occurrences of t:

```
$ echo -e "ca\n
cat\n
catt\n
c\n
catterpillar" | awk '/cat*/'
```

The output on execution of this code is as follows:

```
ca
cat
catt
catterpillar
```

To match as long a string as possible between (and), we can use closure as follows:

```
$ awk '/\(.*\)/'   dot_regex.txt
```

The output on execution of the preceding program is as follows:

```
(that is cool)
(this)
```

A summary of closure operations is as follows:

Pattern	Matches
A*	Matches the null string, A, or AA, and so on
AB*C	Matches AC, ABC, or ABBC, and so on
AB.*C	Matches AB followed by zero or more other characters followed by C as ABC, ABBC, or XAB78478XC, and so on
[0-9]*	Matches zero or more numbers
[0-9][0-9]*	Matches one or more numbers
^A*	Matches any line
^A*	Matches any line starting with A*
^AA*	Matches any line starting with one A as A, AA, or AAA, and so on

Positive closure

The positive closure or plus (+) means that the item immediately preceded by + is matched one or more times. For example, the ca+t would match cat and caat, whereas ca*t would match all three, as follows:

```
$ echo -e "cat\n
ct\n
caat\n
cbt" | awk '/ca+t/'
```

The output on execution of the preceding code is as follows:

```
cat
caat
```

A summary of positive closure (+) is as follows:

Pattern	Matches
A+	Matches the single A, AA, or AAA, and so on
AB+C	Matches ABC, ABBC, or ABBBC, and so on
[0-9]+	Matches one or more numbers
[0-9][0-9]+	Matches two or more numbers
^A+	Matches any line beginning with one or more A letters
^A\+	Matches any line starting with A+
^AA+	Matches any line starting with two AA as AA or AAA, and so on
AB+C	Matches ABC, ABBC, or ABBBC, and so on
(AB)+C	Matches ABC, ABABC, ABABABC, and so on
[A-Z]+	Matches any string of one or more uppercase letters

Zero or one

The zero or one operator (?) matches occurrences of the preceding character zero or one time. For example, we use ? to mark the e as an optional character to match the Jean or Jan string, as follows:

```
$ echo -e "Jean\nJan\nJeean" | awk '/Je?an/'
```

The output on execution of the preceding code is as follows:

```
Jean
Jan
```

A summary of the unary operator for repetition is as follows:

Pattern	Matches
A?	Matches the single A or null string
AB?C	Matches AC or ABC

Repetition ranges with interval expressions

We can use interval expressions to specify a minimum, maximum, or exact number of occurrences to match the preceding regular expression. The unary operator for repetition can specify a minimum number of occurrences, but we cannot specify the maximum number of occurrences of the preceding expression with them.

Interval expressions were not originally available in AWK. They were added as part of the POSIX standard to make AWK and `egrep` consistent with each other. In GAWK, they are available with version 4.0 and above.

Let's create a file to illustrate the interval expression:

```
vi interval_regex.txt
a1b
a12b
a123b
a1234b
a12345b
a1233456b
a111b
a111111b
cababababt
cababt
```

A single number in brackets

A single number in brackets, {n}, matches exactly n occurrence of the preceding expression. For example, the following regular expression matches the line consisting of exactly 5 digits between a and b:

```
$ awk '/a[0-9]{5}b/' interval_regex.txt
```

The output on execution of the preceding code is as follows:

```
a12345b
```

If from the `emp.dat` file, you want to print all the lines in which an employee's phone number had the 9 repeated twice, we can write the regular expression as follows:

```
$ awk '/[9]{2}/' emp.dat
```

The output on execution of the preceding code is as follows:

```
Amit    Sharma   9911887766   amit@yahoo.com   M   lgs   2350
John    Kapur    9911556789   john@gmail.com   M   hr    2200
Billy   Chabra   9911664321   bily@yahoo.com   M   lgs   1900
```

A single number followed by a comma in brackets

A single number followed by a comma in brackets, {n, }, means that the preceded regular expression is repeated at least n number of times. For example, to match the occurrence of the minimum 3 numbers between a and b in a line, we can use the following:

```
$ awk '/a[0-9]{3,}b/' interval_regex.txt
```

The output on execution of the preceding code is as follows:

```
a123b
a1234b
a12345b
a1233456b
a111b
a111111b
```

Two numbers in brackets

If there are two numbers, n and m, in brackets, then it means that the preceded item must be matched at least n times but not more than m times. The values of n and m must be non-negative and smaller than 255. For example, to match the occurrence of a minimum of 2 numbers and a maximum of 6 numbers between a and b in a line, we can use the following regular expression:

```
$ awk '/a[0-9]{2,6}b/' interval_regex.txt
```

The output on execution of the preceding code is as follows:

```
a12b
a123b
a1234b
a12345b
a111b
a111111b
```

In interval expression, the preceding regular expression should be a single-character regular expression, or if it is a string, it must be enclosed in a bracketed regular expression. For example:

```
$ awk '/(ab){2,3}/'  interval_regex.txt
```

The output on execution of the preceding code is as follows:

```
cababababt
cababt
```

A summary of interval expressions is as follows:

Pattern	Matches
A{3}B	Matches the line with AAAB
A{3,}B	Matches AAAB, AAAAB,or AAAAAB, and so on
A{3,5}B	Matches AAAB, AAAAB, or AAAAAB
{4,8}	Matches any line with {4,8}
X(ab){2}Z	Matches any XababZ

Grouping using parentheses

This is also known as creating sub-expressions. Single-letter repetition can be easily controlled with unary operators or interval expressions, however, if we need to match the repetition of a word or group of characters, then we have to group that regular expression together inside parentheses. It is quite similar to the grouping of expressions as done in math. Parentheses or grouping is used for two operations, that is, concatenation and back-referencing.

Concatenation using alternation operator within parentheses

Parentheses can be used to concatenate regular expressions using the ' | ' alternation operator. In this, we simply place two or more regular expressions separated using the alternation operator pipe, ' | ', within parentheses to match any of them. For example, in the given example we print lines with the Jane, Emily, Ana, or Victor employee name from the emp.dat file, as follows:

```
$ awk '/(Jane|Emily|Ana|Victor)/{ print }' emp.dat
```

The output on execution of the preceding code is as follows:

```
Jane     Kaur     9837432312   jane@gmail.com     F   hr    1800
Ana      Khanna   9856422312   anak@hotmail.com   F   Ops   2700
Victor   Sharma   8826567898   vics@hotmail.com   M   Ops   2500
Emily    Kaur     8826175812   emily@gmail.com    F   Ops   2100
```

Backreferencing in regular expressions – sed and grep

If we group the regular expressions with more than one character and place it inside parentheses, it becomes a sub-expression. This sub-expression is matched and the output of the match is remembered and can be recalled if you find the same pattern occurrence again during the subsequent match operation.

We can recall the remembered pattern with \ followed by a single digit. We can have a maximum of nine different remembered patterns. Each occurrence of (starts a new pattern of a sub-expression. This process of recalling remembered patterns is called the **backreferencing of sub-expressions**.

Sub-expressions are represented by enclosing a regex between parentheses: → **\(regex\)**

A **backreference** is represented by a backslash followed by a digit, where the digit is the sub-expression reference number:→ **\digit**

back-references don't work with AWK or GAWK. GAWK uses the gensub() function for backreferencing. However, backreferencing is a quite useful feature of regular expressions and is frequently used with the grep and sed utilities of Linux, so we'll discuss them in this chapter.

Now, we create a file for practicing back-references, as follows:

```
vi backreference.txt
cat
first example of back-referencing
catcat
example of palindrome
xabax
```

In first example, we will print the line containing the `cat` string followed by the `cat` string again. So, to match the second reference of cat, we use `\1`, as follows:

```
$ grep '\(cat\)\1' backreference.txt --color
```

The output on execution of the preceding command is as follows:

```
catcat
```

To match the five-letter palindrome string in the `backreference.txt` file, we can use the following regular expression:

```
$ grep '\([a-z]\)\([a-z]\)[a-z]\2\1'  backreference.txt --color
```

The output on execution of the preceding code is as follows:

```
first example of backreferencing
xabax
```

Precedence in regular expressions

In regular expressions, the ' | ' alternation operator has the lowest precedence, then concatenation, followed by the +, *, and ? repetition operations as well as brackets, ' { ' and ' } '. As in arithmetic expressions, operators of higher precedence are done before lower ones. Also, parentheses can change how operators are grouped. Due to these conventions, parentheses are often omitted, as follows:

```
$ awk '/Jane|Emily/' emp.dat is same as
$ awk '/(Jane)|(Emily)/' emp.dat
```

The output on execution of the preceding code is as follows:

```
Jane     Kaur     9837432312   jane@gmail.com      F   hr    1800
Emily    Kaur     8826175812   emily@gmail.com     F   Ops   2100
```

In POSIX, AWK, and GAWK, the '*', '+', and '?' operators stand for themselves when there is nothing in the regular expression that precedes them. For example, /+/ matches a literal plus sign:

```
$ echo -e "This is new line
one + one is two
posix regular expression" | awk '/+/{ print }'
```

The output on execution of the preceding code is as follows:

```
one + one is two
```

GAWK-specific regular expression operators

GAWK has some more regular expression operators, in addition to those we've already discussed. The operators described in this section are specific to GAWK and are not available in other AWK implementations. These are basically shorthand character classes that are frequently used, and most of them deal with word matching (here, word refers to a sequence of one or more letters, digits, or underscores). We access them by using the escape character, '\', followed by a letter (here, the escape character adds special meaning to them instead of taking it away).

Let's create a file to practice GAWK-only operators:

```
vi  gopr.txt
start
bigstarting
starting
start end
white space example
e d
end
e_d
e1d
e;d
eNd
white space example with tab
e d
```

Matching whitespaces

Whitespaces matches anything that is considered a whitespace character. It is equivalent to `'[[:space:]]'`.

For example, in the `gopr.txt` file, we match all the lines that contain `'e'` followed by whitespace and `'d'` using the `'\s'` operator. It will print all the lines in which there is a space or tab between `'e'` and `'d'`, as follows:

```
$ awk '/e\sd/'  gopr.txt
```

The output on execution of the preceding code is as follows:

```
e d
e    d
```

Matching not whitespaces

Matches the opposite of `\s`, that is, anything that is not considered whitespace. It is the equivalent of `[^[:space:]]`. For example, if we want to print all the lines that don't contain any whitespace between e and d, then we can use the `\S` shorthand, as follows:

```
$ awk '/e\Sd/' gopr.txt
```

The output on execution of the preceding code is as follows:

```
start end
end
e_d
e1d
e;d
eNd
```

Matching words (\w)

Matching everything that is considered a word character, this can be done using `\w`. It is the equivalent of any letter, digit, or underscore as `[[:alnum:]_]`. Here, the underscore is included because in many programming languages, the underscore is used as a variable or function name. For example:

```
$ awk '/e\wd/' gopr.txt
```

The output on execution of the preceding code is as follows:

```
start end
end
e_d
e1d
eNd
```

Matching non-words

Matches any character that is not considered a word, character, or underscore. It is the opposite of \W and the equivalent of [^[:alum:]_]. For example:

```
$ awk '/e\Wd/' gopr.txt
```

The output on execution of the preceding code is as follows:

```
e d
e;d
e    d
```

Matching word boundaries

Word boundaries are the beginning or end of a word. Here, it also word includes a letter, digit, or underscore.

Matching at the beginning of a word

It matches the beginning of a word. The string followed by \< should be the beginning of the string. It should not be preceded by other characters. For example, \<start will match starting, start, or started, but not restart, as shown here:

```
$ awk '/\<start/'   gopr.txt
```

The output on execution of the given code is as follows:

```
start
starting
start end
```

Matching at the end of a word

Matches a string at the end of a word. The string preceded by '`\>`' should mark the end of the word. It should not be followed by any character. For example, '`start\>`' will match `restart` or `bigstart`, but not starting or started, as follows:

```
$ awk '/start\>/' gopr.txt
```

The output on execution of the preceding code is as follows:

```
start
start end
```

Matching not as a sub-string using

The string enclosed between `\y` and `\y` should not occur as a sub-string of a word in a line. If `\y` is used at the beginning, it matches the empty string at the beginning. If `\y` used at the end, it matches the empty string at the end. For example:

```
$ awk '/\ystart\y/'  gopr.txt
```

The output on execution of the preceding code is as follows:

```
start
start end
```

Matching a string as sub-string only using

This matches the string enclosed between `\B` and `\B` as a sub-string. It is the opposite of `\y`. For example, `\Bstart\B` will match `bigstarting`, but not `start` or `starting`, as follows:

```
$ awk '/\Bstart\B/'  gopr.txt
```

The output on execution of the preceding code is as follows:

```
bigstarting
```

Case-sensitive matching

In bracket expressions, we can use both lowercase and uppercase characters to match the characters for case-insensitive results, but the same is not true for other regular expressions. However, this becomes difficult if you have to match to many characters. Here comes the two built-in string functions of AWK, `tolower()` and `toupper()`. Using these two functions, we can perform case-insensitive match operations.

For example, to match the first name `'John'` of an employee in the `emp.dat` file, we can perform a case-insensitive match using the `tolower()` function, as follows:

```
$ awk 'tolower($1) ~ /john/' emp.dat
```

The output on execution of this code is as follows:

```
John     Kapur    9911556789   john@gmail.com      M    hr     2200
```

Another way to perform a case-insensitive match operation is by setting the `IGNORECASE` bash variable value to `TRUE`.

Escape sequences

When using regular expressions and strings, certain characters cannot be included literally in string constants (`"hello"`) or regular expression constants (`/hello/`). To specify the characters for which there may not be other notations, they are represented as escape sequences. Escape sequences begin with a backslash (`'\'`). For example, it can represent that an `\n` newline character is used, which otherwise cannot be represented in strings or regular expressions. Similarly, `\b` stands for backspace, `\t` stands for tab, and `\/` represents a forward slash. They are quite useful in generating formatted output.

For example, to insert a new line after each line of the `emp.dat` file, we can use the `\n` escape sequence, as follows:

```
$ awk '{ print $0"\n" }' emp.dat
```

The output on execution of the given code is as follows:

```
Jack     Singh    9857532312   jack@gmail.com      M    hr     2000

Jane     Kaur     9837432312   jane@gmail.com      F    hr     1800

Eva      Chabra   8827232115   eva@gmail.com       F    lgs    2100
```

Amit	Sharma	9911887766	amit@yahoo.com	M	lgs	2350
Julie	Kapur	8826234556	julie@yahoo.com	F	Ops	2500
Ana	Khanna	9856422312	anak@hotmail.com	F	Ops	2700
Hari	Singh	8827255666	hari@yahoo.com	M	Ops	2350
Victor	Sharma	8826567898	vics@hotmail.com	M	Ops	2500
John	Kapur	9911556789	john@gmail.com	M	hr	2200
Billy	Chabra	9911664321	bily@yahoo.com	M	lgs	1900
Sam	khanna	8856345512	sam@hotmail.com	F	lgs	2300
Ginny	Singh	9857123466	ginny@yahoo.com	F	hr	2250
Emily	Kaur	8826175812	emily@gmail.com	F	Ops	2100
Amy	Sharma	9857536898	amys@hotmail.com	F	Ops	2500
Vina	Singh	8811776612	vina@yahoo.com	F	lgs	2300

The following table summarizes the most-used escape sequences:

Escape sequence	Meaning
\\	Insert a literal backslash, \
\/	Insert a literal forward slash, /
\"	Insert a double quote, "
\a	Matches alert character (this produces a bell sound)
\b	Insert a backspace
\f	Insert a form feed
\n	Insert a new line
\r	Insert a carriage return
\t	Insert a horizontal tab
\v	Insert a vertical tab
\ddd	Octal value ddd, where ddd stands for 1 to 3 digits between 0 and 7

Finally, we can summarize the regular expressions with the help of the following table:

Regular expression	Meaning
.	Any single character except a new line
^	Beginning of a line
$	End of a line
[...]	Range of characters given within the square brackets
[^..]	A character that is not one of those within the square brackets
*	Match zero or more preceding items
+	Match one or more preceding items
?	Match zero or one preceding items
{n}	Match the preceding item exactly n times
{n,}	Match the preceding item n or more times
{n,m}	Match the preceding item a minimum of n and a maximum of m times
\	Remove the special meaning of the next character (quoted metacharacter)
\(..\)	Back-reference, remembers pattern
\1 ... \9	Back-reference, recalls pattern
( )	Group a part of regular expressions into a sub-expression
(...|...)	Alternation operator, match what is on either the left or right of the pipe symbol
\s	Match any character considered whitespace
\S	Match any character not considered whitespace
\w	Match any character that is a word character (a-zA-Z0-9_)
\W	Match any character that is not a word character
\<	Matches the beginning of a word
\>	Matches the end of a word

Summary

In this chapter, we learned about regular expressions. We learned the regular expression construct using literals and metacharacters. Then, we learned the usage of various different regular expression metacharacters, which are also known as regular expression operators. Finally, we covered some GAWK-specific regular expression metacharacter usage and understood escape sequences and their role in regular expressions.

In the next chapter, we will learn about handling AWK variables and constants while writing AWK programs.

3
AWK Variables and Constants

This chapter will focus on the usage of AWK variables. By the end of the chapter, the reader will understand how to use built-in and user-defined variables while writing AWK programs and command lines. Almost all expressions contain variables. Some of the variables are user-defined, while some are built-in, and others are fields. A variable is a named location that is either a string or a number, or both. User-defined variables in AWK consist of sequences of alphanumeric characters and underscores, with the exception that they do not begin with a digit. All built-in variables have uppercase names. The AWK variable type is not declared, but automatically infers the type from the context. When required, AWK converts a string value to a numeric value and vice versa. This chapter will give you a deep insight into different built-in and environment variables in AWK. We will also see how string and numeric constants can be used to process different fields in data files.

In this chapter, we will cover the following:

- Predefined variables in AWK
- Environment variables in AWK and GAWK
- String and numeric constants
- Conversion between strings and numbers

Built-in variables in AWK

Variables play an important role when creating AWK scripts and programs. They modify the behavior of AWK commands. AWK built-in variables have uppercase names. These built-in variables can be used in all expressions, and can be reset by the user. They are set automatically. The following sections discuss the different built-in variables in AWK.

Field separator

The **field separator** (**FS**) is either a single character or a regular expression. It decides the way AWK splits an input record into fields. The FS is represented by the built-in variable FS, and its default value is a single space. It tells AWK to separate fields across any number of spaces and/or tabs.

Using a single character or simple string as a value of the FS

Fields are normally separated by whitespace sequences (spaces, tabs, and newlines). In this case, leading and trailing whitespaces (spaces or tabs) are stripped from the current input line, and fields are separated by a space or a tab. The AWK default value of the FS is a single space, and AWK normally splits the record into fields in this way.

Like other AWK variables, its value can be changed at any time in a program with the assignment operator =. Usually, the correct time to do this is before any input line has been read, hence it is generally defined in the BEGIN block, although we can define these variables anywhere in the script. When the FS is set to any single character other than blank, then that character becomes the FS.

For example, we know that the /etc/passwd file in Linux stores users' details in seven fields separated by six colon signs (:). If we need to print only usernames from our system, we can use AWK variables as follows:

```
$ awk 'BEGIN { FS=":" } ; {print $1}' /etc/passwd
```

The output of the execution of the preceding code is as follows:

```
root
daemon
bin
sys
sync
games
man
mail
news
uucp
proxy
irc
gnats
nobody
mysql
. . . . . . . . . . .
```

An example of using a string as the FS is as follows:

```
$ echo "Linux is awesome..!" | awk 'BEGIN {FS="is"};{print $2}'
```

The output of the execution of this code is as follows:

```
awesome..!
```

 Note that we can set FS = ":" to any single character or string, but to set a single character or a special character, we specify it within square brackets as FS = "[ ]" (for a single space).

Using regular expressions as values of the FS

If a string is longer than a single character, it is considered as a regular expression while setting the FS. The FS can have any string containing any regular expression. Whenever the match is found for the regular expression, it separates the fields. Multiple FS can be specified within square brackets, as shown in the following example:

```
$ echo "a:b;c,d" | awk 'BEGIN { FS = "[:;,]"} ; {print $1, $2, $3, $4 }'
```

In the preceding example, we specify multiple FS as :, ;, and , .

The output of the execution of this code is as follows:

```
a b c d
```

In our next example, the FS matches the hello phrase:

```
$ echo -e "Hey...! Hello Good Morning\nHey..! hello good morning" | awk
'BEGIN {FS="[Hh]ello"}{print $1}'
```

The output of the execution of this command is as follows:

```
Hey...!
Hey..!
```

The FS retains its value until it is explicitly allotted a new value. We can change the FS value as many times as we want while reading a file. Let us create a file that contains mixed data in which lines four to six have colon-separated fields, while others are separated by spaces, as follows:

```
$ vi  ch3_1.dat
sam 8800554422
#entry
jack:9900334433
vij:7788991122
#exit
ralph 8822334411
```

Now, to switch between two different FS, we can perform the following:

```
$ vi fs1.awk
{
if ($1 == "#entry")
{ FS=":"; }
else if ($1 == "#exit")
{ FS=" "; }
else
{ print $2 }
}

$ awk -f fs1.awk ch3_1.dat
```

The output of the execution of the preceding code is as follows:

```
8800554422
9900334433
7788991122
8822334411
```

The same logic can also be applied in another way, as follows:

```
$ vi fs2.awk

{
  if ( $0 ~ /:/ )
    { FS=":";}
  else
    { FS=" ";}
    print $2
}

$ awk -f fs2.awk ch3_1.dat
```

The output of the execution of the preceding code is as follows:

```
8800554422


7788991122

8822334411
```

We can define the FS either before or after reading the current line. It has no effect on the current input line. Once the defined value is read in the variable, it does not change until we change it ourselves.

Using each character as a separate field

If you want to print or examine each character of a line separately, then you can do this by defining a null string as an FS. In that case, each character in that line will become a separate field, as shown in the following example:

```
$ echo "hello good morning" |awk 'BEGIN {FS =""};{print
$1,$2,$3,$4,$5,$NF}'
```

The output of the execution of the preceding code is as follows:

```
h e l l o g
```

Using the command line to set the FS as -F

We can also define the FS on the command line using option -F. For example:

```
$ awk -F":" '{print $1}' /etc/passwd
```

The output of the execution of this command is as follows:

```
root
daemon
bin
sys
sync
games
man
lp
mail
news
uucp
nobody
.........
```

Output field separator

The default value of the **output field separator** (**OFS**) is space. It is the output equivalent of the FS. We can set any string of characters to be used as the OFS by setting the predefined variable to OFS. The OFS is generated when we put a comma in the print statement to separate the arguments. For example, when we print the field without using a comma, then each of the field values are written contiguously in the output, as follows:

```
$ awk '{print NR"." $1 $3 $4}' emp.dat
```

The output of the execution of this code is as follows:

```
1.Jack9857532312jack@gmail.com
2.Jane9837432312jane@gmail.com
3.Eva8827232115eva@gmail.com
4.Amit9911887766amit@yahoo.com
5.Julie8826234556julie@yahoo.com
6.Ana9856422312anak@hotmail.com
7.Hari8827255666hari@yahoo.com
8.Victor8826567898vics@hotmail.com
9.John9911556789john@gmail.com
10.Billy9911664321bily@yahoo.com
11.Sam8856345512sam@hotmail.com
```

```
12.Ginny9857123466ginny@yahoo.com
13.Emily8826175812emily@gmail.com
14.Amy9857536898amys@hotmail.com
15.Vina8811776612vina@yahoo.com
```

On the other hand, when we use comma to separate fields in the output, each field value is separated by a single space, as follows:

```
$ awk '{print NR"." $1,$3,$4}' emp.dat
```

The output of the execution of the preceding code is as follows:

```
1.Jack 9857532312 jack@gmail.com
2.Jane 9837432312 jane@gmail.com
3.Eva 8827232115 eva@gmail.com
4.Amit 9911887766 amit@yahoo.com
5.Julie 8826234556 julie@yahoo.com
6.Ana 9856422312 anak@hotmail.com
7.Hari 8827255666 hari@yahoo.com
8.Victor 8826567898 vics@hotmail.com
9.John 9911556789 john@gmail.com
10.Billy 9911664321 bily@yahoo.com
11.Sam 8856345512 sam@hotmail.com
12.Ginny 9857123466 ginny@yahoo.com
13.Emily 8826175812 emily@gmail.com
14.Amy 9857536898 amys@hotmail.com
15.Vina 8811776612 vina@yahoo.com
```

We can set the OFS for any single character or any number of characters. Now we will set the value of the OFS as \t: in the BEGIN block; then each field value is separated by a tab and a colon, as follows:

```
$ vi setofs.awk

#!/usr/bin/awk -f
BEGIN { OFS = "\t:" }
{print $1,$3,$4}

$ awk -f setofs.awk emp.dat
```

The output of the execution of the preceding code is as follows:

```
Jack    :9857532312    :jack@gmail.com
Jane    :9837432312    :jane@gmail.com
Eva     :8827232115    :eva@gmail.com
Amit    :9911887766    :amit@yahoo.com
Julie   :8826234556    :julie@yahoo.com
Ana     :9856422312    :anak@hotmail.com
```

```
Hari     :8827255666     :hari@yahoo.com
Victor   :8826567898     :vics@hotmail.com
John     :9911556789     :john@gmail.com
Billy    :9911664321     :bily@yahoo.com
Sam      :8856345512     :sam@hotmail.com
Ginny    :9857123466     :ginny@yahoo.com
Emily    :8826175812     :emily@gmail.com
Amy      :9857536898     :amys@hotmail.com
Vina     :8811776612     :vina@yahoo.com
```

Now we will set the OFS as an ABC string, as follows:

```
$ awk 'BEGIN { OFS="ABC"}{print $1, $2 }' emp.dat
```

The output of the execution of this code is as follows:

```
JackABCSingh
JaneABCKaur
EvaABCChabra
AmitABCSharma
JulieABCKapur
AnaABCKhanna
HariABCSingh
VictorABCSharma
JohnABCKapur
BillyABCChabra
SamABCkhanna
GinnyABCSingh
EmilyABCKaur
AmyABCSharma
VinaABCSingh
```

Similarly, we can use AWK to generate a CSV file, which is a primitive method of creating a flat file database out of a text file. Let us create an AWK file to convert our cars.dat file, which contain five fields, as follows:

```
$ vi txt2csv.awk

BEGIN {
  IFS="\t"
  OFS=","
      }
{ print $1, $2, $3, $4, $5 }

$ awk -f txt2csv.awk cars.dat > cars.csv
```

On execution of this command, it will create a `cars.csv` file in the same directory. The contents of `cars.csv` are as follows:

```
$ cat cars.csv
maruti,swift,2007,50000,5
honda,city,2005,60000,3
maruti,dezire,2009,3100,6
chevy,beat,2005,33000,2
honda,city,2010,33000,6
chevy,tavera,1999,10000,4
toyota,corolla,1995,95000,2
maruti,swift,2009,4100,5
maruti,esteem,1997,98000,1
ford,ikon,1995,80000,1
honda,accord,2000,60000,2
fiat,punto,2007,45000,3
```

This is mainly useful when we want to generate a formatted report. We can set the `OFS` as a sequence of characters, such as a comma followed by a space and so on.

Record separator

The **record separator** (**RS**) defines the input `RS` for AWK and its default value is set as a single new line. As with other AWK variables, we can redefine the `RS` as a new value. While defining the new input `RS`, it needs to be enclosed in quotation marks as a string constant in the `BEGIN` block. For example, let us set the new input record separator as a single dot (`.`) for the employee database `emp.dat` file as follows:

```
$ awk 'BEGIN { RS="."}{ print}' emp.dat
```

The output of the execution of this code is as follows:

```
Jack Singh 9857532312 jack@gmail
com M hr 2000
Jane Kaur 9837432312 jane@gmail
com F hr 1800
Eva Chabra 8827232115 eva@gmail
com F lgs 2100
Amit Sharma 9911887766 amit@yahoo
com M lgs 2350
Julie Kapur 8826234556 julie@yahoo
com F Ops 2500
Ana Khanna 9856422312 anak@hotmail
com F Ops 2700
Hari Singh 8827255666 hari@yahoo
```

```
com M Ops 2350
Victor Sharma 8826567898 vics@hotmail
com M Ops 2500
John Kapur 9911556789 john@gmail
com M hr 2200
. . . . . . . . . . . .
. . . . . . . . . . . .
```

RS, when assigned a null value, matches an empty line to separate multiline records in a file. Now let us create a file that contains the following information so that we can look at how the RS works when it is set to null—that is, RS=" ":

```
$ vi label.dat

Jack
9988776655
jack@gmail.com
Sam
8855991122
sam@gmail.com

$ vi   rs1.awk
#!/usr/bin/awk -f

BEGIN { RS=""; OFS="\t" }
{print $1,$2,$3 }

$ awk -f rs1.awk label.dat
```

The output of the execution of the preceding code is as follows:

```
Jack    9988776655     jack@gmail.com
Sam     8855991122     sam@gmail.com
```

It is important to note that you can arrange for whole files to be treated as a single record by setting the RS to a value that you know will not occur in the input file. So, most of the time we can set a null character as the separator (RS = "\0") as shown in the following example:

```
$ awk 'BEGIN { RS="\0" }{print $8}' emp.dat
```

Outputting the record separator

The default value of the **output record separator** (**ORS**) is a single newline by default. We assign new values to the variable ORS to change how records are separated. It is also used to create a formatted output. Let us say that we want to print each line separated by a sequence of special character asterisks, as follows:

```
$ vi   ors.awk

#!/usr/bin/awk -f
BEGIN {
ORS="\n********************************************************\n"
}
{ print $0 }

$ awk -f ors.awk emp.dat
```

The output of the execution of the preceding code is as follows:

```
Jack     Singh    9857532312   jack@gmail.com       M   hr    2000
**********************************************************************
Jane     Kaur     9837432312   jane@gmail.com       F   hr    1800
**********************************************************************
Eva      Chabra   8827232115   eva@gmail.com        F   lgs   2100
**********************************************************************
Amit     Sharma   9911887766   amit@yahoo.com       M   lgs   2350
**********************************************************************
Julie    Kapur    8826234556   julie@yahoo.com      F   Ops   2500
**********************************************************************
Ana      Khanna   9856422312   anak@hotmail.com     F   Ops   2700
**********************************************************************

.........
.........
```

To separate each record in a file by two newlines, we can set ORS to "\n\n". For example:

```
$ awk 'BEGIN { ORS="\n\n" } {print}' emp.dat
```

The output of the execution of this code is as follows:

```
Jack     Singh    9857532312   jack@gmail.com       M   hr    2000

Jane     Kaur     9837432312   jane@gmail.com       F   hr    1800

Eva      Chabra   8827232115   eva@gmail.com        F   lgs   2100

Amit     Sharma   9911887766   amit@yahoo.com       M   lgs   2350
```

Julie	Kapur	8826234556	julie@yahoo.com	F	Ops	2500
Ana	Khanna	9856422312	anak@hotmail.com	F	Ops	2700
Hari	Singh	8827255666	hari@yahoo.com	M	Ops	2350

. . . .
. . . .

If we set `ORS` to an empty string, then the output records are not separated at all. Take the following example:

```
$ awk 'BEGIN { ORS="" } {print}' emp.dat
```

The output of the execution of this code is as follows:

```
Jack Singh 9857532312 jack@gmail.com M hr 2000Jane Kaur 9837432312
jane@gmail.com F hr 1800Eva Chabra 8827232115 eva@gmail.com F lgs 2100Amit
Sharma 9911887766 amit@yahoo.com M lgs 2350Julie Kapur 8826234556
julie@yahoo.com F Ops 2500Ana Khanna 9856422312 anak@hotmail.com F Ops
2700Hari Singh 8827255666 hari@yahoo.com M Ops 2350Victor Sharma 8826567898
vics@hotmail.com M Ops 2500John Kapur 9911556789 john@gmail.com M hr
2200Billy Chabra 9911664321 bily@yahoo.com M lgs 1900Sam khanna 8856345512
sam@hotmail.com F lgs 2300Ginny Singh 9857123466 ginny@yahoo.com F hr
2250Emily Kaur 8826175812 emily@gmail.com F Ops 2100Amy Sharma 9857536898
amys@hotmail.com F Ops 2500Vina Singh 8811776612 vina@yahoo.com F lgs 2300
```

NR and NF

NR and NF are set each time a new record is read.

AWK sets the variable `NR` whenever a new record from input file is read. It's value represent the number of current input record being processed by AWK. It is generally used to number the records in a file. For example, to print the number of records with each record in the output from the `emp.dat` file, we can use it as follows:

```
$ awk '{ print NR "." $0 }' emp.dat
```

The output of the execution of the preceding code is as follows:

1.Jack	Singh	9857532312	jack@gmail.com	M	hr	2000
2.Jane	Kaur	9837432312	jane@gmail.com	F	hr	1800
3.Eva	Chabra	8827232115	eva@gmail.com	F	lgs	2100
4.Amit	Sharma	9911887766	amit@yahoo.com	M	lgs	2350
5.Julie	Kapur	8826234556	julie@yahoo.com	F	Ops	2500
6.Ana	Khanna	9856422312	anak@hotmail.com	F	Ops	2700

7.Hari	Singh	8827255666	hari@yahoo.com	M	Ops	2350
8.Victor	Sharma	8826567898	vics@hotmail.com	M	Ops	2500
9.John	Kapur	9911556789	john@gmail.com	M	hr	2200

```
. . . . . . . . . . . . . . . . . . . . . . . . . .
. . . . . . . . . . . . . . . . . . . . . . . . . .
```

After the last input line is read, NR will contain the number of input records read until that time. Thus, it can be used to print the total number of records processed in the END block to provide a summary. So, we can print the name and phone number of employees in emp.dat as follows:

```
$ vi phonelist.awk

#!/usr/bin/awk  -f

{ print $1, "\t:" $3 }
END     {
        print ""
        print "Total no. of records processed : ", NR
        }

$ awk -f phonelist.awk emp.dat
```

The output of the execution of the preceding code is as follows:

```
Jack      :9857532312
Jane      :9837432312
Eva       :8827232115
Amit      :9911887766
Julie     :8826234556
Ana       :9856422312
Hari      :8827255666
Victor    :8826567898
John      :9911556789
Billy     :9911664321
Sam       :8856345512
Ginny     :9857123466
Emily     :8826175812
Amy       :9857536898
Vina      :8811776612

Total no. of records processed : 15
```

We can use NR to make AWK examine only a certain number of lines. For example, to print the lines after the first five lines in the emp.dat file, we can use NR as follows:

```
$ vi read_line_after_5.awk

#!/usr/bin/awk -f

{
if ( NR > 5 )
{ print NR, $0 }
}

$ awk -f read_line_after_5.awk emp.dat
```

The output of the execution of the preceding code is as follows:

```
6  Ana     Khanna   9856422312  anak@hotmail.com   F  Ops  2700
7  Hari    Singh    8827255666  hari@yahoo.com     M  Ops  2350
8  Victor  Sharma   8826567898  vics@hotmail.com   M  Ops  2500
9  John    Kapur    9911556789  john@gmail.com     M  hr   2200
10 Billy   Chabra   9911664321  bily@yahoo.com     M  lgs  1900
11 Sam     khanna   8856345512  sam@hotmail.com    F  lgs  2300
12 Ginny   Singh    9857123466  ginny@yahoo.com    F  hr   2250
13 Emily   Kaur     8826175812  emily@gmail.com    F  Ops  2100
14 Amy     Sharma   9857536898  amys@hotmail.com   F  Ops  2500
15 Vina    Singh    8811776612  vina@yahoo.com     F  lgs  2300
```

We can also print lines selectively using NR. In the following example we print the record number 2 and the record number 4 selectively, as follows:

```
$ awk 'NR==2||NR==4{print NR, $0 }' emp.dat
```

The output of the execution of this code is as follows:

```
2  Jane  Kaur    9837432312  jane@gmail.com   F  hr   1800
4  Amit  Sharma  9911887766  amit@yahoo.com   M  lgs  2350
```

We can also print a range of line numbers with NR by specifying the first record number, followed by a comma, followed by the last record number that you want to process, as follows:

```
$ awk 'NR==5,NR==10{print NR, $0 }' emp.dat
```

The output of the execution of this code is as follows:

```
5 Julie    Kapur    8826234556   julie@yahoo.com    F   Ops   2500
6 Ana      Khanna   9856422312   anak@hotmail.com   F   Ops   2700
7 Hari     Singh    8827255666   hari@yahoo.com     M   Ops   2350
8 Victor   Sharma   8826567898   vics@hotmail.com   M   Ops   2500
9 John     Kapur    9911556789   john@gmail.com     M   hr    2200
10 Billy   Chabra   9911664321   bily@yahoo.com     M   lgs   1900
```

NF is reset when $0 changes or when a new field is created. The NF variable defines the number of fields for the current input line. We can use NF to check whether the record has the number of fields that we expect or not. We can also use NF to refer to fields by prefixing it with the $ field operator so that $NF will always print the last field of the current input record. $(NF -1) will access the second to last field of each record, and so on. For example, the employee database file emp.dat contains the salaries of employees in USD; we can print that value using NF as follows:

```
$ vi nf1.awk

#!/usr/bin/awk -f

{ print "No. of fields : ", NF," and last field :",$(NF) }

$ awk -f nf1.awk emp.dat
```

The output of the execution of the preceding code is as follows:

```
No. of fields :  7  and last field : 2000
No. of fields :  7  and last field : 1800
No. of fields :  7  and last field : 2100
No. of fields :  7  and last field : 2350
No. of fields :  7  and last field : 2500
No. of fields :  7  and last field : 2700
No. of fields :  7  and last field : 2350
No. of fields :  7  and last field : 2500
No. of fields :  7  and last field : 2200
No. of fields :  7  and last field : 1900
No. of fields :  7  and last field : 2300
No. of fields :  7  and last field : 2250
No. of fields :  7  and last field : 2100
No. of fields :  7  and last field : 2500
No. of fields :  7  and last field : 2300
```

Sometimes, it is useful to know how many fields there are in a line. We can modify the script operation on a number of fields. Let us create a file that contains a different number of fields in multiple lines, as follows:

```
$ vi varying_fields.dat

Jack Singh 9857532312 jack@gmail.com M hr 2000
Jane 9837432312 jane@gmail.com F hr 1800
Eva Chabra 8827232115 eva@gmail.com F lgs 2100
Amit 9911887766 amit@yahoo.com M lgs 2350
Julie Kapur 8826234556 julie@yahoo.com F Ops 2500
Ana 9856422312 anak@hotmail.com F Ops 2700
```

Say that we want to print the username and phone number for each employee. To do this, we can print the field number 1 and field number 3 for the record that has a total number of seven fields. For the records with six fields, we can print the field number 1 and field number 2 as follows:

```
$ vi nf2.awk

#!/usr/bin/awk -f

{
if (NF == 7)
{
    print $1, $3;
}
else if (NF == 6)
{
    print $1, $2;
}
}

$ awk -f nf2.awk varying_fields.dat
```

The output of the execution of the preceding code is as follows:

```
Jack 9857532312
Jane 9837432312
Eva 8827232115
Amit 9911887766
Julie 8826234556
Ana 9856422312
```

There is a limit of 99 fields in a single line in AWK.

FILENAME

FILENAME is set each time a new file is read. It stores the name of the current input file being read. This can be used when multiple files need to be parsed by AWK. When no data files are given on the command line, AWK reads from stdin and FILENAME is set to "-". In that case, you have to enter records in standard input, and once you are done, press *Ctrl +* *C* to stop reading from stdin. Let us begin with a very basic example:

```
$ awk 'END{print FILENAME}' cars.dat
```

The output of the execution of this command is as follows:

```
cars.dat
```

Now we will process the two files, cars.dat and emp.dat, and print some data from these files, as follows:

```
$ vi filename.awk

#!/usr/bin/awk -f

BEGIN   { f1="";
          f2="";
        }
{
if ( FILENAME == "cars.dat" )
{
print NR, $1,"\t", $2 ;
f1=FILENAME;
}
else
{
print;
f2=FILENAME;
}
}
END    {
print "First file processed is ", f1;
print "Second file processed is ", f2;
}

$ awk -f filename.awk cars.dat emp.dat
```

The output of the execution of the preceding code is as follows:

```
1 maruti     swift
2 honda      city
3 maruti      dezire
4 chevy      beat
5 honda      city
6 chevy      tavera
7 toyota      corolla
8 maruti      swift
9 maruti      esteem
10 ford      ikon
11 honda      accord
12 fiat       punto
Jack     Singh    9857532312   jack@gmail.com     M   hr    2000
Jane     Kaur     9837432312   jane@gmail.com     F   hr    1800
Eva      Chabra   8827232115   eva@gmail.com      F   lgs   2100
Amit     Sharma   9911887766   amit@yahoo.com     M   lgs   2350
Julie    Kapur    8826234556   julie@yahoo.com    F   Ops   2500
Ana      Khanna   9856422312   anak@hotmail.com   F   Ops   2700
Hari     Singh    8827255666   hari@yahoo.com     M   Ops   2350
Victor   Sharma   8826567898   vics@hotmail.com   M   Ops   2500
John     Kapur    9911556789   john@gmail.com     M   hr    2200
Billy    Chabra   9911664321   bily@yahoo.com     M   lgs   1900
Sam      khanna   8856345512   sam@hotmail.com    F   lgs   2300
Ginny    Singh    9857123466   ginny@yahoo.com    F   hr    2250
Emily    Kaur     8826175812   emily@gmail.com    F   Ops   2100
Amy      Sharma   9857536898   amys@hotmail.com   F   Ops   2500
Vina     Singh    8811776612   vina@yahoo.com     F   lgs   2300
First file processed is   cars.dat
Second file processed is   emp.dat
```

Environment variables in AWK

Like other programming environments, AWK also has environment variables. In this section, we will discuss the different environment variables available to users in the AWK programming language.

ARGC and ARGV

The ARGC and ARGV variables are used to pass arguments to the AWK script from the command line.

ARGC specifies the total number of arguments passed to the AWK script on the command line. It always has a value of 1 or more, as it counts the program name as the first argument.

The AWK script filename specified using the -f option is not counted as an argument. If we declare any variable on the command line, it is counted as an argument in GAWK:

```
$ awk 'BEGIN { print "No of arguments =", ARGC }' one two three four
```

The output of the execution of the preceding command is as follows:

```
No of arguments = 5
```

ARGV is an array that stores all the arguments passed to the AWK command, starting from index 0 through to ARGC. ARGV[0] always contains AWK.

In the following example, we show how ARGV and ARGC work. Here, ARGV[0] will store the AWK:

```
$ vi arguments.awk

BEGIN    {
             print "Total no. of arguments =", ARGC
             for ( i=0; i<ARGC; i++ )
             printf "ARGV[%d] = %s\n", i, ARGV[i]
}

$ awk -f arguments.awk a1 a2 a3 a4
```

The output of the execution of the preceding code is as follows:

```
Total no. of arguments = 5
ARGV[0] = awk
ARGV[1] = a1
ARGV[2] = a2
ARGV[3] = a3
ARGV[4] = a4
```

The variable assignment using the -v option is also not counted in the command-line argument; however, normal variable assignment is counted in the command-line argument, and is accessible through ARGV. For example:

```
$ awk -v A=10 -f arguments.awk B=20 one two three
```

The output of the execution of this code is as follows:

```
Total no. of arguments = 5
ARGV[0] = awk
ARGV[1] = B=20
ARGV[2] = one
ARGV[3] = two
ARGV[4] = three
```

In the next example, we pass arguments to the script in the format `- - argument_name argument_value`. The AWK script will accept the employee's first name, `empfname`, and salary, `empsal`, as arguments. If we use `- - name Amit 4000` as an argument for the AWK script, it will set the salary as `4000` for the employee name `Amit` as follows:

```
$ vi argc_argv.awk

BEGIN {
    OFS="\t"
    for ( i=0; i<ARGC; i++ )
    {
        if ( ARGV[i]=="--name")
        {
            empfname=ARGV[i+1];
            empsal=ARGV[i+2];
            delete ARGV[i]
            delete ARGV[i+1]
            delete ARGV[i+2]
        }
    }
}
{
if ( $1==empfname)
    print $1,$2,$3,$4,$5,$6,empsal
else
    print $0;
}

$ awk -f argc_argv.awk --name Amit 4000 emp.dat
```

The output of the execution of the preceding code is as follows:

```
Jack     Singh    9857532312   jack@gmail.com      M    hr      2000
Jane     Kaur     9837432312   jane@gmail.com      F    hr      1800
Eva      Chabra   8827232115   eva@gmail.com       F    lgs     2100
Amit     Sharma   9911887766     amit@yahoo.com     M    lgs     4000
Julie    Kapur    8826234556   julie@yahoo.com     F    Ops     2500
Ana      Khanna   9856422312   anak@hotmail.com    F    Ops     2700
```

Hari	Singh	8827255666	hari@yahoo.com	M	Ops	2350
Victor	Sharma	8826567898	vics@hotmail.com	M	Ops	2500
John	Kapur	9911556789	john@gmail.com	M	hr	2200
Billy	Chabra	9911664321	bily@yahoo.com	M	lgs	1900
Sam	khanna	8856345512	sam@hotmail.com	F	lgs	2300
Ginny	Singh	9857123466	ginny@yahoo.com	F	hr	2250
Emily	Kaur	8826175812	emily@gmail.com	F	Ops	2100
Amy	Sharma	9857536898	amys@hotmail.com	F	Ops	2500
Vina	Singh	8811776612	vina@yahoo.com	F	lgs	230

CONVFMT and OFMT

CONVFMT is used to control number-to-string conversion—that is, when a number is converted to a string, AWK will use the CONVFMT format to decide how to print the values. CONVFMT has its default value set as %.6g, which implies a total of six characters, including both sides of a dot in a number. This variable was added in POSIX-compliant AWK. We can print the value contained in the format specifier CONVFMT variable with the help of the following command:

```
$ awk 'BEGIN { print "Conversion Format =", CONVFMT}'
```

The output of the execution of this command is as follows:

```
Conversion Format = %.6g
```

When we use g as the format specifier, it counts all the characters on both sides of the dot. For example, %.4g means a total of 4 characters will be printed, including characters on both sides of the dot.

When we use f as the format specifier, it counts only the characters on the right side of the dot. For example, %.4f means 4 characters will be printed on the right side of the dot. The total number of characters on the left side of the dot does not matter.

When we use d as the format specifier, it converts the characters into an integer format. For example, %d means the all the characters before the dot will be printed and no character on the right side of the dot will be printed. This converts all numbers to strings in an integer format.

The following example AWK script convfmt.awk explains how the output can be formatted when using various CONVFMT values (for g, f, and d as format specifiers):

```
$ vi convfmt.awk
```

```
BEGIN    {
    A=123.123456789
    print "---Default CONVFMT---";
    printf "%s\n", A;
    print "====================";
    CONVFMT="%.4g";
    print "---%.4g as CONVFMT---";
    printf "%s\n", A;
    print "====================";

    CONVFMT="%.8g";
    print "---%.8g as CONVFMT---";
    printf "%s\n", A;
    print "====================";
    CONVFMT="%2.2f";
    print "---%.2.2f as CONVFMT---";
    printf "%s\n", A;
    print "====================";
    CONVFMT="%d";
    print "---%d as CONVFMT---";
    printf "%s\n", A;
    print "====================";
    }

$ awk -f convfmt.awk
```

The output of the execution of the preceding code is as follows:

```
---Default CONVFMT---
123.123
====================
---%.4g as CONVFMT---
123.1
====================
---%.8g as CONVFMT---
123.12346
====================
---%.2.2f as CONVFMT---
123.12
====================
---%d as CONVFMT---
123
====================
```

With CONVFMT, we use the printf command for printing the output, as we did in the previous example. However, if you want to use a print statement, then first you have to force it to be converted into numbers by adding zero and then suffix it with an empty string " " to force it to convert into a string before printing the same output as print A+0" ".

Before CONVFMT was introduced by POSIX, OFMT was used to serve the purpose of string-to-number conversion. It uses the print statement to perform the same job of controlling the conversion of numeric values to a strings.

The following example explains the same use of format specifiers %f, %g, and %d with the OFMT command:

```
$ vi ofmt.awk

BEGIN    {
    A=123.123456789
    print "---Default OFMT---";
    print A;
    print "====================";

    OFMT="%.4g";
    print "---%.4g as OFMT---";
    print A;
    print "====================";

    OFMT="%.8g";
    print "---%.8g as OFMT---";
    print A;
    print "====================";

    OFMT="%2.2f";
    print "---%.2.2f as OFMT---";
    print A;
    print "====================";

    OFMT="%d";
    print "---%d as OFMT---";
    print A;
    print "====================";
    }

$ awk -f ofmt.awk
```

The output of the execution of the preceding command is as follows:

```
---Default OFMT---
123.123
====================
---%.4g as OFMT---
123.1
====================
---%.8g as OFMT---
123.12346
====================
---%.2.2f as OFMT---
123.12
====================
---%d as OFMT---
123
====================
```

It is important to note that the numbers that are integers are always converted to strings that are integers, irrespective of the set values of CONVFMT and OFMT.

RLENGTH and RSTART

The match function searches for a given string/pattern/regular expression in the input string and returns a positive value when a successful match occurs. It sets the two special variables, RSTART and RLENGTH, that indicate where a regular expression begins and ends:

- RSTART: This stores the starting location of the search string/pattern
- RLENGTH: This stores the length of the search string/pattern

The contents of the RLENGTH or RSTART variable are set/changed when the match function is invoked.

In the following example, we use the match function to search for a pattern and print all that is present before and after the pattern—as well as the pattern itself, separately—as follows:

```
$ vi match.awk

BEGIN    {
    regex="Singh";
    }
{
```

```
    if (match($0,regex))
    {
        before=substr($0,1,RSTART-1);
        pattern=substr($0,RSTART,RLENGTH);
        after=substr($0,RSTART+RLENGTH);
        printf("BEFORE : %s, PATTERN : %s, AFTER : %s\n",before,pattern,
after);
    }
}

$ awk -f match.awk emp.dat
```

The output of the execution of the preceding code is as follows:

```
BEFORE : Jack      , PATTERN : Singh, AFTER :     9857532312  jack@gmail.com
M    hr       2000
BEFORE : Hari      , PATTERN : Singh, AFTER :     8827255666  hari@yahoo.com
M    Ops      2350
BEFORE : Ginny     , PATTERN : Singh, AFTER :     9857123466  ginny@yahoo.com
F    hr       2250
BEFORE : Vina      , PATTERN : Singh, AFTER :     8811776612  vina@yahoo.com
F    lgs      2300
```

FNR

The FNR is set each time a new record is read. It useful when dealing with multiple input files. It provides the access to the number of current input records relevant to the current input file. Whereas NR continues to grow between multiple files, it continues to incrementally grow from the last NR number value of the previous file until the last record of the last file is processed.

In the following example, we print the NR and FNR values while processing two files consecutively, as follows:

```
$ vi  fnr.awk

BEGIN   {
        print "Example to show both NR and FNR difference..!"
    }
{
    printf "FILENAME=%s  NR=%s  FNR=%s\n", FILENAME, NR, FNR;
}
END     {
    printf "END Block: NR=%s FNR=%s\n", NR, FNR
```

```
}

$ awk -f fnr.awk label.dat cars.dat
```

The output of the execution of the preceding code is as follows:

```
Example to show both NR and FNR difference..!
FILENAME=label.dat   NR=1   FNR=1
FILENAME=label.dat   NR=2   FNR=2
FILENAME=label.dat   NR=3   FNR=3
FILENAME=label.dat   NR=4   FNR=4
FILENAME=label.dat   NR=5   FNR=5
FILENAME=label.dat   NR=6   FNR=6
FILENAME=label.dat   NR=7   FNR=7
FILENAME=cars.dat    NR=8   FNR=1
FILENAME=cars.dat    NR=9   FNR=2
FILENAME=cars.dat    NR=10  FNR=3
FILENAME=cars.dat    NR=11  FNR=4
FILENAME=cars.dat    NR=12  FNR=5
FILENAME=cars.dat    NR=13  FNR=6
FILENAME=cars.dat    NR=14  FNR=7
FILENAME=cars.dat    NR=15  FNR=8
FILENAME=cars.dat    NR=16  FNR=9
FILENAME=cars.dat    NR=17  FNR=10
FILENAME=cars.dat    NR=18  FNR=11
FILENAME=cars.dat    NR=19  FNR=12
END Block: NR=19 FNR=12
```

ENVIRON and SUBSET

The environment variable is an associative array containing the values of environment variables for the current process. The index of the array stores the environment variable name, and the elements are the values of particular environment variables. It is also helpful when we want to access the shell environment variable in our AWK script.

For example, the array element ENVIRON["HOME"] will contain the value of the HOME environment variable, ENVIRON["PATH"] will contain the value of the PATH environment variable, and so on. In the following example, we print all the available environment variables and their values:

```
$ vi  environ.awk

BEGIN   {
    OFS="="
    for( v in ENVIRON )
```

```
    print v, ENVIRON[v];
    }

$ awk -f envion.awk
```

The output of the execution of this code is as follows:

```
DBUS_SESSION_BUS_ADDRESS=unix:path=/run/user/1000/bus,guid=4a2603b5563ee1ba
fd07d8135a7469af
SHLVL=1
SYSTEMD_NSS_BYPASS_BUS=1
GNOME_DESKTOP_SESSION_ID=this-is-deprecated
PWD=/home/shiwang/Desktop/AWK-BOOK-PAKT/WORK-DONE/CHAPTER3
GDMSESSION=default
QT_QPA_PLATFORMTHEME=qgnomeplatform
XDG_CURRENT_DESKTOP=GNOME
JOURNAL_STREAM=8:23337
XDG_DATA_DIRS=/usr/share/gnome:/usr/local/share/:/usr/share/
SHELL=/bin/bash
GDM_LANG=en_US.UTF-8
QT_LINUX_ACCESSIBILITY_ALWAYS_ON=1
COLORTERM=truecolor
PATH=/usr/local/bin:/usr/bin:/bin:/usr/local/games:/usr/games
XDG_SESSION_ID=2
XDG_MENU_PREFIX=gnome-
GPG_AGENT_INFO=/run/user/1000/gnupg/S.gpg-agent:0:1
INVOCATION_ID=35b0bb46651e4656a87f4117d7526ff4
LS_COLORS=rs=0:di=01;34:ln=01;36:mh=00:pi=40;33:so=01;35:do=01;35:bd=40;33;
01:cd=40;33;01:or=40;31;01:mi=00:su=37;41:sg=30;43:ca=30;41:tw=30;42:ow=34;
42:st=37;44:ex=01;32:*.tar=01;31:*.tgz=01;31:*.arc=01;31:*.arj=01;31:*.taz=
01;31:*.lha=01;31:*.lz4=01;31:*.lzh=01;31:*.lzma=01;31:*.tlz=01;31:*.txz=01
;31:*.tzo=01;31:*.t7z=01;31:*.zip=01;31:*.z=01;31:*.Z=01;31:*.dz=01;31:*.gz
=01;31:*.lrz=01;31:*.lz=01;31:*.lzo=01;31:*.xz=01;31:*.zst=01;31:*.tzst=01;
31:*.bz2=01;31:*.bz=01;31:*.tbz=01;31:*.tbz2=01;31:*.tz=01;31:*.deb=01;31:*
.rpm=01;31:*.jar=01;31:*.war=01;31:*.ear=01;31:*.sar=01;31:*.rar=01;DESKTOP
_SESSION=default
DBUS_STARTER_BUS_TYPE=session
SSH_AGENT_PID=969
SSH_AUTH_SOCK=/tmp/ssh-sGgTcGoku7YG/agent.916
GTK_MODULES=gail:atk-bridge
QT_ACCESSIBILITY=1
HOME=/home/shiwang
TERM=xterm-256color
AWKLIBPATH=/usr/lib/x86_64-linux-gnu/gawk
SESSION_MANAGER=local/debian:@/tmp/.ICE-unix/916,unix/debian:/tmp/.ICE-
unix/916
USERNAME=shiwang
LANG=en_US.UTF-8
```

```
XDG_RUNTIME_DIR=/run/user/1000
LOGNAME=shiwang
XDG_SESSION_TYPE=x11
XDG_VTNR=2
XDG_SESSION_DESKTOP=default
VTE_VERSION=4601
DBUS_STARTER_ADDRESS=unix:path=/run/user/1000/bus,guid=4a2603b5563ee1bafd07
d8135a7469af
WINDOWPATH=2
_=/usr/bin/awk
USER=shiwang
DISPLAY=:0
AWKPATH=.:/usr/share/awk
XAUTHORITY=/run/user/1000/gdm/Xauthority
XDG_SEAT=seat0
WINDOWID=20971526
MANAGERPID=901
```

SUBSEP is known as a **subscript separator**, and is used to separate the indices of a multidimensional array. It has the default value of \034, which is a nonprinting character. You can control this character value by using the SUBSEP variable.

In the following example, we change the value of the SUBSEP variable to : to separate the indices of the multidimensional array as follows:

```
$ vi subsep.awk

BEGIN {
SUBSEP=":";
item[1,1]=100;
item[1,2]=200;
item[2,1]=300;
item[2,2]=400;
for (x in item)
print "Index",x,"contains",item[x];
}

$ awk -f subsep.awk
```

The output of the execution of the preceding code is as follows:

```
Index 1:1 contains 100
Index 1:2 contains 200
Index 2:1 contains 300
Index 2:2 contains 400
```

Do not enclose any index within quotes or the SUBSEP variable will not work. For example, say that we slightly modify the previous example and place the index within double quotes, as follows:

```
$ vi mod_subsep.awk

BEGIN {
SUBSEP=":";
item["1,1"]=100;
item["1,2"]=200;
item[2,1]=300;
item[2,2]=400;
for (x in item)
print "Index",x,"contains",item[x];
}


$ awk  -f  mod_subsep.awk
```

The output of the execution of the preceding code is as follows:

```
Index 1:1 contains 100
Index 1:2 contains 200
Index 2:1 contains 300
Index 2:2 contains 400
```

FIELD (POSITIONAL) VARIABLE ($0 and $n)

The fields of the current input line are called $1 and $2, through $NF. $0 represents the whole newline. Fields share the properties of other variables. These field variables can be used in arithmetic or string operations and can also be used for assignment. For example, to display the content of the cars.dat file line by line, we can use the following command:

```
$ awk '{print $0}' cars.dat
```

This can also be performed as follows:

```
$ awk '{print $1, $2,$3,$4,$5 }' cars.dat
```

The second command will change the spacing between the fields to a single space, otherwise the result remains the same.

We can modify the field value for each line using these positional parameters. For example, if we want to put DEZIRE for each row in the second column and delete the third row, we put it as follows:

```
$ awk '{$2="DEZIRE";$3="";print}' cars.dat
```

The output of the execution of the preceding code is as follows:

```
maruti DEZIRE  50000 5
honda DEZIRE   60000 3
maruti DEZIRE   3100 6
chevy DEZIRE   33000 2
honda DEZIRE   33000 6
chevy DEZIRE   10000 4
toyota DEZIRE  95000 2
maruti DEZIRE   4100 5
maruti DEZIRE  98000 1
ford DEZIRE   80000 1
honda DEZIRE   60000 2
fiat DEZIRE   45000 3
```

Environment variables in GAWK

In this section, we discuss the various GAWK-specific variables. They are not available in the original AWK distribution. However, on modern Linux systems, generally these options will work because AWK is set as a symbolic link to the GAWK executable.

ARGIND

ARGIND represents the index in the ARGV array to retrieve the current file being processed. When we operate with one file in AWK script, the ARGIND will be 1, and ARGV[ARGIND] will return the filename that is currently being processed.

In the following example, we print the value of ARGIND and the current filename using ARGV[ARGIND] as follows:

```
$ vi argind.awk

END    {
    print "ARGIND : ", ARGIND;
    print "Current Filename : ", ARGV[ARGIND];
```

```
}
```

```
$ awk -f argind.awk
```

The output of the execution of the preceding code is as follows:

```
ARGIND :   1
Current Filename :   cars.dat
```

We have printed the value stored in ARGIND in the END block here so that it is not printed in a loop when each line of cars.dat is processed. So, we can say that the value stored in the FILENAME variable is always equal to ARGV[ARGIND].

ERRNO

The ERRNO variable stores the error message as a string if the redirection (I/O) operation fails while using the getline command. These errors happen mostly while performing read operations or during a close operation. GAWK clears the ERRNO before opening each command-line input file.

We will be using AWK's built-in getline command to read the input from the file to understand how the ERRNO variable works. The getline command returns 1 if it finds a record and 0 if it encounters the end of file. If an error occurs when it is getting the record, for example if the file could not be read or found, then it returns -1. In this scenario, GAWK will set ERRNO to a string explaining the error.

For example, let's create the following AWK script to check whether the employee's first name is Eva, and to make getline read from dummy-file.txt if the employee with this first name is found. As, there is no such file, ERRNO will store the error message, which is displayed using a print statement, as follows:

```
$ vi erro.awk

{
x=getline < "dummy-file.txt"
if ($1 == "Eva")
{
    print "Trying to read from file : dummy-file.txt"
    if ( x == -1 )
        print ERRNO
    else
        print $0;
```

```
   }
}

$ awk -f err.awk emp.dat
```

The output of the execution of the preceding code is as follows:

```
Trying to read from file : dummy-file.txt
No such file or directory
```

FIELDWIDTHS

The FIELDWIDTHS variable is used to process fixed-width columns in the input. It takes a space-separated list of columns to tell GAWK how to split the input with fixed column boundaries. If we use FIELDWIDTH in our AWK program, it overrides the value of FS and FPAT for field splitting.

For example, let us take the sample cars database file cars.dat. It has five columns of data. The first column is 16 characters wide, the second is 12, the third and fourth columns are also 12 characters wide, and the last column is a single character wide. So, we can use the FIELDWIDTHS variable to print the fields, as follows:

```
$ awk 'BEGIN { FIELDWIDTHS="16 12 12 12 1"}{print $1 $2 $3 $4 $5}' cars.dat
```

The output of the execution of the preceding code is as follows:

```
maruti          swift       2007        50000       5
honda           city        2005        60000       3
maruti          dezire      2009        3100        6
chevy           beat        2005        33000       2
honda           city        2010        33000       6
chevy           tavera      1999        10000       4
toyota          corolla     1995        95000       2
maruti          swift       2009        4100        5
maruti          esteem      1997        98000       1
ford            ikon        1995        80000       1
honda           accord      2000        60000       2
fiat            punto       2007        45000       3
```

The preceding AWK command is the equivalent of printing the whole line using `$0`. Now, let us apply this `FIELDWIDTHS` variable to the output of the Linux/Unix `w` utility. In this example, we will take the input from the `w` command and convert the fourth field values, which represent the CPU idle time in seconds. Finally, we will print the first two fields and the calculated idle time as follows:

```
$ vi fieldwidth.awk

BEGIN   { FIELDWIDTHS = "9 6 10 6 7 7 35" }
NR > 2 {
    idle = $4
    sub(/^ +/, "", idle)    # strip leading spaces
    if (idle == "")
        idle = 0
    if (idle ~ /:/) {        # hh:mm
        split(idle, t, ":")
        idle = t[1] * 60 + t[2]
    }
    if (idle ~ /days/)
        idle *= 24 * 60 * 60

    print $1, $2, idle
}

$ w | awk -f fieldwidth.awk
```

The output of the execution of the preceding command is as follows:

```
shiwang    tty2    0
```

IGNORECASE

The `IGNORECASE` variable is used to make the GAWK program case-insensitive or case-sensitive. By default, `IGNORECASE` is set to `0`, making the GAWK program case-sensitive. When we set `IGNORECASE` to `1`, the GAWK program becomes case-insensitive. This has a major affect on regular expression and string comparisons.

In the following example, we are looking for the records containing the string `chabra`, with a lowercase `c` in the employee database file `emp.dat`. However, the last name begins with a capital letter, and hence only `chabra` is there:

```
$ awk '/chabra/{print}' emp.dat
```

Upon the execution of the preceding code, we will not get any output. Now, we set IGNORECASE to 1, and again print the records containing chabra. It will do a case-insensitive pattern match as follows:

```
$ awk 'BEGIN{IGNORECASE=1}/chabra/ {print}' emp.dat
```

The output of the execution of the preceding code is as follows:

```
Eva      Chabra   8827232115   eva@gmail.com      F   lgs    2100
Billy    Chabra   9911664321   bily@yahoo.com     M   lgs    1900
```

In the next example, we will demonstrate how the IGNORECASE value works for both strings and for regular expressions. Let us create a script to print the details of those employees whose first names begin with Ja or whose last names are kapur in the employee database file emp.dat:

```
$ vi ignorecase.awk

BEGIN    {
    IGNORECASE=1;
    }
{
    if ( $2 == "kapur" ) print $0;
    if ( $1 ~ "ja" ) print $0;
}

$ awk -f ignorecase.awk emp.dat
```

The output of the execution of the preceding code is as follows:

```
Jack     Singh    9857532312   jack@gmail.com     M   hr     2000
Jane     Kaur     9837432312   jane@gmail.com     F   hr     1800
Julie    Kapur    8826234556   julie@yahoo.com    F   Ops    2500
John     Kapur    9911556789   john@gmail.com     M   hr     2200
```

PROCINFO

The PROCINFO variable is an associative array containing information about the process, such as the process ID number, error number, group ID, real and effective UID numbers, and so on.

For example, if we set the FIELDWIDTHS to a certain value, then the FS will be FIELDWIDTHS. Using PROCINFO, we can print many details of the current instance of AWK program as follows:

```
$ vi procinfo.awk

BEGIN { FIELDWIDTHS = "16"}
END {
printf "Process id of awk program is     : %s\n", PROCINFO["pid"];
printf "User ID of user running awk is   : %s\n", PROCINFO["uid"];
printf "Group ID of awk program is      : %s\n", PROCINFO["gid"];
printf "Field Splitter set of awk is     : %s\n", PROCINFO["FS"];
printf "Version no. of awk program is    : %s\n", PROCINFO["version"];
}

$ awk -f procinfo.awk cars.dat
```

The output of the execution of the preceding code is as follows:

```
Process id of awk program is : 4316
User ID of user running awk is : 1000
Group ID of awk program is : 1000
Field Splitter set of awk is : FIELDWIDTHS
Version no. of awk program is : 4.1.4
```

These were the main environment variables used in AWK and GAWK. There are other environment variables, but they are not in our current scope of learning.

String constants

A string constant is a sequence of zero or more characters enclosed in double quotation marks. A string constant can be of any length, and they can have any of the possible 8-bit ASCII characters. These string constants can be stored in variables or appear literally as string constants, such as "River" or " ".

For example, if we want to print those records from cars.dat that contain the maruti string in the first field, we have to enclose the maruti string in double quotes while performing the match as follows:

```
$ awk '$1 == "maruti" {print}' cars.dat
```

The output of the execution of the preceding code is as follows:

```
maruti          swift           2007            50000           5
maruti          dezire          2009            3100            6
maruti          swift           2009            4100            5
maruti          esteem          1997            98000           1
```

- **Null string**: The string that contains no character is known as a null string, such as "".

- **Substring**: The contiguous sequence of zero or more characters within a string is known as a substring. Hence, every string contains a null string.

Any nonempty string value in AWK is true in the case of expression evaluation, and the null string is false. For example:

```
$ vi strings.awk

BEGIN {

if ( "0" )
    print "string 0";
if ("one")
    print "string one"
if ("")
    print "empty string"
}

$ awk -f strings.awk
```

The output of the execution of the preceding code is as follows:

```
string 0
string one
```

Numeric constants

A numeric constant stands for a number. It can be an integer, a decimal fraction, or a number in an exponential notation. Some examples of numeric constant values are as follows:

- *100*
- *1.10*
- *1.05e+2*
- *1.05e-1*

Any nonzero numeric value in AWK is true in the case of expression evaluation, and zero is false. For example:

```
$ vi numeric.awk

BEGIN{
if ( 1 )
    print "numeric 1 "
if ( 1.234 )
    print "numeric 1.234"
if ( 1.234e )
    print "numeric 1.234e"
if ( 0 )
    print "false"
}

$ awk -f numeric.awk
```

The output of the execution of the preceding code is as follows:

```
numeric 1
numeric 1.234
numeric 1.234e
```

Conversion between strings and numbers

The conversion to string and numeric values occurs automatically in AWK as per demand. When any expression is built using any operator and operand, if the expression has a numeric value but the operator demands a string value, then the numeric value is automatically converted into a string and vice versa. If a numeric value appears in a string concatenation, it is converted to a string.

For example, in the following example, variables a and b are converted to strings first and then concatenated together. The resulting string is again converted back to number 45, in which 4 is further added, and we get the output of the number 49:

```
$ vi str2num.awk

BEGIN    {
    a=4; b=5;
    print ( a b ) + 4 ;
    }

$ awk -f str2num.awk
```

The output of the execution of the preceding code is as follows:

```
49
```

Any string can be forcefully converted to a number by adding a 0 to it, as follow:

```
$ awk 'BEGIN{a="hello";print a+0 }'
```

The output of the execution of this code is as follows :

```
0
```

Any number can be forcefully converted to a string by adding "" (an empty string) to it as follows:

```
$ awk 'BEGIN{a=5; print a+"" }'
```

The output of the execution of this command will be like this:

```
5
```

Summary

In this chapter, we learned about the different types of variables that are available in AWK. We learned how to use built-in variables and environment variables in AWK programs. Then we learned about the usage of environment variables specific to GAWK. Finally, we looked at the string constants and numeric constants from an AWK perspective, and at how the conversion of string to numeric values, and numeric to string values, takes place in AWK.

In our next chapter, we will learn about how to handle arrays in AWK programs.

4
Working with Arrays in AWK

An array is a variable that is used to store a set of values (strings or numbers). These values, or independent elements, are accessed by their index in the array. Indexes are stored in square brackets and may be either numbers or strings. This chapter focuses on how arrays are implemented in AWK.

In this chapter, we will cover the following topics:

- One-dimensional arrays in AWK
- Assigning and accessing elements in arrays
- Referring to array elements
- Processing arrays using loops
- Creating an array using a `split` function
- Delete operations in arrays
- Multidimensional array implementation in AWK

One-dimensional arrays

The AWK language provides one-dimensional arrays for storing strings and numbers. An array name could be any valid variable name. One variable name cannot be used as both an array and a variable at the same time in the same program.

Arrays in AWK are extremely powerful in comparison to traditional arrays that we use in other programming languages. Arrays in AWK are associative—that is, each array is a collection of a pair: an index and its corresponding array element value. In associative arrays, indexes are not essentially required to be in order, one can use either a string or a number as an array index. An array size can expand or shrink at runtime and is not statically defined.

Its syntax is as follows:

$$arr[index] = value$$

The different elements of the array syntax used here are explained in the following list:

- `arr`: This is the name of the array
- `index`: This is the index of the array
- `value`: This is any value assigned to the element of the array

The following are some examples of associative arrays in AWK:

```
arr["apple"] = red
arr["grape" ] = green
arr[ "lemon" ] = yellow
arr[ 10 ] = number
arr[ pineapple ] = fruit
```

In the preceding declaration, index `10` is automatically converted to a string and the order of assigning elements to the array is also independent. Those indexes that are not double quoted, such as `pineapple`, are automatically converted to string values.

Assignment in arrays

Array elements can be assigned values like any other AWK variables, as follows:

$$arr[index] = value$$

In the following example, we take the `cars` database file `cars.dat`. Here, we make the record number the index to the array and store each record as a value to the corresponding array element. The system variable `NR` is used as the index for the array as it gets incremented for each record. In the end, we print the array elements using a `for` loop as follows:

```
$ vi basic_array.awk

{
arr[NR] = $0
}
END{
    for ( x=1; x<= NR; x++)
        print "index : "x, "value :"arr[x]
}

$ awk  -f  basic_array.awk  cars.dat
```

The output of the execution of the preceding code is as follows:

```
index : 1 value :maruti      swift      2007      50000      5
index : 2 value :honda       city       2005      60000      3
index : 3 value :maruti      dezire     2009      3100       6
index : 4 value :chevy       beat       2005      33000      2
index : 5 value :honda       city       2010      33000      6
index : 6 value :chevy       tavera     1999      10000      4
index : 7 value :toyota      corolla    1995      95000      2
index : 8 value :maruti      swift      2009      4100       5
index : 9 value :maruti      esteem     1997      98000      1
index : 10 value :ford        ikon       1995      80000      1
index : 11 value :honda       accord     2000      60000      2
index : 12 value :fiat        punto      2007      45000      3
```

Let us create a sample database file, `marks.dat`, that contains the marks of students in a class as follows:

```
$ vi marks.txt

ram 80 78 60 85 72
amit 64 67 69 61 62
vijay 90 98 92 96 97
satvik 81 74 72 79 80
akshat 67 80 74 60 72
rishi 85 80 82 76 84
tushar    70 82 68 79 6
```

Now, we will use this database to calculate the average mark of each student and the assignment of grades. We will also calculate the average scoring of the whole class:

```
$ vi marks_summary.awk

BEGIN { OFS = "\t"
    print "====================";
    printf "Name\tAvg\tGrade\n";
    print "====================";
}
{
    student_total = 0
    for ( x=2; x <=NF; x++ )
        student_total += $x
# calculate average
    avg = student_total / (NF -1)
    student_avg[NR] = avg
# determine grade of student
    if ( avg >= 90 ) grade = "Excellent"
    else if ( avg >=80 ) grade = "Very Good"
    else if ( avg >=70 ) grade = "Good"
    else if ( avg >=60 ) grade = "Satisfactory"
    else grade = "Fail"
    print $1, avg, grade
}
END    {
# calculate the average of marks scored by whole class
    for ( x =1; x <= NR; x++ )
        class_avg_total += student_avg[x]
    class_avg = class_avg_total / NR
    print "====================";
    print "Class Average: ", class_avg
}

$ awk -f marks_summary.awk  marks.txt
```

The output of the execution of the preceding code is as follows:

```
====================
Name    Avg     Grade
====================
ram     75      Good
amit    64.6    Satisfactory
vijay   94.6    Excellent
satvik  77.2    Good
akshat  70.6    Good
```

```
rishi   81.4   Very Good
tushar  71.8   Good
====================
Class Average: 76.4571
```

Accessing elements in arrays

The ideal way to access an array element is to refer to that element via its index, as follows:

arr[index]

Here, `arr` is the name of an array, and `index` is the index of the desired element of the array that we want to access.

The following is a simple example of assigning and accessing AWK arrays:

```
$ vi arr_access.awk

BEGIN {
        arr[30] = "volvo"
        arr[10] = "bmw"
        arr[20] = "audi"
        arr[50] = "toyota"
        arr["car"] = "ferrari"
        arr[70] = "renault"
        arr[40] = "ford"
        arr[80] = "porsche"
        arr[60] = "jeep"
        print "arr[10]  : ", arr["10"]
        print "arr[car] : ", arr["car"]
        print "arr[80]  : ", arr["80"]
        print "arr[30]  : ", arr["30"]
}

$ awk  -f  arr_access.awk
```

The output of the execution of the preceding code is as follows:

```
arr[10]  : bmw
arr[car] : ferrari
arr[80]  : porsche
arr[30]  : volvo
```

In the preceding example, we can see that the array indexes are not in sequence. They don't begin with zero or one array indexes can be string also, as we have used `car` as index. We don't initialize or even define the array in AWK. We don't need to specify the total size before using it. The naming convention is similar to that of an AWK variable.

If a referenced array element has no stored value, or it has not been assigned any value yet, it will give a null string (" ") as output. The same is true if we try to access a deleted element of an array—it will be assigned a null string value.

If we refer to an array element that does not exist, then AWK automatically creates that array element with the given index and assigns a null string as its value. So, we should never check whether an element exists in an AWK associative array by checking whether the value is empty, because it will automatically create the array element as a null string value at the time of checking itself. For example:

```
$ vi check_arry.awk

BEGIN {
    if ( a["apple"] != "")
    print "a[apple] has some value : " a["apple"];
    else
    print "a[apple] is empty"
    }

$ awk -f check_arry.awk
```

The output of the execution of the preceding code is as follows:

```
a[apple] is empty
```

Referring to members in arrays

We can directly display the value stored in an array element using the `print` command, or we can assign it to another variable for further processing inside a AWK program as follows:

```
$ vi arr_var_assign.awk

BEGIN    {
    arr[10] = "maruti"
    arr[20] = "audi"
    print "arr[10] : " arr[10]
    x=arr[20]
```

```
    print "x : " x
    }

$ awk  -f  arr_var_assign.awk
```

The output of the execution of the preceding code is as follows:

```
arr[10] : maruti
x : audi
```

To check whether a particular index exists in an array, we use the `if` condition within the operator to build the conditional expression syntax, as shown in the following syntactical phrase. It will return true (1), if the index exists in the array; otherwise, it will return false (0):

if(index in array)

In the following example, we show you how the `if` condition works when checking for the existence of an array's index. Here, we declare an array, `arr`, of five elements, with the index as 10, 20, 30, 40, and 50, respectively. Then, we check for the existence of the index value 60 in the `arr[60]` array using the keyword `in`. If the index value is found, it prints its corresponding element; otherwise, it prints that the index is not found, as follows:

```
$ vi arr_member_check.awk

BEGIN    {
    arr[10] = "bmw"
    arr[20] = "audi"
    arr[30] = "volvo"
    arr[40] = "ford"
    arr[50] = "toyota"

    if ( 60 in arr )
        print "arr index 60 contains : ", arr[60];
    else
        print "arr index 60 not found";
    if ( 50 in arr )
        print "arr index 50 contains : ", arr[50];
    else
        print "arr index 50 not found";
    }

$ awk -f arr_member_check.awk
```

The output of the execution of the preceding code is as follows:

```
arr index 60 not found
arr index 50 contains :  toyota
```

Processing arrays using loops

If we have to access all the array elements, we can use a loop that executes once for each element of the array. In other programming languages, where indexes are sequentially numbered, a simple for loop construct is used to access the elements of array. Here, AWK has an associative array, so we use a special type of `for` loop to go through all the indexes of an array. Its syntax is as follows, followed by a listed explanation of the elements involved:

for (var in array)

body of loop

- `var`: This is any variable name, which is set to the index of the corresponding array element.
- `in`: This is a keyword.
- `array`: This is an array name.
- `body of loop`: This is a list of AWK statements that are to be executed. If you want to execute more than one action, it needs to be enclosed within braces. The loop will execute until there is an index element in the array.

For example, let's consider this simple loop example that iterates through all the elements in the `arr` array and prints them as follows:

```
$ vi arr_forloop.awk

BEGIN {
    arr[10] = "bmw"
    arr[20] = "audi"
    arr[30] = "volvo"
    arr[40] = "ford"
    arr[50] = "toyota"
    arr[60] = "jeep"
    arr[70] = "renault"
    arr[80] = "porsche"
    for ( v in arr)
```

```
            print v, arr[v];
    }

$ awk  -f  arr_forloop.awk
```

The output on the execution of the preceding code is as follows:

```
10 bmw
20 audi
30 volvo
40 ford
50 toyota
60 jeep
70 renault
80 porsche
```

In the following example, we take the `cars` database file `cars.dat`. Here, we make the record number the index to the array and store each record as the value of the corresponding array element. The system variable `NR` is used as the index for the array as it gets incremented for each record. In the end, we print the array elements using this special `for` loop where we don't have to take care of the index element, as follows:

```
$ vi arr_forloop2.awk

{
arr[NR] = $0;
}
END {
for ( v in arr )
    print "arr["v"] : ",arr[v]
}

$ awk  -f  arr_forloop2.awk  cars.dat
```

The output of the execution of the preceding code is as follows:

```
arr[1] :   maruti    swift     2007     50000     5
arr[2] :   honda     city      2005     60000     3
arr[3] :   maruti    dezire    2009     3100      6
arr[4] :   chevy     beat      2005     33000     2
arr[5] :   honda     city      2010     33000     6
arr[6] :   chevy     tavera    1999     10000     4
arr[7] :   toyota    corolla   1995     95000     2
arr[8] :   maruti    swift     2009     4100      5
arr[9] :   maruti    esteem    1997     98000     1
```

```
arr[10]  :   ford        ikon      1995    80000    1
arr[11]  :   honda       accord    2000    60000    2
arr[12]  :   fiat        punto     2007    45000    3
```

Using the split() function to create arrays

The built-in `split()` function can parse any string into elements of an array. The `split(string, arr, fs)` function splits the string value of `str` into fields and stores them in the `arr` array. The number of fields produced is returned as the value of the `split` function. The string value of the third argument, `fs`, determines the field separator. The syntax of `split()` functions is as follows, followed by a listed explanation of the elements involved:

$$n = split\ (str,\ arr,\ fs)$$

- `str`: This is the input string to be parsed into the elements of the named `arr`.
- `arr`: This is the name of the array.
- `fs`: This is the separator character based on which the array elements are split. If the separator is not given, the elements are split based on the `fs` as the separator. The separator can be a single character of the regular expression.
- `n`: This is the index of the array, starting at `1` and going up to `n`.

The following example illustrates the basic usage of `split` to create an array:

```
$ vi arr_basic_split.awk

BEGIN    {
    z= split( "10/20/30/40", arr, "/")
    for ( i in arr )
        print "arr["i"] : ",arr[i]
    }

$ awk -f arr_basic_split.awk
```

The output of the execution of the preceding code is as follows:

```
arr[1]  :   10
arr[2]  :   20
arr[3]  :   30
arr[4]  :   40
```

In the following example, we break a single record using a space as a separator. z will contain the number of elements in the array. Using the value returned by the split() function, we write a loop to read all the elements of this arr array as follows:

```
$ vi arr_using_split.awk

BEGIN    {
    name = "Ranvijay Singh is a good boy"
    z= split( name, arr, " ")
    for ( i in arr )
        print i, arr[i]
    }

$ awk  -f  arr_using_split.awk
```

The output of the execution of the preceding code is as follows:

```
1 Ranvijay
2 Singh
3 is
4 a
5 good
6 boy
```

The split() function can also be used to clear the array as follows:

$$split\ ("",\ array)$$

In the preceding example, split call there is no data to split out, and the function simply clears the array and then returns.

Delete operation in arrays

The delete command is used to remove the individual element from an array. Once an element from an AWK array is deleted, we cannot obtain its value any longer. The syntax of the delete statement is as follows:

$$delete\ arr[index];$$

In the following example, we delete the array element with the `car` index and print all the remaining elements using the `for` loop, as follows:

```
$ vi arr_delete.awk

BEGIN    {
    arr[10] = "maruti"
    arr[20] = "audi"
    arr["car"] = "ford"
    arr[30] = "ferrari"
    arr[40] = "porsche"
    delete arr["car"]
    for ( v in arr )
        print v,arr[v]
}

$ awk -f arr_delete.awk
```

The output of the execution of the preceding code is as follows:

```
10 maruti
20 audi
30 ferrari
40 porsche
```

The following `for` loop command removes all elements from an `arr` array:

$$for\ (v\ in\ arr)$$
$$delete\ arr[v]$$

Now, we delete all the elements of the array using the loop and print the array elements again. It will not display anything as all elements in the array are deleted, as follows:

```
$ vi arr_del_forloop.awk

BEGIN    {
    arr[10] = "maruti"
    arr[20] = "audi"
    arr["car"] = "ford"
    arr[30] = "ferrari"
    arr[40] = "porsche"
    for ( v in arr )
        delete arr[v]
    for ( v in arr )
```

```
        print arr[v]
    }

$ awk  -f  arr_del_forloop.awk
```

It will not give any output of the execution of the preceding code, since all elements of the arrays are deleted and the `arr` array is now empty.

Once an element is deleted, a subsequent loop iteration used to scan the array will not report that element, and using the `in` operator to check for the existence of that element will return zero—that is, false. For example, in the following code, we delete an array element and then use the `if` conditional statement to check for its existence:

```
delete arr[20]
if ( 20 in arr )
    print "index 20 found"
else
    print "20 not found"
```

Deleting an element is not the same as assigning it a null value string (the empty string " "). For example:

```
arr[20] = " "
if ( 20 in arr )
print "20 is array, although arr[20] is empty"
```

Also, if we try to delete an element that does not exist, it is not treated as an error. Furthermore, if you want to delete all the elements of the array in a single command, we can use the `delete` command without any subscripts, as follows:

```
$ vi arr_delall.awk

BEGIN    {
    arr[10] = "maruti"
    arr[20] = "audi"
    arr["car"] = "ford"
    arr[30] = "ferrari"
    arr[40] = "porsche"
    delete arr
    print "List of elements in array is : "
    for ( v in arr )
        print arr[v]
}

$ awk -f arr_delall.awk
```

The output of the execution of the preceding code is as follows:

```
List of elements in array is :
```

Hence, if you want to delete all the elements of an array, using the `delete` statement alone is much more efficient than using an equivalent loop to delete each element one at a time. This form of `delete` statement is also supported by most types of implementation of AWK, such as MAWK, NAWK, and so on.

Deleting all elements from an array does not change its type and make it available for use as a regular variable. For example, the following code will throw the error and not work:

```
$ vi arr_delete_error.awk

BEGIN    {
    arr[10] = "audi";
    delete arr;
    arr = "bmw";
    print arr;
    }

$ awk  -f  arr_delete_error.awk
```

The output of the execution of the preceding code is as follows:

```
awk: arr_delete_err.awk:4: fatal: attempt to use array `arr' in a scalar
context
```

Multidimensional arrays

AWK supports one-dimensional arrays only. However, we can simulate multidimensional arrays using one-dimensional arrays. Let us create a multidimensional array as follows:

```
$ vi multi_arr1.awk

BEGIN{
    arr["1,1"] = 10
    arr["1,2"] = 20
    arr["2,1"] = 30
    arr["2,2"] = 40
    arr["3,1"] = 50
    arr["3,2"] = 60
    for ( v in arr )
```

```
        print "Index ",v, " contains "arr[v]
}

<strong>$ awk -f multi_arr1.awk
```

The output of the execution of the preceding code is as follows:

```
Index  1,1  contains 10
Index  1,2  contains 20
Index  2,1  contains 30
Index  2,2  contains 40
Index  3,1  contains 50
Index  3,2  contains 60
```

In the preceding example, we have given the `arr["1,1"]` array as the index. It is not two indexes, as would be the case in a true multidimensional array in other programming languages. It is just one index with the `"1,1"` string. So, AWK concatenates the index value and makes them a single string index in the case of multidimensional arrays as well. Hence, we are actually storing the value `10` at a single-dimensional array with the `1,1` index.

If we have not used double quotes to enclose indexes of the array, then the indexes are separated by the AWK variable `SUBSEP`, which has the default value of the nonprintable character `\034`. We can set this value of `SUBSEP` to any character of our choice, which will be output when we print array indexes. In the following example, we set `SUBSEP` to `:` to separate the indexes of the array, as follows:

```
$ vi multi_arr2.awk

BEGIN{
    SUBSEP = ":"
    arr["1,1"] = 10
    arr["1,2"] = 20
    arr["2,1"] = 30
    arr["2,2"] = 40
    arr[3,1] = 50
    arr[3,2] = 60
    for ( v in arr )
        print "Index ",v, " contains "arr[v]
}

$ awk -f multi_arr2.awk
```

The output of the execution of the preceding code is as follows:

```
Index  1,1  contains 10
Index  1,2  contains 20
Index  2,1  contains 30
Index  2,2  contains 40
Index  3:1  contains 50
Index  3:2  contains 60
```

So, for a multidimensional array, the best practice is to put the indexes in double quotes or to use the SUBSEP variable without enclosing them in double quotes, but not both together in the same AWK program.

In the preceding example, we have used the same for loop to print the multidimensional arrays because, in reality, AWK does not have multidimensional arrays or elements—it is just a multidimensional way of accessing a single-dimensional array. Hence, looping over a multidimensional array is the same process as would be used with one-dimensional arrays:

for (v in arr)

print v, arr[v]

The multidimensional array syntax also supports the testing for array membership using the "in" operator with if expression. The only thing that needs to be taken care of here is that the subscripts should be placed inside the parentheses. In the following example, we put the subscripts within parentheses to check for the existence of the index inside the array. This actually tests whether the "2 SUBSEP 1" subscript exists in the specified array:

```
$ vi multi_arr3.awk

BEGIN{
    SUBSEP = ":"
    arr[1,1] = 10
    arr[1,2] = 20
    arr[2,1] = 30
    arr[2,2] = 40
    arr[3,1] = 50
    arr[3,2] = 60
    if ( (2 SUBSEP 1) in arr )
        print "arr[2,1] is : " arr[2,1]
    else
        print "index not found"
}

$ awk  -f  multi_arr3.awk
```

The output of the execution of the preceding code is as follows:

```
arr[2,1] is : 30
```

The delete operation in a multidimensional array is the same as in a single-dimensional array. For example:

```
$ vi muti_arr4.awk

BEGIN{
    SUBSEP = ":"
    arr[1,1] = 10
    arr[1,2] = 20
    arr[2,1] = 30
    arr[2,2] = 40
    arr[3,1] = 50
    arr[3,2] = 60
    delete arr    # delete arrays using single delete command
    print "Now printing array if exists...!"
    for ( v in arr )
        print arr[v]

    arr[i,j] = 100
    print arr[i,j]
    delete arr[i,j]    # delete arrays using indexes
}

$ awk  -f  multi_arr4.awk
```

The output of the execution of the preceding code is as follows:

```
Now printing array if exists...!
100
```

Summary

In this chapter, we learned about arrays. We learned that AWK provides one-dimensional associative arrays (arrays indexed by string values). We also learned how array elements are referenced using `arr[index]`, and that it creates the element if it does not exist. Then we used the `for` loop to scan through all the individual elements of an array, and tested the array membership using the `in` operator with the `if` expression. We used the `split` function to create an array. We also learned how to delete an individual element or a whole array using the `delete` command. Finally, we covered how AWK simulates multidimensional arrays by separating subscript values with commas. In this index, values are concatenated into a single string, separated by the value of `SUBSEP`.

In the next chapter, we will learn about how to do pretty printing in AWK using formatted reports, and we will learn how to create one ourselves. We will also look at how to use redirection in AWK.

5
Printing Output in AWK

In most programming languages, the most common task is to display or print the output after processing the input. Inside AWK, we have two statements, `print` and `printf`, to accomplish the task of generating output. The `print` statement generates a simple output, while `printf` is used to generate formatted output or reports. These statements can be used together; the output comes in the order that they were used. In this chapter, we focus on basic and formatted printing (pretty printing). In the end, we will also cover I/O redirections to files instead of printing the output on screen.

In this chapter, we will cover the following topics:

- Basic printing using the `print` statement
- Using an output separator with the `print` statement
- Pretty printing with `printf`
- Using escape sequences
- Printing with a format specifier
- Printing with optional parameters
- Redirecting output to a file

The print statement

So far, we have been using `print` statements mainly to produce simple yet standardized output. With a `print` statement, we specify the expressions to print as a list separated by commas. The output is separated by single spaces, followed by a newline. The `print` statement has two forms:

```
print expr1, expr2, ......, exprn
print (expr1, expr2, ........., exprn)
```

Both print the string value of each expression separated by the **Output Field Separator** (**OFS**); the default is a single space followed by the **Output Record Separator** (**ORS**); the default is newline. Using parentheses is necessary if an expression uses the > relational operator to mark its differentiation from redirection operator. Here expression could be any AWK expression or any constant string, or number, or field of current input record (like $1, $2, ... and so on). Numeric values are automatically converted to string, and then printed. For example, if we want to print the first two fields from the `car` database using a simple `print` statement, we can print as follows:

```
$ awk '{ print $1 $2 }' cars.dat
```

The output on execution of the preceding code is as follows:

```
marutiswift
hondacity
marutidezire
chevybeat
hondacity
chevytavera
toyotacorolla
marutiswift
marutiesteem
fordikon
hondaaccord
fiatpunto
```

In the preceding example output, you will find the field one is immediately printed after print two without any space in between because we didn't use the comma there. To print the field values separated by space we have to use the comma as follows:

```
$ awk '{ print $1, $ 2 }' cars.dat
```

The output on execution of the preceding code is as follows:

```
maruti swift
honda city
maruti dezire
chevy beat
honda city
chevy tavera
toyota corolla
maruti swift
maruti esteem
ford ikon
honda accord
fiat punto
```

The simple `print` statement is an abbreviation for `print $0`. It prints the current input record as show in the following example:

```
$ awk '{ print }' cars.dat
```

Or it can be represented in different way:

```
$ awk '{ print $0 }' cars.dat
```

The output on execution of the preceding code is as follows:

```
maruti        swift      2007      50000      5
honda         city       2005      60000      3
maruti        dezire     2009      3100       6
chevy         beat       2005      33000      2
honda         city       2010      33000      6
chevy         tavera     1999      10000      4
toyota        corolla    1995      95000      2
maruti        swift      2009      4100       5
maruti        esteem     1997      98000      1
ford          ikon       1995      80000      1
honda         accord     2000      60000      2
fiat          punto      2007      45000      3
```

To print a blank line, that is, an empty line with newline only, we use the following:

```
$ awk '{print $0;print " "}' cars.dat
```

The output on execution of the preceding code is as follows:

maruti	swift	2007	50000	5
honda	city	2005	60000	3
maruti	dezire	2009	3100	6
chevy	beat	2005	33000	2
honda	city	2010	33000	6
chevy	tavera	1999	10000	4
toyota	corolla	1995	95000	2
maruti	swift	2009	4100	5
maruti	esteem	1997	98000	1
ford	ikon	1995	80000	1
honda	accord	2000	60000	2
fiat	punto	2007	45000	3

To print a fixed string, we enclose it in double quotes as follows:

```
$ awk '{print $1 ":" $2}' cars.dat
```

The output on execution of the preceding code is as follows:

```
maruti:swift
honda:city
maruti:dezire
chevy:beat
honda:city
chevy:tavera
toyota:corolla
maruti:swift
maruti:esteem
ford:ikon
honda:accord
fiat:punto
```

Role of output separator in print statement

When we print multiple fields separated by comma using `print` command, it uses OFS and ORS built-in variable values to decide how to print the fields and rows. Output field separator is stored in the OFS variable and output record separator is stored in the ORS variable. By default OFS is set to single space and ORS is set to a single newline. We can change these values anytime as required, but the usually best place to assign new values to OFS and ORS is in the BEGIN statement. For example, in the following example we print all the fields of `car` database with a colon between them as separator, and the two newlines after each processing record as follows:

```
$ vi output_separator.awk

BEGIN  { OFS = ":"
     ORS = "\n\n"
     }
{ print $1,$2,$3,$4,$5 }

$ awk  -f  output_separator.awk  cars.dat
```

The output on execution of the preceding code is as follows:

```
maruti:swift:2007:50000:5

honda:city:2005:60000:3

maruti:dezire:2009:3100:6

chevy:beat:2005:33000:2

honda:city:2010:33000:6

chevy:tavera:1999:10000:4

toyota:corolla:1995:95000:2

maruti:swift:2009:4100:5

maruti:esteem:1997:98000:1

ford:ikon:1995:80000:1

honda:accord:2000:60000:2

fiat:punto:2007:45000:3
```

We can also modify the values of OFS and ORS using the -v command-line option before the names of input files in the awk command. For example, we achieve the same output as in the previous example using the -v command-line option for setting OFS to colon and ORS to double newlines:

```
$ awk -v OFS=":" -v ORS="\n\n" '{print $1,$2,$3}' cars.dat
```

The output on execution of the preceding code is as follows:

```
maruti:swift:2007

honda:city:2005

maruti:dezire:2009

chevy:beat:2005

honda:city:2010

chevy:tavera:1999

toyota:corolla:1995

maruti:swift:2009

maruti:esteem:1997

ford:ikon:1995

honda:accord:2000

fiat:punto:2007
```

 printf doesn't use the OFS and ORS variables. It uses only the specified format specifier to print the field values and to separate them; we have to use escape sequences to format the output as desired.

Pretty printing with the printf statement

Most of the programs we have written so far have used the `print` command to display the output. Sometimes, the columns don't line up properly with the `print` statement. So, to have more control over output formatting we have to use a `printf` statement. It is very flexible and is used to generate formatted output. It is similar to the C language's `printf` statement, with only one exception: the absence of a `*` format specifier. Like the `print` statement, it can be used with parentheses or without parentheses, as follows:

```
printf format, expr1, expr2, expr3 ......... exprn
printf ( format, expr1, expr2, expr3 ......... exprn )
```

The main difference between `print` and `printf` is the format argument. It is an expression whose value is taken as a string; it specifies how to output each of the other arguments. It is also known as **format string**. The format string consists of a percentage sign (`%`) followed by a format specifier.

It does not automatically append a newline in its output. To add a newline, we have to add an escape sequence `\n` in the format string. This format string consists of the format specifier, some string, and some special characters. We will be discussing these special characters and format control characters in the coming section in detail. The argument (expressions) lists are outputted as per the given format specifier. The two most common format specifiers used are `s` for strings and `d` for decimal numbers.

In the following example, we print the header inside the `BEGIN` statement using the `printf` command, followed by the first and third field of each processed record. Here we have used the `\n` character to add a new line and `\t` for a tab between fields, as follows:

```
$ vi printf_example.awk

BEGIN    { printf "FNAME     EMAIL_ID\n"
      printf "================\n"
    }
{
    printf "%s\t%s\n", $1, $4
}

END    { printf "================\n" }
$ awk -f printf_example.awk emp.dat
```

The output on execution of the preceding code is:

```
FNAME     EMAIL_ID
=================
Jack      jack@gmail.com
Jane      jane@gmail.com
Eva       eva@gmail.com
Amit      amit@yahoo.com
Julie     julie@yahoo.com
Ana       anak@hotmail.com
Hari      hari@yahoo.com
Victor    vics@hotmail.com
John      john@gmail.com
Billy     bily@yahoo.com
Sam       sam@hotmail.com
Ginny     ginny@yahoo.com
Emily     emily@gmail.com
Amy       amys@hotmail.com
Vina      vina@yahoo.com
=================
```

Escape sequences for special character printing

As we use a simple string with `printf`, we can use any escape sequences to print control characters that are difficult to represent. These are special characters that do not represent their literal meaning when used inside a string; instead they represent something special that would otherwise be difficult to represent as such. Most of the escape sequences consist of at least two characters, the first of which is a backslash character \, which is used to escape or mark a special character.

The following table lists the special characters that form the escape sequences with special meanings inside `printf`:

Special character	Description
\n	Newline
\t	Tab
\v	Vertical tab
\b	Backspace

\r	Carriage return
\f	Form feed
\<any character>	That character
\'	Single quotation
\"	Double quotation
\\	Backslash character

The following are a few more special characters:

- **Horizontal tab**: In the following example, we use \t to put a horizontal tab between the fields of the employee database in the output. Here, it does not represent backslash followed by t; instead, it represents a special meaning of the horizontal tab. It will print the employee's first name, followed by a horizontal tab, and then the employee's phone number:

```
$ awk '{ printf "%s\t%s", $1,$3 }' emp.dat
```

The output of the preceding code is as follows:

```
Jack      9857532312Jane      9837432312Eva      8827232115Amit
9911887766Julie     8826234556Ana      9856422312Hari
8827255666Victor    8826567898John     9911556789Billy
9911664321Sam       8856345512Ginny    9857123466Emily
8826175812Amy       9857536898Vina     881177661
```

- **Newline**: In the previous example, we used a horizontal tab (\t) as the field delimiter; however, after processing one record, the subsequent record is printed without giving any newline character. It instructs the awk program to print each record in a newline. To insert the newline character after each record, we have to use \n, as shown in the following example:

```
$ awk '{ printf "%s\t%s\n", $1,$3 }' emp.dat
```

The output on execution of the preceding code is as follows:

```
Jack      9857532312
Jane      9837432312
Eva       8827232115
Amit      9911887766
Julie     8826234556
Ana       9856422312
```

```
Hari     8827255666
Victor   8826567898
John     9911556789
Billy    9911664321
Sam      8856345512
Ginny    9857123466
Emily    8826175812
Amy      9857536898
Vina     8811776612
```

- **Vertical tab**: The vertical tab was used to speed up the printer's vertical movement in olden times. Some printers used these special tab belts with various tab spots to align the content on paper. Although nowadays it is not used, it still exists in many programming languages. In the next example, we use a vertical tab after each field to print the first field of each record on the employee database, as follows:

```
$ awk '{printf "%s\v", $1}' emp.dat
```

The output on execution of the preceding code is:

```
Jack
    Jane
        Eva
            Amit
                Julie
                    Ana
                        Hari
                            Victor
                                John
                                    Billy
                                        Sam
                                            Ginny
                                                Emily
                                                    Amy
                                                        Vina
```

- **Backspace**: The backspace special character erases the last character of the previous string. In the following example, we print four strings and delete the last character from each string except the last string. In the last string, in place of the backspace escape sequence, we have put a newline \n escape sequence, as follows:

```
$ awk 'BEGIN{ printf "TEST 1\bTEST 2\bTEST 3\bTEST 4\n"}'
```

The output of the preceding code is as follows:

```
TEST TEST TEST TEST 4
```

- **Carriage return**: Carriage return means returning to the start of the current line without advancing downward. Its name is adopted from the printer's carriage. In the following example, after printing every string , we do a carriage return using the \r escape sequence. This prints the next value on top of the current printed value. This means that in the final output we get the last string only, as it was the last thing to be printed on top of all the previous strings:

```
$ awk 'BEGIN{ printf "TEST 1\rTEST 2\rTEST 3\rTEST 4\n"}'
```

The output on execution of the preceding code is as follows:

```
TEST 4
```

- **Form feed**: Form feed, in the good old days, was used to advance downward to the next page. It was used as a page separator, but now it is also used to separate two sections. Text editors such as MS Word use it to insert a page break. It is represented by a backslash followed by f (as \f), as shown in the following example:

```
$ awk '{printf "%s\f", $1}' emp.dat
```

The output of the preceding code is as follows:

```
Jack
    Jane
        Eva
            Amit
                Julie
                    Ana
                        Hari
                            Victor
                                John
                                    Billy
                                        Sam
                                            Ginny
                                                Emily
                                                    Amy
                                                        Vina
```

Different format control characters in the format specifier

Format specifiers begin with a percentage character (%) and end with a format control character. It tells the `printf` statement how to output an item. The format control character decides what kind of value to print. The rest of the format specifier is made up of optional modifiers that control field width. The following are the format control characters used in format specifiers with `printf` in AWK:

- `%c`: It prints a single character. If the argument is a number, then its corresponding ASCII character is printed. If a string is given as the argument, then only the first character of that string is printed. For example, if we give 65 to `printf` for printing, it outputs the letter A, which is the ASCII equivalent of 65:

  ```
  $ awk 'BEGIN { printf "ASCII representation of 65 = character
  %c\n", 65 }'
  ```

  The output on execution of the preceding code is as follows:

  ```
  ASCII representation of 65 = character A
  ```

- `%d` and `%i`: They print only the integer part of a decimal number. Both control letters are equivalent. For example, on giving 21.33 as the argument and format control character as `%d` or `%i`, only the integer part (21) of the decimal number is printed:

  ```
  $ awk 'BEGIN { printf "Integer part of 21.33 = %d\n", 21.33 }'
  ```

  Or it can be written as:

  ```
  $ awk 'BEGIN { printf "Integer part of 21.33 = %i\n", 21.33 }'
  ```

  The output is as follows:

  ```
  Integer part of 21.33 = 21
  ```

- `%e` and `%E`: This format control character prints a number in scientific (exponential) notation. The exponential form represented here is *[-]d.dddddde[+-]dd*. For example, the same number 21.33 with total four significant figures, three of which follow the decimal point, is represented using `%4.3e` as follows:

  ```
  $ awk 'BEGIN { printf "21.33 = %4.3e\n", 21.33 }'
  ```

The output on execution of the preceding code is:

```
21.33 = 2.133e+01
```

And if we use E in place of e:

```
$ awk 'BEGIN { printf "21.33 = %4.3E\n", 21.33 }'
```

The output will be as follows:

```
21.33 = 2.133E+01
```

- %f: Prints a number in floating-point notation. The floating form represented here prints up to six decimal places by default, in the form *dddd.dddddd*. For example, the same 21.33 number in floating-point representation is written as:

```
$ awk 'BEGIN { printf "21.33 = %f\n", 21.33 }'
```

The output on execution of the preceding code is as follows:

```
21.33 = 21.330000
```

- %g and %G: Prints the number in floating point notation or scientific notation, whichever is shortest. If the result is printed in scientific notation, it uses E and not e. It suppresses non-significant zeros. For example, 21.33 when using %g and %G is printed as follows:

```
$ awk 'BEGIN { printf "21.33 = %g\n", 21.33 }
```

   Or it can be written as:

```
$ awk 'BEGIN { printf "21.33 = %G\n", 21.33 }'
```

The output on execution of the preceding code is as follows:

```
21.33 = 21.33
```

- %o: It prints an unsigned octal number. For example, the octal representation of 21 is printed as:

```
$ awk 'BEGIN { printf "Octal representation of 21 = %o\n", 21 }'
```

The output on execution of the preceding code is as follows:

```
Octal representation of 21 = 25
```

- `%u`: It prints an unsigned decimal integer. For example, we can print `21.33` in unsigned decimal integer notation as follows:

```
$ awk 'BEGIN { printf "Unsigned decimal representation of 21.33 =
%u\n", 21.33 }'
```

The output on execution of the preceding code is:

```
Unsigned decimal representation of 21.33 = 21
```

- `%s`: It prints a string. Any literal passed as argument is printed as such. For example:

```
$ awk 'BEGIN { printf "%s\n", "0800 AM, What a beautiful
morning..?" }'
```

The output on execution of the preceding code is as follows:

```
0800 AM, What a beautiful morning..?
```

- `%x` and `%X`: Prints an unsigned hexadecimal integer. `%x` prints the lowercase letters `a` through `f`, and `%X` prints uppercase `A` through `F`. For example, we can get hexadecimal characters in lowercase using small `x` and hexadecimal characters in uppercase using capital `X` as follows:

```
$ vi printf_hex.awk

BEGIN    {
    printf "Lower Case Letters using: x\n"
    for ( i = 1 ; i <= 15; ++i )
    printf "%x ", i
    printf "\nUpper Case Letters using: X\n"
    for ( i = 1 ; i <= 15; ++i )
    printf "%X ", i
    printf "\n"
    }

$ awk  -f  printf_hex.awk
```

The output on execution of the preceding code is as follows:

```
Lower Case Letters using: x
1 2 3 4 5 6 7 8 9 a b c d e f
Upper Case Letters using: X
1 2 3 4 5 6 7 8 9 A B C D E F
```

- `%%`: This prints a single percentage character (`%`) and no argument is required for it to function. For example, if want to put a percentage symbol anywhere with the `printf` statement, we can put it as follows:

```
$ awk 'BEGIN { printf "Percentage = 21.33 %%\n"}'
```

The output of the preceding code is:

```
Percentage = 21.33 %
```

The following table summarizes the use of different control characters in format specifiers:

Character	Description
`%c`	Prints the ASCII character.
`%d`	Prints the decimal integer.
`%i`	Prints the decimal integer (Added in POSIX).
`%e`	Prints a number in exponential floating-point (scientific) notation format.
`%f`	Prints a number in fixed floating-point format.
`%g`	Prints a number in either scientific notation or floating-point notation, whichever is shorter, with trailing zeros removed.
`%o`	Prints an unsigned octal value.
`%u`	Prints an unsigned decimal integer.
`%s`	Prints a string.
`%x`	Prints an unsigned hexadecimal number. Uses *a-f* for *10* to *15*.
`%X`	Prints an unsigned hexadecimal number. Uses *A-F* for *10* to *15*.
`%%`	Prints a single percentage symbol (`%`).

Format specification modifiers

Each format specification begins with a % and ends with a character that determines the conversion, known as format control letter. In between, it may contain optional modifiers that control how much of the item's value is printed or how much of total space it gets. The following are the possible modifiers that may appear in a printf format specifier.

Printing with fixed column width

To create a fixed-column-width report, we have to specify a number immediately after the % in the format specifier. This number shows the minimum number of characters to be printed. This is the width (minimum size) of the field. If the input in the field becomes large, it automatically grows to prevent information loss. If the input string is smaller than the specified number, spaces are added to the left.

The following example displays the basic use of printf with fixed column width using the number specified immediately after the %. We have added headers inside the BEGIN statement to make the output more readable, as follows:

```
$ vi printf_width.awk

BEGIN {
    printf "%6s\t%6s\t%10s\t%17s\t%3s\t%3s\t%6s\n",
    "FName","LName","ContactNo.","EmailId","Sex","Dpt","Salary"
    printf "-----------------------------------------------------------
---------------\n"
        }
{
    printf "%6s\t%6s\t%10d\t%17s\t%3s\t%3s\t%4d\n", $1,$2,$3,$4,$5,$6,$7
}

$ awk -f printf_width.awk emp.dat
```

The output on execution of the preceding code is as follows:

FName	LName	ContactNo.	EmailId	Sex	Dpt	Salary
Jack	Singh	9857532312	jack@gmail.com	M	hr	2000
Jane	Kaur	9837432312	jane@gmail.com	F	hr	1800
Eva	Chabra	8827232115	eva@gmail.com	F	lgs	2100
Amit	Sharma	9911887766	amit@yahoo.com	M	lgs	2350
Julie	Kapur	8826234556	julie@yahoo.com	F	Ops	2500
Ana	Khanna	9856422312	anak@hotmail.com	F	Ops	2700

Hari	Singh	8827255666	hari@yahoo.com	M	Ops	2350
Victor	Sharma	8826567898	vics@hotmail.com	M	Ops	2500
John	Kapur	9911556789	john@gmail.com	M	hr	2200
Billy	Chabra	9911664321	bily@yahoo.com	M	lgs	1900
Sam	khanna	8856345512	sam@hotmail.com	F	lgs	2300
Ginny	Singh	9857123466	ginny@yahoo.com	F	hr	2250
Emily	Kaur	8826175812	emily@gmail.com	F	Ops	2100
Amy	Sharma	9857536898	amys@hotmail.com	F	Ops	2500
Vina	Singh	8811776612	vina@yahoo.com	F	lgs	2300

If the input string has more characters than what we've specified as the exact width, the whole string will be printed; the output will be zigzag and not what we applied. So, we have to put exactly as many characters as we want to print.

Space is added to the left. Let us say we print `hello` as an eight-character string. Then three spaces will be added on the left, as follows:

```
$ awk 'BEGIN{printf "%8s", "hello\n"}'
```

The output on execution of the preceding code is:

```
hello
```

The whole string is printed even if we specify a smaller character width. For example, now we extend the `hello` string used in the previous example to `hello world`, as follows:

```
$ awk 'BEGIN{printf "%8s", "hello world\n"}'
```

The output on execution of the preceding code is as follows:

```
hello world
```

To align the header and other multiple `printf` statements, sometimes we need to go through several rounds of trial and error.

Using the minus modifier (-) for left justification

In previous examples, the empty spaces were added on the left of the input string. However, this not the general output we use. To add the spaces to the right of the string, we have to make the string left justified. If the input string is less than the number of characters specified, we put a minus symbol (–) immediately after the %. This will print characters to the left and spaces will be added to the right.

For example, in the employee database emp.dat, we print the first name of the employee using a left-justified expression in printf, with a minus symbol immediately followed by a percentage % sign. To print each processed record in separate line, we append backslash n:

```
$ awk '{printf "|%-10s|\n", $1 }' emp.dat
```

The output is as follows:

```
|Jack      |
|Jane      |
|Eva       |
|Amit      |
|Julie     |
|Ana       |
|Hari      |
|Victor    |
|John      |
|Billy     |
|Sam       |
|Ginny     |
|Emily     |
|Amy       |
|Vina      |
```

Printing with fixed width – right justified

As we have seen in the previous example, to add an empty space on the right side, we used a minus symbol (–) immediately after %. If we do not put any symbol after %, it makes the string right justified. The empty spaces are kept on the left side instead of the right.

For example, in the employee database emp.dat we print the first name of the employee again but this time using the right justified expression in printf with no symbol following the percentage % sign, as follows:

```
$ awk '{printf "|%10s|\n", $1 }' emp.dat
```

The output on execution of the preceding code is as follows:

```
|      Jack|
|      Jane|
|       Eva|
|      Amit|
|     Julie|
|       Ana|
|      Hari|
```

```
|   Victor|
|    John|
|   Billy|
|     Sam|
|   Ginny|
|   Emily|
|     Amy|
|    Vina|
```

Using hash modifier (#)

This works with format control letters. For %o octal notation it adds a leading zero in the output. For %x and %X hexadecimal format control characters it adds a leading 0x or 0X, respectively for a nonzero result. For %e, %E, %f, and %F, the result always contains a decimal point. For %g and %G, trailing zeros are not removed from the result. The following example illustrates the workings of a hash (#) modifier:

```
$ vi printf_hash_modifier.awk

BEGIN   {
        printf "Octal representation = %#o\n", 10
    printf "Hexadecimal representation = %#X\n", 10
    printf "Trailing zeros in %% g = %#g\n", 10
}

$ awk -f printf_hash_modifier.awk
```

The output on execution of the preceding code is as follows:

```
Octal representation = 012
Hexadecimal representation = 0XA
Trailing zeros in % g = 10.0000
```

Using plus modifier (+) for prefixing with sign/symbol

If we want to prefix all the numeric values, whether they are positive or negative, rather then an optional modifier we put a plus (+) symbol after percentage (%) symbol instead. Positive values will have a plus (+) prefix in output, and negative values will have (−) prefix in output.

For example, we can prefix the salary of all employees in the employee database `emp.dat` using the plus (+) symbol as follows:

```
$ awk '{ printf "%s\t%+d\n", $1, $7}' emp.dat
```

The output on execution of the preceding code is as follows:

```
Jack      +2000
Jane      +1800
Eva       +2100
Amit      +2350
Julie     +2500
Ana       +2700
Hari      +2350
Victor    +2500
John      +2200
Billy     +1900
Sam       +2300
Ginny     +2250
Emily     +2100
Amy       +2500
Vina      +2300
```

Printing with leading zeros as modifier:

Till now, we have seen that default values are right justified with space added to the left. For right justified with spaces, we added – immediately after the percentage % sign.

If we want to prefix the output with 0's in front of the number instead of space, add a zero (0) before the number. For example, if we want to print the leading zeros in the salary field of the employee database, we put 0 in front of percentage % sign (format identifier) as follows:

```
$ vi printf_leading_zero.awk

BEGIN    {
    printf "|%-.4s|%-.2s|\n", "FNAME", "SALARY"
    printf "|=====|=====|\n"
    }
    {
    printf "|%-.4s|%-.3d|\n", $1, $7
    }

$ awk -f printf_leading_zero.awk emp.dat
```

The output on execution of the preceding code is as follows:

```
|FNAM|SA|
|=====|=====|
|Jack|2000|
|Jane|1800|
|Eva|2100|
|Amit|2350|
|Juli|2500|
|Ana|2700|
|Hari|2350|
|Vict|2500|
|John|2200|
|Bill|1900|
|Sam|2300|
|Ginn|2250|
|Emil|2100|
|Amy|2500|
|Vina|2300|
```

Printing with prefix sign/symbol

To add any symbol or special character as prefix before the field value, we had to add that symbol before a percentage sign. This will make the prefix to be added to all the values of that corresponding field. In the following example, we use employee database file `emp.dat` and put the dollar ($) symbol before the last field, which contains the salary of users in USD, as follows:

```
$ vi printf_symbol.awk

BEGIN    {
    printf "|%-10s|%-8s|\n",  "FNAME","SALARY"
    printf "|==========|========|\n"
    }
    {
    printf "|%-10s|$%-7d|\n", $1,$7
    }

$ awk -f printf_symbol.awk emp.dat
```

The output on execution of the preceding code is as follows:

```
|FNAME      |SALARY   |
|==========|========|
|Jack      |$2000    |
|Jane      |$1800    |
|Eva       |$2100    |
|Amit      |$2350    |
|Julie     |$2500    |
|Ana       |$2700    |
|Hari      |$2350    |
|Victor    |$2500    |
|John      |$2200    |
|Billy     |$1900    |
|Sam       |$2300    |
|Ginny     |$2250    |
|Emily     |$2100    |
|Amy       |$2500    |
|Vina      |$2300    |
```

Dot precision as modifier

A dot/period followed by an integer indicates the precision to use when printing. The meaning of precision differs by control letter:

- %d, %i, %o, %u, %x, and %X: Minimum number of digits to print in output
- %e, %E, %f, and %F: Number of digits to print on the right of the decimal point in output
- %g and %G: Prints the maximum number of significant digits in output
- %s: Prints maximum number of characters from the string that should print

The following example shows how a dot is used as modifier for format control character. We will use a number 201.33 and print it using .1 and .4 dot precision with different format control characters as follows:

```
$ vi printf_precision.awk

BEGIN    {
    print "====Using .1 precision===="
    printf ".1d -> %.1d\n", 201.33
    printf ".1e -> %.1e\n", 201.33
    printf ".1f -> %.1f\n", 201.33
    printf ".1g -> %.1g\n", 201.33
    print "====Using .4 precision===="
```

```
    printf ".4d -> %.4d\n", 201.33
    printf ".4e -> %.4e\n", 201.33
    printf ".4f -> %.4f\n", 201.33
    printf ".4g -> %.4g\n", 201.33
    }

$ awk -f printf_precison.awk
```

The output on execution of the preceding code is as follows:

```
====Using .1 precision====
.1d -> 201
.1e -> 2.0e+02
.1f -> 201.3
.1g -> 2e+02
====Using .4 precision====
.4d -> 0201
.4e -> 2.0133e+02
.4f -> 201.3300
.4g -> 201.3
```

Positional modifier using integer constant followed by $ (N$):

First we specify percentage (%) sign, then an integer constant followed by $ is a positional specifier and finally format control character. By using positional specifier, we can apply the format specification to the specific argument, otherwise by default format specification is applied to arguments in the order given in format string.

For example, lets print the following message `Hello World`, first without any positional specifier, as follows:

```
$ awk 'BEGIN { printf "%s %s\n", "Hello", "World"}'
```

The output on execution of the preceding code is as follows:

```
Hello World
```

Now we print the same message with positional modifier. This time, we make the first format specifier application to the second argument, and the second format specifier application to the first argument, as follows:

```
$ awk 'BEGIN { printf "%2$s %1$s\n", "Hello", "World"}'
```

The output on execution of the preceding code is as follows:

```
World Hello
```

Redirecting output to file

Till now we have been sending the output of `print` and `printf` commands to `stdout`, that is, the screen. However, we can also redirect the output to files by using the redirection operator. Redirection is done after the `print` command. It is the same as we do in shell commands using redirection operator.

There are three forms of output redirection:

- Output to file
- Output appended to a file
- Output through a pipe to another command

Redirecting output to a file (>)

This redirection operator (>) prints the items into the output file. Its syntax is as follows:

```
print items > demo
```

In this type of redirection, if the output file named `demo` exists, then it is erased before the first output is written to it. Subsequent write operations to the same file within the same AWK command do not overwrite the content, but append to it. If the output file does not it creates it. For example, with the employee database file, `emp.dat`, we generate a report with headers columns, as follows:

```
$ vi printf_redirection1.awk

BEGIN {
    printf "-----------------------------------------------------
-------------------\n"> "emp_report"
    printf "|%-6s\t|%-6s\t|%-10s\t|%-17s\t|%-3s\t|%-3s\t|%-6s|\n",
    "FName","LName","ContactNo.","EmailId","Sex","Dpt","Salary" >
"emp_report"
    printf "-----------------------------------------------------
-------------------\n"> "emp_report"
    }
{
```

```
    printf "|%-6s\t|%-6s\t|%-10d\t|%-17s\t|%-3s\t|%-3s\t|%-6d|\n",
$1,$2,$3,$4,$5,$6,$7> "emp_report"
}
END    {
    printf "----------------------------------------------------------
-----------------\n"> "emp_report"
    }

$ awk -f printf_redirection1.awk emp.dat
```

On execution of preceding code, a file with the name emp_report will get created in the same directory containing the AWK program script. We can view the content of report generated as follows:

```
$ cat emp_report
```

```
------------------------------------------------------------------------
-----
|FName    |LName     |ContactNo.   |EmailId           |Sex    |Dpt
|Salary|
------------------------------------------------------------------------
-----
|Jack     |Singh     |9857532312   |jack@gmail.com    |M      |hr
|2000  |
|Jane     |Kaur      |9837432312   |jane@gmail.com    |F      |hr
|1800  |
|Eva      |Chabra    |8827232115   |eva@gmail.com     |F      |lgs
|2100  |
|Amit     |Sharma    |9911887766   |amit@yahoo.com    |M      |lgs
|2350  |
|Julie    |Kapur     |8826234556   |julie@yahoo.com   |F      |Ops
|2500  |
|Ana      |Khanna    |9856422312   |anak@hotmail.com  |F      |Ops
|2700  |
|Hari     |Singh     |8827255666   |hari@yahoo.com    |M      |Ops
|2350  |
|Victor   |Sharma    |8826567898   |vics@hotmail.com  |M      |Ops
|2500  |
|John     |Kapur     |9911556789   |john@gmail.com    |M      |hr
|2200  |
|Billy    |Chabra    |9911664321   |bily@yahoo.com    |M      |lgs
|1900  |
|Sam      |khanna    |8856345512   |sam@hotmail.com   |F      |lgs
|2300  |
|Ginny    |Singh     |9857123466   |ginny@yahoo.com   |F      |hr
|2250  |
|Emily    |Kaur      |8826175812   |emily@gmail.com   |F      |Ops
```

```
|2100    |
|Amy          |Sharma      |9857536898      |amys@hotmail.com      |F      |Ops
|2500    |
|Vina         |Singh       |8811776612      |vina@yahoo.com        |F      |lgs
|2300    |
------------------------------------------------------------------------
-----
```

The following program puts the details of cars from the `cars.dat` database into two files: `expensive_cars` if the price of cars is greater than 3 lakh, and `budget_cars` if price of cars is less than 3 lakh:

```
$ awk '$5 > 3 {print $0 > "expensive_cars"}' cars.dat

$ awk '$5 <= 3 {print $0 > "budget_cars"}' cars.dat
```

Filenames can be variables or expressions, as shown in the following example:

```
$ awk '{ print($0) > ( $5 >3 ? "expensive_cars" : "budget_cars" )}'
cars.dat
```

 The filenames have to be enclosed in double quotes, otherwise AWK treats them as uninitialized variables.

Appending output to a file (>>)

This redirection operator appends the output to file. It's syntax is as follows:

```
print items >> demo
```

In this type of redirection, items are appended into the preexisting output file named `demo`. Here, while performing the redirection the output file is not erased. If the output file does not exist, then it is created. For example, now we append the content at the end of the file (`emp_report`) created using the `printf_rediection1.awk` using redirection operator (`>>`), as follows:

```
$ vi printf_append.awk

BEGIN    {
    printf "=========employee database ends here============\n"
>>"emp_report"
```

```
    }
```

```
$ awk -f printf_append.awk
```

On execution of preceding code, it will append the line in the existing file, emp_report, which was created in the previous example.

Sending output on other commands using pipe (|)

We can send the output of print command to another program using pipe instead of sending it to a file. For example, we can sort the first name of employees from the emp.dat file by piping the output of the first column to the sort command, and then storing it in a file. We will first display the names in alphabetical order, and in the next example we will store them in a file instead of printing on screen, as follows:

```
$ awk '{ printf "%s\n", $1 | "sort" }' emp.dat
```

The output on execution of the preceding code is as follows:

```
Amit
Amy
Ana
Billy
Emily
Eva
Ginny
Hari
Jack
Jane
John
Julie
Sam
Victor
Vina
```

The following stores the result in file names.sorted instead of displaying on screen, as follows:

```
$ awk '{ printf "%s\n", $1 | "sort > names.sorted" }' emp.dat
```

On execution of the preceding code a file called names.sorted in same directory, which contains the AWK script.

Special file for redirecting output (/dev/null, stderr)

Linux/Unix programs use three streams available to them for reading input and writing output, named standard input, standard output, and standard error. These open streams (open files or pipes) are known as **file descriptors**. By default, these streams are connected to a keyboard for input and a screen for output. There are the two different ways of writing an error message to standard error in AWK programs.

In the following example, error message is first send to another shell process cat using pipe, which further send it to standard error stream using file descriptors (1 and 2) as follows :

```
$ awk 'BEGIN{ print "Error message!" | "cat 1>&2" }'
```

The output on execution of the preceding code is as follows:

```
Error message!
```

The following example illustrates another method of writing an error message to standard error in AWK programs. Here, the error message is redirected to special device file "/dev/stderr" as follows :

```
$ awk 'BEGIN{ print "Error message!" > "/dev/stderr" }'
```

Output on execution of preceding command is as follows:

```
Error message!
```

Closing files and pipes

If the same filename or the same shell command is used more than once during AWK program execution, the file is opened for the first time only. The file is opened and the first record is read from that file, subsequently if the same file is used then another record is read from it and so on.

So, in order to re-read that file from the beginning, it becomes necessary to close that file first. The `close()` function makes this possible .The `close(expr)` function is used to close a file or pipe referenced using `expr`. The string value of `expr` should be the same as the string used to create/open the file or pipe used. Closing of files is necessary if we want to write a file and use it later in the same program. The operating system also defines a limit on the number of files and pipes that can be opened at the same time. This `close()` function returns value zero if close succeeds, or -1 if it fails.

The following is an example of opening and closing a file. Here we first create a file to store the output of `print` command, and then we subsequently close the file using `close` command, as follows:

```
$ awk 'BEGIN{print "Error message!" > "temp" ; close("temp")}
```

In our next example, we use the `close()` function to a command instead of a file. Here, we first store the `date` command in a variable named `cmd` to avoid any typing errors while closing the command. The same variable name is used again to store another shell command `sort`. Here, `sort` command output is given to getline command using co-process operator, which is then displayed on our screen line by line using print $0 statement. Then, this `sort` command is also closed using the `close()` function after processing the `cars.dat` file, as shown in the following code:

```
$ vi close.awk

BEGIN {
  cmd = "date"
  cmd |& getline
  print "DATE: ", $0
  close(cmd)
  cmd = "sort cars.dat"
  while (( cmd |& getline ) > 0 )
      print $0
  close(cmd);
  print "End of File..!"
}

$ awk -f close.awk
```

The output on execution of the preceding code is as follows:

```
DATE: Sat Mar 10 00:17:08 IST 2018
chevy beat 2005 33000 2
chevy tavera 1999 10000 4
fiat punto 2007 45000 3
ford ikon 1995 80000 1
honda accord 2000 60000 2
honda city 2005 60000 3
honda city 2010 33000 6
maruti dezire 2009 3100 6
maruti esteem 1997 98000 1
maruti swift 2007 50000 5
maruti swift 2009 4100 5
toyota corolla 1995 95000 2
End of File..!
```

Summary

In this chapter, we learned to use `print()` and `printf()` for finer control over output. We began with OFS and ORS for formatting the output, which was followed by introduction to escape sequences in `printf` for printing special characters. Then we learned how AWK uses format-control characters for different data types, and optional modifiers for modifying the behavior of format control characters. Finally, we covered how the output from both `print` and `printf` can be redirected to files and pipes. In the end, we learned the importance of the `close()` function to close open files and pipes.

In the next chapter, we will learn about different types of expressions in AWK programming language and how they form the core logic of a program.

6
AWK Expressions

Expressions are the basic building blocks of any programming language. They form its core logic. Expressions evaluate to a value that we can test, print, or pass to any function. They are also used to assign a new value to a variable. AWK expressions are made up of operators and operands, which consist of constants, variables, regular expressions, and function calls.

In this chapter, we will cover the following topics:

- AWK variables and constants
- Expressions using binary arithmetic operators
- Expressions using assignment operations
- Expressions using increment and decrement operators
- Expressions using relational operators
- Expressions using logical operators
- Expressions using ternary operators
- Unary arithmetic expressions
- Exponential expressions
- String concatenation
- Regular expression operators

AWK variables and constants

This sections describes the different types of AWK variables and constants available in the AWK programming language.

AWK variables give names to values for use or reference later in another part of the program. AWK variables are case sensitive. The AWK variable name should begin with an alphabet and the rest of the characters can be numbers, letters, or underscore. AWK keywords cannot be used as variable names. Variables are assigned new values using assignment operators, increment operators, and decrement operators. AWK also has some built-in variables, which have special meaning; however, they can be used and assigned like other variables. All built-in variables of AWK are named in uppercase.

Inside AWK, we don't have to declare a variable to use it. Also, there is no need to initialize an AWK variable explicitly. Variables are automatically initialized to empty strings; if the variable is a number, it is initialized to zero upon conversion. And if we wish to initialize an AWK variable, then the best place to do it is in the BEGIN section, which is executed only once.

An AWK constant is the simplest type of expression, which always has the same value. There are three types of constants, namely string, numeric, and regexp constants. Numeric constants represent numbers; this can be an integer, a decimal fraction, or an exponential notation. In AWK, all numbers are in decimal representation (base 10) by default. String constants represent a sequence of characters enclosed in double quotes. Strings in AWK can be of any length and they can have any of the possible 8-bit ASCII characters. A regular expression constant is a regex expression enclosed in forward slashes. Most regular expressions in AWK are built using constants but sometimes they can be built using expressions.

Now we will study operators that make use of the values provided by constants and variables in building expressions.

Arithmetic expressions using binary operators

AWK supports almost all basic arithmetic operators for building arithmetic expressions. These operators are binary operators; that is, they operate on two variables and are very similar to C language expressions. All these arithmetic operators follow the normal precedence rule. AWK supports the following arithmetic operators.

Addition (p + q):

This is represented by a plus (+) symbol, which adds two or more numbers. These numbers could be variables or constants. For example, we can add two numbers after assigning them to two variables as follows:

```
$ awk 'BEGIN{ p = 20; q = 30; print "( p + q ) = ",( p + q )}'
```

The output on execution of this code is as follows:

```
( p + q ) =   50
```

Now, we will use the `marks.txt` sample file to calculate the sum of marks obtained by a student using the arithmetic operator, as follows:

```
$ vi sum.awk

BEGIN    {
    printf "%-6s\t%-7s\t%-7s\t%-7s\t%-7s\t%-7s\t%-5s\n", "Name",
"Eng","Hindi","Maths","Science","Arts","Total"
    }
    {
    sum = $2+$3+$4+$5+$6;
    printf "%-6s\t%-7d\t%-7d\t%-7d\t%-7d\t%-7d\t%-5d\n",
$1,$2,$3,$4,$5,$6,sum
    }

$ awk -f sum.awk marks.txt
```

Output:

Name	Eng	Hindi	Maths	Science	Arts	Total
ram	80	78	60	85	72	375
amit	64	67	69	61	62	323
vijay	90	98	92	96	97	473
satvik	81	74	72	79	80	386
akshat	67	80	74	60	72	353
rishi	85	80	82	76	84	407
tushar	70	82	68	79	60	359

Subtraction (p – q):

This is represented by a minus (–) symbol, which subtracts two or more numbers. These number also could be variables or constants. For example, we can subtract two numbers after assigning them to two variables as follows:

```
$ awk 'BEGIN{ p = 20; q = 30; print "( p - q ) = ",( p - q )}'
```

The output on execution of this code is as follows :

```
( p - q ) = -10
```

Multiplication (p * q):

This is represented by an asterisk (*) symbol, which multiplies two or more numbers. These numbers could be variables or constants. For example, we can multiply two numbers after assigning them to two variables:

```
$ awk 'BEGIN{ p = 20; q = 30; print "( p * q ) = ",( p * q )}'
```

Output:

```
( p * q ) =  600
```

Division (p / q):

This is represented by a forward slash (/) symbol, which divides two or more numbers. These numbers can also be variables or constants. For example, we can divide two numbers after assigning them to two variables as follows:

```
$ awk 'BEGIN{ p = 20; q = 30; print "( p / q ) = ",( p / q )}'
```

The output is as follows:

```
( p / q ) =  0.666667
```

Modulus (p % q):

This is represented by the percentage (%) symbol, which gives the remainder after division of one number by another number. When computing the remainder of p % q, the quotient is rounded toward zero to an integer. These numbers can be variables or constants. For example, we can find the modulo of two numbers after assigning them to two variables as follows:

```
$ awk 'BEGIN{ p = 20; q = 30; print "( p % q ) = ",( p % q )}'
```

Output:

```
( p % q ) =  20
```

Using the `marks.txt` file, we can find the average number of marks scored by students in a class as follows:

```
$ vi average.awk

BEGIN   {
    printf "%-6s\t%-7s\t%-7s\t%-7s\t%-7s\t%-7s\t%-5s\t%-4s\n", "Name",
"Eng","Hindi","Maths","Science","Arts","Total","avg"
    }
    {
    sum = $2+$3+$4+$5+$6;
    avg = sum/5
    printf "%-6s\t%-7d\t%-7d\t%-7d\t%-7d\t%-7d\t%-5d\t%-4d\n",
$1,$2,$3,$4,$5,$6,sum,avg
    }

$ awk -f average.awk marks.txt
```

The output on execution of the preceding code is:

```
Name      Eng     Hindi    Maths     Science  Arts     Total     avg
ram       80      78       60        85       72       375       75
amit      64      67       69        61       62       323       64
vijay     90      98       92        96       97       473       94
satvik    81      74       72        79       80       386       77
akshat    67      80       74        60       72       353       70
rishi     85      80       82        76       84       407       81
tushar    70      82       68        79       60       359       71
```

The `print` command outputs a floating-point number on divide and an integer for the rest. Numbers are automatically converted into strings when needed. Unlike other programming languages, AWK does not support types for variables.

The following table summarizes binary arithmetic operators:

Operator	Meaning	Expression	Result
+	Addition	12+5	17
−	Subtraction	12−5	7
*	Multiplication	12*5	60
/	Division	12/5	2.4
%	Modulo	12%5	2

Assignment expressions

An assignment is an expression that stores a value in a variable. The simplest assignment operator is =, the equals sign. It stores the value of the right-hand-side operand as such. The assignment statement syntax is as follows:

<variable> or <field> or <array> = <constant> or <expression> or

The basic variable assignment is represented by the equals sign, =. Whatever value was assigned earlier is forgotten and the new value is assigned. For example, we assign a value to variable x=10 as follows:

```
$ awk 'BEGIN{ x=10; print "Number x is : ", x}'
```

The output on execution of the preceding code is as follows:

```
Number x is :   10
```

Assignment can store string values as well. For example, now we declare a variable message and store the string Welcome to Awk Programming. To store this string, we use two more variables and then concatenate them as follows:

```
$ vi assign.awk

BEGIN    {
    greet = "Welcome " ;
    lang = "Awk Programming";
    message = greet "to " lang;
    print message
    }

$ awk -f assign.awk
```

The output on execution of the preceding code is as follows:

```
Welcome to Awk Programming
```

Variables do not have any permanent types. A variable's type is whatever value we have assigned to it on the right-hand side. In the following program, the demo variable is assigned a numeric value at first and then it is reassigned a string value, as follows:

```
$ vi reassign.awk

BEGIN    {
    demo = 10;
```

```
    print demo;
    demo = "Hello";
    print demo;
    }

$ awk -f reassign.awk
```

The output on execution of the preceding code is as follows:

```
10
Hello
```

We can write multiple assignments together in AWK. In the following example, we store the value 10 in three variables—x, y, and z—together x = 10, y = 10, z = 10:

```
$ awk 'BEGIN{x=y=z=10; printf "x = %d, y = %d, z = %d \n" ,x ,y ,z}'
```

The output on execution of the preceding code is as follows:

```
x = 10, y = 10, z = 10
```

Besides simple assignment operations, we can use = with some arithmetic operators as well, to perform both the assignment and arithmetic operations one after another using shorthand notation. We will discuss this in the following section.

Shorthand addition (+=):

It is represented by +=. The following example illustrates this:

```
$ awk 'BEGIN { count = 100; count += 5; print "Counter = ", count}'
```

The output on execution of the preceding code is as follows:

```
Counter =   105
```

Shorthand subtraction (-=):

It is represented by −=. The following example illustrates this:

```
$ awk 'BEGIN { count = 100; count -= 5; print "Counter = ", count}'
```

The output on execution of the preceding code is as follows:

```
Counter =   95
```

Shorthand multiplication (*=):

Represented by `*=`. The following example illustrates this:

```
$ awk 'BEGIN { count = 100; count *= 5; print "Counter = ", count}'
```

The output is as follows:

```
Counter =   500
```

Shorthand division (/=):

It is represented by `/=`. The following example illustrates this:

```
$ awk 'BEGIN { count = 100; count /= 5; print "Counter = ", count}'
```

The output is:

```
Counter =   20
```

Shorthand modulo (%=):

It is represented by `%=`. The following example illustrates it:

```
$ awk 'BEGIN { count = 100; count %= 5; print "Counter = ", count}'
```

The output on execution of the preceding code is as follows:

```
Counter =   0
```

Shorthand exponential (^=):

This is represented by `^=`:

```
$ awk 'BEGIN { count = 2; count -= 5; print "Counter = ", count}'
```

The output on execution of the preceding code is as follows:

```
Counter =   -3
```

Shorthand exponential (=):**

It is represented by `**=`. The following example illustrates this:

```
$ awk 'BEGIN { count = 100; count **= 5; print "Counter = ", count}'
```

The output on execution is as follows:

```
Counter =   10000000000
```

AWK assignment operators summary table:

Operator	Meaning
`Variable += increment`	Add increment to variable
`Variable -= decrement`	Subtract decrement from variable
`Variable *= coefficient`	Multiply variable by coefficient
`Variable /= divisor`	Divide variable by divisor
`Variable %= modulus`	Set the variable to its remainder by modulus
`Variable ^= power`	Raise the variable to the power specified (POSIX-compliant)
`Variable **= power`	Raise the variable to the power specified

Increment and decrement expressions

AWK also supports the increment ++ and decrement -- operators; they increase or decrease the value of a variable by one. Both operators are similar to the operators in C. These operators can only be used with a single variable and, thus, only before or after the variable. They are the short forms of some common operations of adding and subtracting.

Pre-increment:

It is represented by the plus plus (++) symbol prefixed to the variable. It increments the value of an operand by one. Let's say we have a variable, `var`; to pre-increment its value, we write `++var`. It first increments the value of operand and then returns the incremented value. In the following example, we use two variables, `p` =5 and `q` = ++p. Here, first the value is incremented and then it is assigned. So, the pre-increment sets both the operands `p` and `q` to 6. It is equivalent to p=p+1 and then q=p, as follows:

```
$ vi pre-increment.awk

BEGIN    {
    p = 5;
    q = ++p;
    printf "p = %d, q = %d\n", p,q
    }

$ awk -f pre-increment.awk
```

The output on execution of the preceding code is as follows:

```
p = 6, q = 6
```

Post-increment:

This one is represented by plus plus (++) symbol postfixed to the variable. It also increments the value of an operand by one. Let's say we have a variable, `var`; to post-increment its value, we write `var++`. It first returns the value of the operand and then increments its value. In the following example, we use two variables, `p =5` and `q = p++`, for assignment. Here, first the assignment takes place and then the value is incremented. So, post-increment sets p to 6 and q to 5. It is equivalent to `q=p` and then `p=p+1`, as follows:

```
$ vi post-increment.awk

BEGIN   {
    p = 5;
    q = p++;
    printf "p = %d, q = %d\n", p,q
    }

$ awk -f post-increment .awk
```

The output on execution of the preceding code is as follows:

```
p = 6, q = 5
```

Pre-decrement:

It is represented by the minus minus (--) symbol prefixed to the variable. It decrements the value of an operand by 1. Let's say we have a variable, `var`; to pre-decrement its value, we write `--var`. It first decrements the value of the operand and then returns the decremented value. In the following example, we use two variables, `p =5` and `q = --p`. The value is first decremented and then assigned. So , pre-decrement sets both the operands p and q to 4. It is equivalent to `p=p-1` and then `q=p`:

```
$ vi pre-decrement.awk

BEGIN   {
    p = 5;
    q = --p;
    printf "p = %d, q = %d\n", p,q
    }

$ awk -f pre-decrement.awk
```

The output is as follows:

```
p = 4, q = 4
```

Post-decrement:

This too is represented by minus minus (- -) symbol postfixed to the variable. It decrements the value of an operand by one. Let's say we have a variable, `var`; to post-decrement its value, we write `var- -`. It first returns the value of the operand and then it decrements its value. In the following example, we use two variables, `p` =5 and `q` = `p--`, for assignment. Here, first the assignment takes place and then the value is decremented. So, post-decrement sets `p` to 4 and `q` to 5. It is equivalent to `q=p` and then `p=p-1`, as follows:

```
$ vi post-decrement.awk

BEGIN    {
    p = 5;
    q = p--;
    printf "p = %d, q = %d\n", p,q
    }

$ awk -f post-decrement.awk
```

The output on execution of the preceding code is as follows:

```
p = 4, q = 5
```

Example to display users with login shells (who can log in to the system):

Here we use the post-increment unary operator to count the number of login shells in the body block and print its result inside the END block. The body block of this script includes a pattern match, so the code is executed only if the last field of the line contains the pattern `/bin/bash`, as follows:

```
$ vi count_login_users.awk

BEGIN    {
    FS=":"
    }
    $NF ~ /bash/{ n++ }
END    {
    print n
    }

$ awk  -f count_login_users.awk /etc/passwd
```

The output on execution of the preceding code is as follows:

```
2
```

Relational expressions

Relational expressions are built using relational operators, also known as **conditional** or **comparison operators**. These operators are used to test conditions, like `if` or `while`. Relational expressions compare strings or numbers for relationships such as equality, greater than , less than, and so on.

These expressions return 1 if the condition evaluates to true and 0 if false. When comparing operands of different types, numeric operands are converted to strings using a built-in variable (using `CONVFMT`). Strings are compared character to character.

Equal to (==):

This relational operator is represented by the equals symbol repeated twice (`==`). It returns true if both operands are equal; otherwise it returns false. Here, we have to make sure not to mistype the `==` operator by forgetting to put one `=` character. In this case, the AWK code still remains valid but the program does not do what it was intended to do, resulting in a semantic error. Syntactically, the program will be correct, though.

In this example, we use the equal to (`==`) condition to print info of all employees from the `emp.dat` database who belong to the logistics department:

```
$ awk 'BEGIN{ OFS="\t"} $6 == "lgs" {print $0}' emp.dat
```

The output on execution of the preceding code is as follows:

```
Eva      Chabra   8827232115   eva@gmail.com      F   lgs   2100
Amit     Sharma   9911887766   amit@yahoo.com     M   lgs   2350
Billy    Chabra   9911664321   bily@yahoo.com     M   lgs   1900
Sam      khanna   8856345512   sam@hotmail.com    F   lgs   2300
Vina     Singh    8811776612   vina@yahoo.com     F   lgs   2300
```

In the following example, we use the equal to (`==`) condition to print all lines from the `/etc/passwd` file that have the same USER ID and GROUP ID. This AWK script prints the line only if `$3` (USER ID) and `$4` (GROUP ID) are equal:

```
$ awk -F: '$3==$4{ print }' /etc/passwd
```

The output on execution of the preceding code is:

```
root:x:0:0:root:/root:/usr/bin/zsh
daemon:x:1:1:daemon:/usr/sbin:/usr/sbin/nologin
bin:x:2:2:bin:/bin:/usr/sbin/nologin
sys:x:3:3:sys:/dev:/usr/sbin/nologin
lp:x:7:7:lp:/var/spool/lpd:/usr/sbin/nologin
mail:x:8:8:mail:/var/mail:/usr/sbin/nologin
news:x:9:9:news:/var/spool/news:/usr/sbin/nologin
uucp:x:10:10:uucp:/var/spool/uucp:/usr/sbin/nologin
proxy:x:13:13:proxy:/bin:/usr/sbin/nologin
www-data:x:33:33:www-data:/var/www:/usr/sbin/nologin
```

In this example, we use the equal to (==) condition to print information about all those users without a comment field (field number 5) in the /etc/passwd file:

```
$ awk -F":" '$5 == "" { print }' /etc/passwd
```

The output on execution of the preceding code is as follows:

```
Debian-exim:x:107:111::/var/spool/exim4:/bin/false
uuidd:x:108:113::/run/uuidd:/bin/false
ntp:x:112:114::/home/ntp:/bin/false
messagebus:x:118:120::/var/run/dbus:/bin/false
Debian-snmp:x:121:125::/var/lib/snmp:/bin/false
sshd:x:126:65534::/var/run/sshd:/usr/sbin/nologin
chromeuser:x:1000:1000::/home/chromeuser:/sbin/nologin
```

Not equal to (!=):

This relational operator is represented by an exclamation symbol followed by an equals symbol (!=). It returns true if both operands are unequal; otherwise it returns false. In the following example we use the not equal to (!=) conditions to print info of all employees from the emp.dat database who do not belong to logistic department, as follows:

```
$ awk 'BEGIN{ OFS="\t"} $6 != "lgs" {print $0}' emp.dat
```

The output is as follows:

```
Jack    Singh    9857532312    jack@gmail.com      M    hr     2000
Jane    Kaur     9837432312    jane@gmail.com      F    hr     1800
Julie   Kapur    8826234556    julie@yahoo.com     F    Ops    2500
Ana     Khanna   9856422312    anak@hotmail.com    F    Ops    2700
Hari    Singh    8827255666    hari@yahoo.com      M    Ops    2350
Victor  Sharma   8826567898    vics@hotmail.com    M    Ops    2500
John    Kapur    9911556789    john@gmail.com      M    hr     2200
Ginny   Singh    9857123466    ginny@yahoo.com     F    hr     2250
```

| Emily | Kaur | 8826175812 | emily@gmail.com | F | Ops | 2100 |
| Amy | Sharma | 9857536898 | amys@hotmail.com | F | Ops | 2500 |

In the following example, we declare two variables, a and b, and then check them for equality using the not equal comparison operator:

```
$ awk 'BEGIN{ a=5; b =6 ; if ( a != b ) print "true" }'
```

The output on execution of the preceding code is as follows:

```
true
```

Less than (<):

This relational operator is represented by < symbol. It returns true if the operand on left-hand side is less than the operand on right-hand side; otherwise it returns false. For strings it compares them character by character; that is, the first character on the left-hand-side string is compared with the first character on the right-hand-side string, and so on. For example, string 10 is less than 9. If a string is sub-string of another, then it is smaller than the longer string:

```
$ awk 'BEGIN{ a="10"; b = "9" ; if ( a < b ) print "true" }'
```

The output on execution of the preceding code is :

```
true
```

In the following example, again the value stored inside the variable "a" is compared to the value stored inside variable "b", character by character as follows :

```
$ awk 'BEGIN{ a="tall"; b = "taller" ; if ( a < b ) print "true" }'
```

The output on execution of the preceding code is as follows:

```
true
```

In the following AWK command also compares the value stored between two variables "a" and "b", however it will not give any output because if the condition is false, it does not print anything.

```
$ awk 'BEGIN{ a="xabc"; b = "abc" ; if ( a < b ) print "true" }'
```

In the following example, we use < condition to print the details of employees from the emp.dat database whose salary is less than 2000 dollars:

```
$ awk '$7 < 2000 { print }' emp.dat
```

The output on execution of the preceding code is as follows:

```
Jane  Kaur   9837432312 jane@gmail.com F hr 1800
Billy Chabra 9911664321 bily@yahoo.com M lgs 1900
```

Less than or equal to (<=):

This relational operator is represented by the <= symbol. It returns true if the left-hand-side operand is less than or equal to the right-hand-side operand; otherwise it returns false.

In the following example, we use <= condition to print the details of employees from emp.dat database whose salary is less than or equal to 2000 dollars:

```
$ awk '$7 <= 2000 { print }' emp.dat
```

The output on execution of the preceding code is as follows:

```
Jack  Singh  9857532312 jack@gmail.com M hr 2000
Jane  Kaur   9837432312 jane@gmail.com F hr 1800
Billy Chabra 9911664321 bily@yahoo.com M lgs 1900
```

Greater than (>):

This relational operator is represented by >. It returns)">true if the left operand is greater than or equal to the right operand; otherwise it returns false.

In the following example, we use the > condition to print the details of employees from emp.dat whose salary is more than 2000 dollars:

```
$ awk '$7 > 2000 { print }' emp.dat
```

The output is as follows:

```
Eva     Chabra   8827232115  eva@gmail.com      F   lgs   2100
Amit    Sharma   9911887766  amit@yahoo.com     M   lgs   2350
Julie   Kapur    8826234556  julie@yahoo.com    F   Ops   2500
Ana     Khanna   9856422312  anak@hotmail.com   F   Ops   2700
Hari    Singh    8827255666  hari@yahoo.com     M   Ops   2350
Victor  Sharma   8826567898  vics@hotmail.com   M   Ops   2500
John    Kapur    9911556789  john@gmail.com     M   hr    2200
Sam     khanna   8856345512  sam@hotmail.com    F   lgs   2300
Ginny   Singh    9857123466  ginny@yahoo.com    F   hr    2250
```

```
Emily    Kaur     8826175812   emily@gmail.com     F   Ops   2100
Amy      Sharma   9857536898   amys@hotmail.com    F   Ops   2500
Vina     Singh    8811776612   vina@yahoo.com      F   lgs   2300
```

In the following example, we use the > condition to display the uid (and complete record) from the /etc/passwd file that has the highest value in the USER ID field. Here, we declare a variable maxuid to store the largest number from field three and corresponding user details in variable userinfo. In the end, we print the value stored in the maxid and userinfo variables:

```
$ vi maxuid.awk

BEGIN   {
    FS = ":"
    }
$3 > maxuid { maxuid=$3; userinfo=$0 };
END     {
    print maxuid, userinfo
    }

$ awk -f maxuid.awk /etc/passwd
```

The output on execution of the preceding code is as follows:

```
65534 nobody:x:65534:65534:nobody:/nonexistent:/usr/sbin/nologin
```

Greater than or equal to (>=):

This relational operator is represented by >=. It returns =)">true if the left-hand-side operand is greater than or equal to the right-hand-side operand; otherwise it returns false.

In the following example, we use >= to print the details of employees from emp.dat whose salary is greater than or equal to 2000 dollars:

```
$ awk '$7 >= 2000 { print }' emp.dat
```

The output on execution of the preceding code is as follows:

```
Jack     Singh    9857532312   jack@gmail.com      M   hr    2000
Eva      Chabra   8827232115   eva@gmail.com       F   lgs   2100
Amit     Sharma   9911887766   amit@yahoo.com      M   lgs   2350
Julie    Kapur    8826234556   julie@yahoo.com     F   Ops   2500
Ana      Khanna   9856422312   anak@hotmail.com    F   Ops   2700
Hari     Singh    8827255666   hari@yahoo.com      M   Ops   2350
Victor   Sharma   8826567898   vics@hotmail.com    M   Ops   2500
John     Kapur    9911556789   john@gmail.com      M   hr    2200
Sam      khanna   8856345512   sam@hotmail.com     F   lgs   2300
```

```
Ginny    Singh    9857123466    ginny@yahoo.com      F    hr     2250
Emily    Kaur     8826175812    emily@gmail.com      F    Ops    2100
Amy      Sharma   9857536898    amys@hotmail.com     F    Ops    2500
Vina     Singh    8811776612    vina@yahoo.com       F    lgs    2300
```

AWK table for string comparison:

Expression	Result
`"abc" >= "xyz"`	False
`1.8 != "+2"`	True
`"2e1" < "3"`	True
`a=2;b="2" a == b`	True

AWK table for relational operators:

Operator	Description	Expression	Result
`==`	Is equal to	`p==q`	True if `p` is equal to `q`
`!=`	Is not equal to	`p!=q`	True if `p` is not equal to `q`
`>`	Is greater than	`p>q`	True if `p` is greater than `q`
`<`	Is less than	`p<q`	True if `p` is less than `q`
`>=`	Is greater than or equal to	`p>=q`	True if `p` is greater than or equal to `q`
`<=`	Is less than or equal to	`p<=q`	True if `p` is less than or equal to `q`

Logical or Boolean expressions

Boolean expressions are also known as **logical expressions**. It is a combination of comparison expressions or matching expressions, using the Boolean operators together with parentheses to control nesting. There are three Boolean operators, namely or (||), and (&&), and not (!). The truth value of Boolean expression is calculated by combining the truth values of the component expressions.

Boolean expressions are used to combine two or more conditional expressions. They return numeric value 1 if true and 0 if false.

Logical AND (&&): This operator is represented by the `&&` symbol. Its syntax is:

expr1 && expr2

It evaluates to true if both expressions *expr1* and *expr2* evaluate to true; otherwise it returns false. Also *expr2* is evaluated if and only if *expr1* evaluates to true. For example, we print those records from the employee database `emp.dat` whose salary is greater than 2500 and gender is female:

```
$ awk '$5 == "F" && $7 > 2500 { print }awk' emp.dat
```

The output on execution of the preceding code is as follows:

```
Ana Khanna 9856422312 anak@hotmail.com F Ops 2700
```

Similarly, if you want to check whether a number is octal or not, you can use the logical AND (`&&`) operator as follows:

```
$ vi octalcheck.awk

BEGIN    {
    num = 4;
    if (num >= 0 && num &lt;= 7)
    printf "%o is an octal number\n", num
    }

$ awk -f octalcheck.awk
```

The output on execution of the preceding code is:

```
4 is an octal number
```

In the following example, we use >= and && conditions to print those user details from `/etc/passwd` file where `USER ID >= 100` and the user's shell is `/bin/bash`:

```
$ awk -F ":" '$3 >=100 && $NF == "/bin/bash" ' /etc/passwd
```

The output on execution of the preceding code is as follows:

```
postgres:x:116:119:PostgreSQL
administrator,,,:/var/lib/postgresql:/bin/bash
couchdb:x:124:129:CouchDB Administrator,,,:/var/lib/couchdb:/bin/bash
practice:x:1001:1001:,,,:/home/practice:/bin/bash
```

Logical OR (| |):

This operator is represented by the | | symbol. Its syntax is:

$$expr1 \; | \; | \; expr2$$

It evaluates to true if either of the expressions *expr1* or *expr2* evaluates to true (nonzero or non-empty); else it returns false. Also, *expr2* is evaluated if and only if *expr1* evaluates to false. For example, we print those records from `emp.dat` whose gender is female or salary is greater than or equal to 2500 USD:

```
$ awk '$5 == "F" || $7 >= 2500 { print }' emp.dat
```

The output on execution of the preceding code is as follows:

```
Jane     Kaur      9837432312    jane@gmail.com      F    hr     1800
Eva      Chabra    8827232115    eva@gmail.com       F    lgs    2100
Julie    Kapur     8826234556    julie@yahoo.com     F    Ops    2500
Ana      Khanna    9856422312    anak@hotmail.com    F    Ops    2700
Victor   Sharma    8826567898    vics@hotmail.com    M    Ops    2500
Sam      khanna    8856345512    sam@hotmail.com     F    lgs    2300
Ginny    Singh     9857123466    ginny@yahoo.com     F    hr     2250
Emily    Kaur      8826175812    emily@gmail.com     F    Ops    2100
Amy      Sharma    9857536898    amys@hotmail.com    F    Ops    2500
Vina     Singh     8811776612    vina@yahoo.com      F    lgs    2300
```

Similarly, if we want to check for the existence of whitespace character anywhere, we use the logical OR (| |) operator:

```
$ vi whitespacecheck.awk

BEGIN    {
    char = "\n"
    if ( char == " " || char == "\n" || char == "\t" )
    print "Character is whitespace"
    }

$ awk -f whitespacecheck.awk
```

The output on execution of the preceding code is as follows:

```
Character is whitespace
```

Logical NOT (!):

This operator is represented by the ! symbol. Its syntax is:

! expr1

It returns the logical compliment of *expr1*. If *expr1* evaluates to true, it returns zero; else it returns one. For example, we print the records from emp.dat whose gender is not female, as follows:

```
$ awk '! ( $5 == "F"){print} ' emp.dat
```

The output on execution of the preceding code is:

```
Jack     Singh    9857532312  jack@gmail.com      M   hr    2000
Amit     Sharma   9911887766  amit@yahoo.com      M   lgs   2350
Hari     Singh    8827255666  hari@yahoo.com      M   Ops   2350
Victor   Sharma   8826567898  vics@hotmail.com    M   Ops   2500
John     Kapur    9911556789  john@gmail.com      M   hr    2200
Billy    Chabra   9911664321  bily@yahoo.com      M   lgs   1900
```

Similarly, if want to check whether a string is empty or not, we can use a logical NOT operator as follows:

```
# vi emptystring_check.awk

BEGIN    {
    str ="";
    if ( ! length(str))
    print "String is empty"
    }

$ awk -f emptystring_check.awk
```

The output on execution of the preceding code is as follows:

```
String is empty
```

In the following example, we print only the first line of any file. It emulates the Linux command head -1. Here, we use negation with the NR built-in variable to print the line as follows:

```
$ awk '!( NR >1 )' emp.dat
```

The output is:

```
Jack     Singh    9857532312  jack@gmail.com      M   hr    2000
```

Ternary expressions

Ternary expressions are also known as **conditional expressions**. They are a special kind of expression that has three operands. In this expression, we use one expression's value to select one of two other expressions. It works the same way as in C language. Its syntax is as follows:

conditional exp1 ? Statement 1 : statement 2

If conditional expression *exp1* returns true, then *Statement1* gets executed; otherwise, *statement2* gets executed. For example, here we use two variables and find largest number from two given numbers as follows:

```
$ vi ternary.awk

BEGIN    {
    p = 10; q=20
    ( p > q )? max=p: max =q
    print max
    }

$ awk -f ternary.awk
```

The output on execution of the preceding code is as follows:

```
20
```

In the following example, we prefix each line with a number, but we only print the numbers if the line is not blank. We use the NF built-in variable to find out whether the line in the file is empty or not, and then use the ternary expression to print the line number followed by the line itself, as follows:

```
$ awk '{print (NF? ++a " : " $0 :"")}' emp.dat
```

The output on execution of the preceding code is:

```
1 : Jack    Singh    9857532312  jack@gmail.com      M   hr    2000
2 : Jane    Kaur     9837432312  jane@gmail.com      F   hr    1800
3 : Eva     Chabra   8827232115  eva@gmail.com       F   lgs   2100
4 : Amit    Sharma   9911887766  amit@yahoo.com      M   lgs   2350
5 : Julie   Kapur    8826234556  julie@yahoo.com     F   Ops   2500
6 : Ana     Khanna   9856422312  anak@hotmail.com    F   Ops   2700
7 : Hari    Singh    8827255666  hari@yahoo.com      M   Ops   2350
8 : Victor  Sharma   8826567898  vics@hotmail.com    M   Ops   2500
9 : John    Kapur    9911556789  john@gmail.com      M   hr    2200
```

```
10 : Billy    Chabra    9911664321    bily@yahoo.com       M    lgs    1900
11 : Sam      khanna    8856345512    sam@hotmail.com      F    lgs    2300
12 : Ginny    Singh     9857123466    ginny@yahoo.com      F    hr     2250
13 : Emily    Kaur      8826175812    emily@gmail.com      F    Ops    2100
14 : Amy      Sharma    9857536898    amys@hotmail.com     F    Ops    2500
15 : Vina     Singh     8811776612    vina@yahoo.com       F    lgs    2300
```

Unary expressions

An operator that accepts a single operand is called a **unary operator**, and expressions built using unary operator are called **unary expressions**. Increment and decrement operators also fall under this category.

Unary plus:

It is represented by a single plus (+) symbol. It multiplies a single operand by +1. In the following example, we assign a variable p with value −5. On applying the unary plus operator to the variable, it multiplies the variable p with +1 and again stores the result inside p, as follows:

```
$ awk 'BEGIN{ p = -5; p = +p; print "p = ",p }'
```

The output on execution of the preceding code is as follows:

```
p =  -5
```

Unary minus:

It is represented by a single minus (−) symbol. It multiplies a single operand by −1. In the following example, we assign a variable p with value −5. On applying the unary minus operator, it multiplies the variable p by −1 and again stores the result inside p:

```
$ awk 'BEGIN{ p = -5; p = -p; print "p = ",p }'
```

The output on execution of the preceding code is as follows:

```
p =  5
```

Let us apply the unary minus operator on the salary column of emp.dat and see how it negates the values stored in that column:

```
$ awk '{print -$7}' emp.dat
```

The output on execution of the preceding code is as follows:

```
-2000
-1800
-2100
-2350
-2500
-2700
-2350
-2500
-2200
-1900
-2300
-2250
-2100
-2500
-2300
```

Summary table for unary and post/pre-increment operators

Operator	Description	Number (p=-5)	Result
+	Multiplies the number by +1	+p	−5
−	Multiplies the number by −1	−p	5
v++	Post-increment	p++	−5
++v	Pre-increment	++p	−4
v−−	Post-decrement	p−−	−5
−−v	Pre-decrement	−−p	−6

Exponential expressions

There are two formats of exponential operators:

Exponential format 1 (^):

This is an exponential operator that raises the value of an operand. For example, the following example raises the value of 5 by the power of 3:

```
$ awk 'BEGIN { a = 5; a = a ^ 3; print "a ^ 3 =",a }'
```

The output on execution of the preceding code is as follows:

```
a ^ 3 = 125
```

Exponential format 2 (**):

This also raises the value of an operand. For example, the following example raises the value of 5 by the power of 3:

```
$ awk 'BEGIN { a = 5; a = a ** 3; print "a ** 3 =",a }'
```

The output on execution of the preceding code is as follows:

```
a ** 3 = 125
```

String concatenation

There is no specific operation to represent string concatenation. Space is a string concatenation operator that is used to merge two strings.

In the following example, we create three string variables to perform concatenation at different locations. In the statement, str3 contains the concatenated value of str1 and str2. Each print statement performs string concatenation with a static string value and AWK variable:

```
$ vi string.awk

BEGIN   {
    OFS=","
    str1 = "Good"
    str2 = "Morning"
    num1 = "10"
    str3 = str1 " " str2;
    print "Concatenated string is : " str3
    num1 = num1+1
    print "string to number conversion on addition : " num1
    }

$ awk -f string.awk
```

The output on execution of the preceding code is as follows :

```
Concatenated string is : Good Morning
string to number conversion on addition : 11
```

Since string concatenation does not have a special operator, it is essential to ensure that it happens at the right time with the right string by enclosing the string to concatenate in parentheses. For example, here we create a file using redirection. The filename is given by concatenating two strings. Although in GAWK, there is no need to enclose the string in parentheses for concatenation, in some versions of AWK, it might give some errors if parentheses are absent. So, it is always a good practice to enclose the filename within parentheses, as shown in this example:

```
$ vi str_fname_concatenate.awk

BEGIN    {
    f1="sample"
    f2=".txt"
    print "this is string concatenation example" >(f1 f2)
    }

$ awk -f str_fname_concatenate.awk
```

On execution of this code, a file by name `sample.txt` will be created in the same directory containing the AWK program `str_fname_concatenate.awk`.

Regular expression operators

When we use the `==` condition, AWK looks for an exact match. However, when we use the match operator (~), AWK looks for a partial match. Here, ~ means contains. To match a specific pattern using regular expression, `~` and `!~` are used. Regular expression comparisons are performed using a matching expression built with either of these two operators. The right-hand side of the ~ or ! ~ operator could be a regular expression or string enclosed between forward slashes (/ . . . /).

Match operator (~):

It is represented as a tilde (~) symbol. It matches a pattern in a specific field. Its syntax is as follows:

$$expression \sim /regexpr/$$

It matches if the string value of the expression contains a sub-string matched by regular expression *regexpr*.

For example, if you want to print the records containing `Singh` or `Kapur` in last name field from the employees database `emp.dat`, use the ~ operator as follows:

```
$ awk '$2 ~ /(Singh|Kapur)/ { print }' emp.dat
```

The output on execution of the preceding code is as follows:

```
Jack    Singh   9857532312  jack@gmail.com    M   hr    2000
Julie   Kapur   8826234556  julie@yahoo.com   F   Ops   2500
Hari    Singh   8827255666  hari@yahoo.com    M   Ops   2350
John    Kapur   9911556789  john@gmail.com    M   hr    2200
Ginny   Singh   9857123466  ginny@yahoo.com   F   hr    2250
Vina    Singh   8811776612  vina@yahoo.com    F   lgs   2300
```

In the following example, we print the total number of users who have bash as their default login shell. In this AWK command, if the last field of a line contains the pattern `bash`, the AWK variable `n` gets incremented by one:

```
$ awk -F ':' '$NF ~ /bash/{n++};END { print n}' /etc/passwd
```

The output on execution of the preceding code is:

```
2
```

Not match operator (!~):

It is represented by `!~`. It is the opposite of the ~ operator. It matches the fields that do not contain the specified pattern. Its syntax is as follows:

expression !~ /regexpr/

It matches if the string value of the expression does not contain a sub-string matched by regular expression *regexpr*.

For example, if you want to print the records not containing `Singh` or `Kapur` in the last name field from the employees database `emp.dat`, use `!~` as follows:

```
$ awk '$2 !~ /(Singh|Kapur)/ { print }' emp.dat
```

The output on execution of the preceding code is as follows:

```
Jane     Kaur     9837432312  jane@gmail.com     F   hr    1800
Eva      Chabra   8827232115  eva@gmail.com      F   lgs   2100
Amit     Sharma   9911887766  amit@yahoo.com     M   lgs   2350
Ana      Khanna   9856422312  anak@hotmail.com   F   Ops   2700
Victor   Sharma   8826567898  vics@hotmail.com   M   Ops   2500
```

```
    Billy    Chabra    9911664321    bily@yahoo.com        M    lgs    1900
    Sam      khanna    8856345512    sam@hotmail.com       F    lgs    2300
    Emily    Kaur      8826175812    emily@gmail.com       F    Ops    2100
    Amy      Sharma    9857536898    amys@hotmail.com      F    Ops    2500
```

Regular expression operators:

Operator	Description
~	Match operator
! ~	No match operator

Operators' Precedence

It determines how operators are grouped when different operators appear in a single expression. For example, * has higher precedence than +. So, if we have a + b * c ;it means multiply b and c and then add a to the result. Precedence of operators can be overridden by using parentheses.

This is table of AWK's operator precedence order from **highest to lowest:**

Operator	Description
(…)	Grouping
$	Field reference
++ or − −	Increment, decrement
^ or **	Exponentiation
+, −, !	Unary plus, minus, logical not
*, /, %	Multiplication, division or remainder
+, −	Addition, subtraction
Space	String concatenation
< <= == != > >= >>	Relational operators
~ !~	Match and no match operator
in	Array membership

&&	Logical and
||	Logical or
?:	Ternary operator
= += -= *= /= %= ^= **=	Assignment operators group right to left

Let us take a look at the following table to summarize the meaning of expression operators:

Operation	Operators	Example	Explanation of example
Assignment	= += -= *= /= %= ^=	p += 2	p = p + 2
Ternary	?:	p ? q : r	If p is true then p else q
Logical OR	||	p || q	1 if p or q is true, else 0
Logical AND	&&	p && q	1 if p and q are true else 0
Logical NOT	!	! p	1 if p is zero or null else 0
Match	~	$1 ~ /regex/	1 if first field contains regex else 0
No match	!~	$1 !~ /regex/	1 if first field do not contain regex else 0
Relational	< <= == != >= >	p == q	1 if p is equal to q else 0
Concatenation	Space	"p" "qr"	"pqr", space merges 2 strings
Arithmetic	+ - * / %	p + q	Sum of p and q
Unary plus and minus	+ -	-p	Negative value of p
Exponentiation	^ or **	2 ^ 3	8
Increment, decrement	++ -	++p , p++	Add 1 to p
Grouping	( )	($i)++	Add 1 to the value of ith field

Summary

In this chapter we learned about different types elements of computation, that is, expressions in AWK. We learned how they are made up of different types of constants and variables. Then we learned about building different types of expressions using unary, binary, assignment, arithmetic, and Relational operators. Then we covered the ternary operator and string concatenation. Finally, we understood regular expression operators and their usage, followed by operator precedence.

In the next chapter, we will learn about the usage of different control flow statements in AWK programs.

7
AWK Control Flow Statements

This chapter covers the control structures of the AWK programming language. This includes the different types of conditional and looping statements, such as `if...else`, `do...while`, `switch...case`, and so on available in AWK . The syntax for conditional and looping constructs is very similar to that of C programming language. If you are already familiar with C, then you will find it quite easy, and those who are new to programming will also find it simple and easy to understand.

In this chapter, we will cover the following topics:

- Different conditional constructs
- `if` statement usage
- `switch` statement usage
- The `while` loop construct
- The `for` loop construct
- Different statements affecting flow controls
- `Break` usage
- `Next` usage
- The `exit` statement

Conditional statements

Conditional statements such as `if` and `switch` are used to test expressions and control the flow of execution in AWK programs. All control statements start with special keywords such as `if` and `switch` to differentiate them from simple expressions. Within one conditional statement block, we can have other multiple statements separated by braces, newlines, or semicolons. Such conditional statements are known as **compound statements**.

The if statement

`if` is a conditional statement used to control the flow of a program. AWK supports three types of `if` statements:

- `if`
- `if...else`
- `if...elseif...elseif...`

if

This is a single and simple `if` statement used to test a condition/expression. It executes the actions given in the body part only if the conditional expression is evaluated as true. Its syntax is as follows:

if (conditional-expression)

action

- *if*: The keyword
- *conditional-expression*: This represents the condition to be tested
- *action*: An AWK statement for execution

If two or more actions need to be executed when the condition is true, then those actions should be enclosed in curly braces. The individual AWK action statements should be separated by newlines or semicolons as shown here:

if (conditional-expression)

{ action1;

action2;

.... }

If the conditional expression is true, then all the actions enclosed in the braces are executed in the given order. After the execution of the `if` block, AWK continues to execute the next statement, as shown in the following figure:

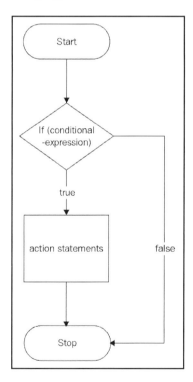

Figure 7.1: An if statement flowchart

Let's understand the working of the `if` statement with some examples. The simplest conditional expression to test is whether a variable is zero or nonzero:

```
$ awk 'BEGIN{ x=0; if ( x ) print x}'
```

On execution of the preceding code, the `print` statement will not be executed, as x is zero:

```
$ awk 'BEGIN{ x=10; if ( x ) print x}'
```

On execution of the preceding code, the value stored inside variable x will be printed as, in the conditional expression, x is nonzero. So, the output is as follows:

```
10
```

We can find out whether a number is even or not using an `if` conditional statement and print the result, as follows:

```
$ awk 'BEGIN{ x=4; if ( x % 2 == 0) print x " is even number" }'
```

The output on execution of the preceding code is:

```
4 is even number
```

In the following example, we will print details of all cars from the `cars.dat` database whose year of manufacturing is 2005 and earlier:

```
$ awk '{ if ( $3 < 2005 )print }' cars.dat
```

The output on execution of the preceding code is as follows:

```
chevy       tavera      1999        10000       4
toyota      corolla     1995        95000       2
maruti      esteem      1997        98000       1
ford        ikon        1995        80000       1
honda       accord      2000        60000       2
```

We can have multiple conditional operators in an `if` statement, as well. In the following example, we will print the details of all the cars that were manufactured is between 2000 and 2007 and have a mileage of less than 40000 kilometers:

```
$ awk '{ if (( $3 >= 2000 && $3 < 2007 ) && ( $4 < 40000 ))print }'
cars.dat
```

The output on execution of the preceding code is as follows:

```
chevy       beat        2005        33000       2
```

If...else

In an `if...else` statement, we can specify a list of actions to be performed if the conditional expression becomes false. The syntax of `if...else` is as follows:

if (conditional-expression)

action1

else

action2

If *conditional-expression* evaluates to true (nonzero), then *action1* is performed, and if *conditional-expression* evaluates to false (zero), then *action2* is performed, as shown in the following figure:

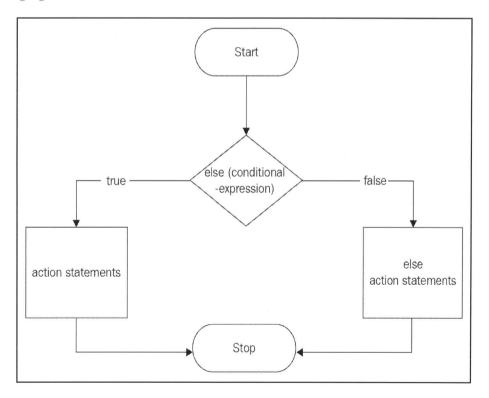

Figure 7.2: An if...else statement flowchart

AWK also has a conditional ternary operator (? :); it is equivalent to the one in C language. It is the same as an if...else statement. The syntax of the ternary operator is as follows:

conditional-expression ? action1 : action2 ;

Let's understand the working of if...else with some examples. The simplest of all conditional expressions to test is whether a variable is zero or nonzero:

```
$ vi check_zero.awk

BEGIN    {
    x = 0;
    if ( x )
    print "x is non-zero"
    else
    print "x is 0"
    }

$ awk -f check_zero.awk
```

On execution of the preceding code, the print statement given in the else block will be executed:

```
x is 0
```

We can find out whether a number is even or not by using an if conditional statement and print the result as follows:

```
$ vi check_even_odd.awk

BEGIN    {
    x = 5;
    if ( x % 2 == 0 )
        printf("%d is even number\n", x)
    else
        printf("%d is odd number\n", x)
    }

$ awk -f check_even_odd.awk
```

The output on execution of the preceding code is as follows:

```
5 is odd number
```

In the following example, we will print the details of all cars from `cars.dat` with the suffix as `OLD MODEL` and the suffix `NEW MODEL` for all others:

```
$ vi car_old_new.awk

{
if ( $3 < 2005 )
    print $0, "\t", "**OLD MODEL**"
else
    print $0, "\t", "NEW MODEL"
}


$ awk -f car_old_new.awk cars.dat
```

The output on execution of the preceding code is as follows:

```
maruti          swift           2007            50000           5           NEW MODEL
honda           city            2005            60000           3           NEW MODEL
maruti          dezire          2009            3100            6           NEW MODEL
chevy           beat            2005            33000           2           NEW MODEL
honda           city            2010            33000           6           NEW MODEL
chevy           tavera          1999            10000           4           **OLD MODEL**
toyota          corolla         1995            95000           2           **OLD MODEL**
maruti          swift           2009            4100            5           NEW MODEL
maruti          esteem          1997            98000           1           **OLD MODEL**
ford            ikon            1995            80000           1           **OLD MODEL**
honda           accord          2000            60000           2           **OLD MODEL**
fiat            punto           2007            45000           3           NEW MODEL
```

We can print even records with the output field separator set as `"="` and odd records the `OFS` set as `"||"`, as follows:

```
$ vi   ifelse1.awk

{
if ( NR%2 )
{
    OFS="=";
    print NR,$1,$2,$3,$4,$5,$6,$7;
}
else
{
    OFS="||";
    print NR,$1,$2,$3,$4,$5,$6,$7;
}
}
```

```
}

$ awk -f ifelse1.awk emp.dat
```

The output on execution of the preceding code is as follows:

```
1=Jack=Singh=9857532312=jack@gmail.com=M=hr=2000
2||Jane||Kaur||9837432312||jane@gmail.com||F||hr||1800
3=Eva=Chabra=8827232115=eva@gmail.com=F=lgs=2100
4||Amit||Sharma||9911887766||amit@yahoo.com||M||lgs||2350
5=Julie=Kapur=8826234556=julie@yahoo.com=F=Ops=2500
6||Ana||Khanna||9856422312||anak@hotmail.com||F||Ops||2700
7=Hari=Singh=8827255666=hari@yahoo.com=M=Ops=2350
8||Victor||Sharma||8826567898||vics@hotmail.com||M||Ops||2500
9=John=Kapur=9911556789=john@gmail.com=M=hr=2200
10||Billy||Chabra||9911664321||bily@yahoo.com||M||lgs||1900
11=Sam=khanna=8856345512=sam@hotmail.com=F=lgs=2300
12||Ginny||Singh||9857123466||ginny@yahoo.com||F||hr||2250
13=Emily=Kaur=8826175812=emily@gmail.com=F=Ops=2100
14||Amy||Sharma||9857536898||amys@hotmail.com||F||Ops||2500
15=Vina=Singh=8811776612=vina@yahoo.com=F=lgs=2300
```

The if...else...if statement

We can also create a multilevel `if...else...if` statement using multiple `if...else` statements. Its syntax is as follows:

if (conditional-expression)

action1

else if (conditional-expression)

action2

else if (conditional-expression)

action3

In multilevel `if...else...if` statement, multiple conditional expressions are used to test whether one of several possible expression is true or not as shown in *Figure 7.3*.

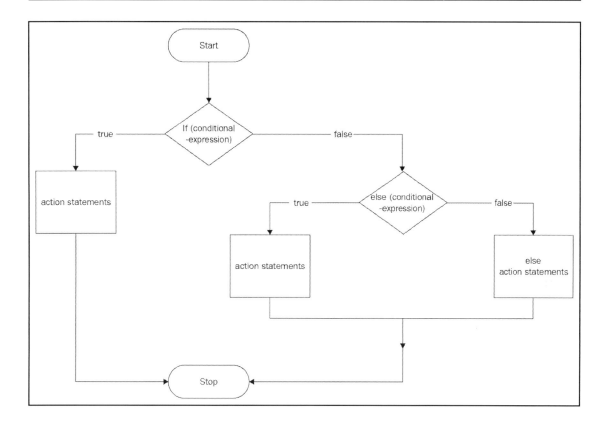

Figure 7.3: An if...else...if statement flowchart

Let's understand the working of if...else...if with some examples. Simplest of all conditional expression to test is if a value is equal to the value stored in a variable use:

```
$ vi if_else_if1.awk

BEGIN    {
    p = 20;
    if ( p == 10 )
    print "p = 10"
    else if ( p == 20 )
    print "p = 20"
    else if ( p == 30 )
    print "p = 30"
    }

$ awk -f if_else_if1.awk
```

The output on execution of the preceding code is as follows:

```
p = 20
```

In the following example, we will use the employee database file `emp.dat` and `print` segregates the email IDs of the same domain. First, we use the `if` conditional expression to identify the email ID of a particular domain using a regular expression match; then, we use a redirection operator to create three separate files of those domains containing the same domain `email _id`, as follows:

```
$ vi if_else_if2.awk

{
    if ( $4 ~ /gmail/ )
    print $4 > "gmail.txt"
    else if ( $4 ~ /yahoo/ )
    print $4 > "yahoo.txt"
    else if ( $4 ~ /hotmail/ )
    print $4 > "hotmail.txt"
}

$ awk -f if_else_if2.awk emp.dat
```

You will get three files in the output on execution of the preceding code in the same directory containing the AWK program `if_else_if2.awk`.

The switch statement (a GAWK-specific feature)

The `switch` statement is a GAWK specific feature which is not available in the default AWK program. It allows the evaluation of an expression and the execution of statements if case match. The `case` statements are checked for a match in the order they are specified. If none of the preceding given `case` statement match is found, then the default section is executed.

The first `switch` expression is evaluated and then the output of expression the is compared with the value given with the `case` statement. Each `case` statement contains a value that could be a numeric, string, or regular expression. The type of constant determines the comparison with `switch` expression result. Type of comparison performed (numeric or string or regular expression) is automatically chosen based on the value used with the `case` statement.

Inside each `case` statement we use `break` statement to stop execution of `switch...case` statement further, otherwise it will go through all the cases till it completes the execution of the `default` block as illustrated in *Figure 7.4*. It's syntax is as follows:

switch (conditional-expression) {

case value or regex :

action1

break

case value or regex :

action2

break

default :

action2

break

}

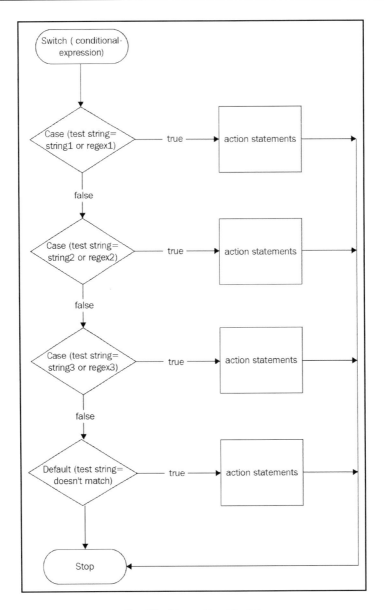

Figure 7.4: switch...case statement flowchart

Let's understand the working of the `switch...case` statement with some examples. The simplest conditional expression to test is if a value is equal to the value stored in a variable use:

```
$ vi switch1.awk

BEGIN    {
    p = "10";
    switch ( p ) {
    case "a" :
        print "p = a"
        break
    case "20" :
        print "p = 20"
        break
    case "10" :
        print "p = 10"
        break
    default :
        print "No match"
        break
    }
    }

$ awk -f switch1.awk
```

The output on execution of the preceding code is as follows:

```
$ p = 10
```

In the following example, we will use the employee database file `emp.dat` and `print` segregates the email ID of the same domain. First, we use the `switch if` conditional-expression to identify the email ID of a particular domain, using a regular expression match, and then we use a redirection operator to create three separate files of the domains containing the same domain `email _id`, as follows:

```
$ vi switch2.awk

{
    switch ( $4 ) {
    case /gmail/ :
        print $4 > "gmail.txt"
        break
    case /yahoo/ :
        print $4 > "yahoo.txt"
        break
    case /hotmail/ :
```

```
        print $4 >  "hotmail.txt"
        break
    default :
        print $4 > "misc_id.txt"
        break
    }
    }

$ awk -f switch2.awk emp.dat
```

You will get three files in the output on execution of the preceding code in the same directory containing the AWK program `switch2.awk`.

Looping statement

A loop is a conditional construct that allows us to perform one or more actions again and again till the condition is true as specified in expression. In AWK we can specify a loop using a `while`, `do` or `for` statement.

The while loop

The `while` is the simplest looping statement in AWK. A `while` statement has a condition and a body. The body contains the action statements that are executed till the condition is true. The condition could be a logical condition or conditional-expression that evaluates to true. First `while` statement tests the condition; if the condition evaluates to true, then it executes the statements specified in the body. Once all the statements specified in the body have been executed, the condition is again tested and, if it is still true, statements in body executes again. This process is repeated as long as the condition is true. If the condition returns false before the first iteration of the loop, the body of the loop never executes and AWK continues with the statements given after the loop, as illustrated in *Figure 7.5*. Its syntax is as follows:

while (condition)

action statement

The description of different keywords and statement used in while loop syntax above, is as follows :

- *while*: This is AWK keyword.
- *condition*: This is the conditional expression of logical conditional.
- *action statement*: This is body of `while` loop. If there is more than one action statement, then actions must be enclosed within curly braces.

The newline is optional after the right parenthesis:

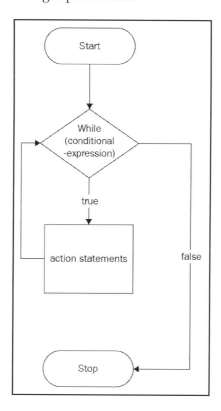

Figure 7.5: A While statement flowchart

Let's understand the working of `while` loop with some examples. In the following example we print the numbers from 1 to 10 number. First, we initialize the counter i to 1, then in `while` statement we put the condition if the counter is less than or equal to 10. If the condition is true, statements given in the body block are executed.

Here, we print the counter value and then increment the counter. When all statements in the body block are executed, the condition is again evaluated, and if it is true, the body block is again executed:

```
$ vi while1.awk

BEGIN    {
    i = 1
    while ( i <=10 )
    {
    print i
    i++
    }
}

$ awk -f while1.awk
```

The output on execution of the preceding code is as follows:

```
1
2
3
4
5
6
7
8
9
10
```

In the following example, we will print four fields of each record, one field per line, from the employee database `emp.dat` to generate labels for employees. The body of the loop is a compound statement containing an action statement and other conditional `if...else...if` statements. First, the value of `i` is initialized to 1. Then the `while` statement tests whether `i` is less than or equal to 4. If this is true, the statements given inside the `while` body are executed.

Then, as the last action statement in the `while` body, `i` is incremented using `i++` and the loop repeats. The loop terminates when `i` attains the value of 5:

```
$ vi while2.awk

{
    i=1
    while ( i<=4 )
    {
```

```
        if ( i == 1 )
        { printf "First Name \t: %s\n", $i }
        else if ( i == 2 )
        { printf "Last Name \t: %s\n", $i }
        else if ( i == 3 )
        { printf "Phone number \t: %s\n", $i }
        else if ( i == 4 )
        { printf "Email id \t: %s\n", $i
          printf "*********************************\n"
        }
        i++
        }
}


$ awk -f while2.awk emp.dat
```

The output on execution of the preceding code is as follows:

```
First Name        : Jack
Last Name         : Singh
Phone number      : 9857532312
Email id          : jack@gmail.com
*********************************
First Name        : Jane
Last Name         : Kaur
Phone number      : 9837432312
Email id          : jane@gmail.com
*********************************
First Name        : Eva
Last Name         : Chabra
Phone number      : 8827232115
Email id          : eva@gmail.com
*********************************
First Name        : Amit
Last Name         : Sharma
Phone number      : 9911887766
Email id          : amit@yahoo.com
*********************************
First Name        : Julie
Last Name         : Kapur
Phone number      : 8826234556
Email id          : julie@yahoo.com
*********************************
First Name        : Ana
Last Name         : Khanna
Phone number      : 9856422312
Email id          : anak@hotmail.com
*********************************
```

```
.........................
.........................
```

In the next example, we will use the `marks.txt` sample file to calculate the total of marks obtained by the student in different subjects. For each line, the program has to add the values of field 2 through to the last field. So, we first initialize `i=2` before entering the loop and test using conditional-expression if it has reached the last field in the record (`I <= NF`). `NF` represents the total number of fields in each record, as follows:

```
$ vi while3.awk

{
    i=2; total=0;
    while ( i <=NF )
    {
    total = total +$i;
    i++;
    }
    print "Student Name : ",$1, "\t", "Total Marks : ", total;
}

$ awk -f while3.awk marks.txt
```

The output on execution of the preceding code is as follows:

```
Student Name :    ram        Total Marks :    375
Student Name :    amit       Total Marks :    323
Student Name :    vijay      Total Marks :    473
Student Name :    satvik     Total Marks :    386
Student Name :    akshat     Total Marks :    353
Student Name :    rishi      Total Marks :    407
Student Name :    tushar     Total Marks :    359
```

do...while loop statement

In the AWK `while` loop, the condition is checked at entry, so it is called an **entry-controlled** loop. The `do...while` loop is an exit-controlled loop; the condition is checked at exit time. The `do...while` loop always executes the body at least once and then repeats the body as long as the condition is true.

It differs from the `while` and `for` in a way; it tests the conditional-expressions at the bottom instead of the top, so it will always execute the body once, even if the condition evaluates to false as illustrated in *Figure 7.6*. Its syntax is as follows:

do

action statements

while (conditional-expression)

Following figure 7.6 illustrates the working of a do-while loop statement in AWK programming:

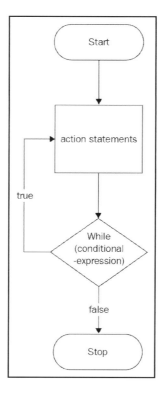

Figure 7.6: A do...while statement flowchart

Here also, newlines are optional after the keyword `do` and after action statements. If `while` appears on the same line as statement, then the only statement should be terminated by a semicolon.

Let's understand the working of the `while` loop with some examples. In the following example the `print` statement is executed only once because we ensure that the conditional-expression evaluates to false. If this were a `while` statement, with the same initialization of counter to 1 and conditional-expression, the body of the loop containing action statements would not be executed once:

```
$ vi dowhile1.awk

BEGIN    {
    counter = 1;
    do
    print "Print this line one time"
    while ( counter != 1 )
}

$ awk -f dowhile1.awk
```

The output on execution of the preceding code is as follows:

```
Print this line one time
```

In the following example, we will use the `marks.txt` sample file to calculate the total of marks obtained by the student in different subjects. For each line, the program has to add the values of field 2 through the to last field. So, we first initialize i=2 before entering the loop. Then it execute the loop body followed by a test using conditional-expression if it has reached last field in record (`I <= NF`). `NF` represents the total number of fields in each record. The output of this program is the same as the `while3.awk` program, but it uses the `do...while` loop construct as follows:

```
$ vi dowhile2.awk

{
    i=2; total=0;
    do
    {
    total = total + $i;
    i++;
    }
    while ( i <= NF )
    print "Student Name : ", $1, "\t", "Total Marks :", total;
```

```
}
```

```
$ awk -f dowhile2.awk marks.txt
```

The output on execution of the preceding code is as follows:

```
Student Name :   ram       Total Marks : 375
Student Name :   amit      Total Marks : 323
Student Name :   vijay     Total Marks : 473
Student Name :   satvik    Total Marks : 386
Student Name :   akshat    Total Marks : 353
Student Name :   rishi     Total Marks : 407
Student Name :   tushar    Total Marks : 359
```

In the following example, we will print four fields of each record, one field per line from
/etc/passwd file to user info from the user database. The body of the loop is a compound
statement containing an action statement and the other conditional if...else...if
statement. First, the value of i is initialized to 1. Then the while statement tests whether i
is less than or equal to 7. If this is true, statements given inside the while body are
executed. Then as last action statement in the while body, i is incremented using i++ and
the loop repeats. The loop terminates when i attains the value of 8:

```
$ vi dowhile3.awk

BEGIN    {
    FS=":"
    }
{
    i=1
    while ( i<=7 )
    {
    if ( i == 1 )
    { printf "User Name \t: %s\n", $i }
    else if ( i == 3 )
    { printf "UID \t\t: %s\n", $i }
    else if ( i == 6 )
    { printf "Home Directory \t: %s\n", $i }
    else if ( i == 7 )
    { printf "Default Shell \t: %s\n", $i
      printf "***********************************\n"
    }
    i++
    }
```

```
    }

    $ awk -f dowhile3.awk /etc/passwd
```

The output on execution of the preceding code is as follows:

```
User Name        : root
UID              : 0
Home Directory   : /root
Default Shell    : /usr/bin/zsh
**********************************
User Name        : daemon
UID              : 1
Home Directory   : /usr/sbin
Default Shell    : /usr/sbin/nologin
**********************************
User Name        : bin
UID              : 2
Home Directory   : /bin
Default Shell    : /usr/sbin/nologin
**********************************
User Name        : sys
UID              : 3
Home Directory   : /dev
Default Shell    : /usr/sbin/nologin
**********************************
User Name        : sync
UID              : 4
Home Directory   : /bin
Default Shell    : /bin/sync
**********************************
User Name        : games
UID              : 5
Home Directory   : /usr/games
Default Shell    : /usr/sbin/nologin
**********************************
User Name        : man
UID              : 6
Home Directory   : /var/cache/man
Default Shell    : /usr/sbin/nologin
**********************************
    . . . . . . . . . .
    . . . . . . . . . .
    . . . . . . . . . .
```

```
************************************
User Name          : practice
UID                : 1001
Home Directory     : /home/practice
Default Shell      : /bin/bash
************************************
```

The for loop statement

The AWK `for` statement functionally works the same as the AWK `while` loop; however, the `for` statement syntax is much easier to use. Its syntax is as follows:

for (initialization; conditional-expression; increment / decrement)

action statements

The description of different keywords and statement used in for loop syntax above is as follows:

- *initialization*: Sets the initial value for the counter variable
- *conditional-expression*: States a condition that is tested at the top of the loop
- *increment/decrement*: Increment/decrement the counter each time at the bottom of the loop, just before testing the *conditional-expression* again

For statement starts by performing *initialization* action, then it checks the *conditional-expression*. If the *conditional-expression* evaluates to true, it executes the action statements specified in body part. Thereafter, it performs *increment* or *decrement* operation. Then it checks the *conditional-expression*, if it is true then AWK again executes the action statement and the *increment/decrement*.

The loop executes as long as the conditional-expression evaluates to true as illustrated in *Figure 7.7*:

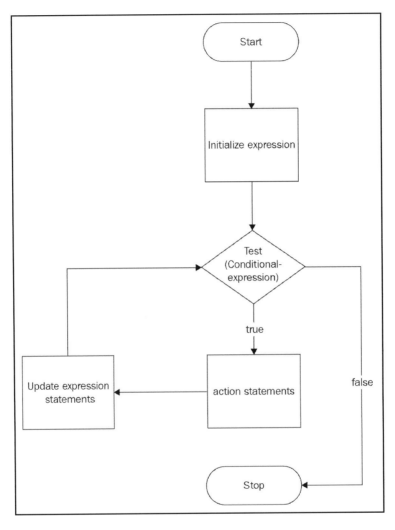

Figure 7.7: A for loop statement flowchart

Let's understand the working of `for` loop with some examples. In the following example, we will print the numbers from 1 to 10. First, we initialize the counter i to 1, then, in the conditional-expression, we put the condition if the counter is less than or equal to 10. If the condition is true, the statements given in the body block are executed.

Here, we print the counter value and then increment the counter. When all statements in the body block are executed, the condition is again evaluated, and, if it is true, the body block is again executed:

```
$ vi for1.awk

BEGIN    {
    for ( i = 1; i <=10; i++ )
    print i
    }

$ awk -f for1.awk
```

The output on execution of the preceding code is as follows:

```
1
2
3
4
5
6
7
8
9
10
```

In the following example, we will print four fields of each record, one field per line, from the employee database emp.dat to generate labels for employees. The body of the for loop is a compound statement containing the action statement and other conditional if...else...if statements. First, the value of i is initialized to 1. Then the for statement tests whether i is less than or equal to 4. If this is true, the action statements given inside the for body are executed. Then, as the last action statement, i is incremented using i++ and the loop repeats. The loop terminates when i attains the value of 5:

```
$ vi for2.awk

{
    for ( i =1; i <10 ; i++ )
    {
    if ( i == 1 )
    { printf "First Name \t: %s\n", $i }
    else if ( i == 2 )
    { printf "Last Name \t: %s\n", $i }
    else if ( i == 3 )
    { printf "Phone number \t: %s\n", $i }
    else if ( i == 4 )
```

```
    { printf "Email id \t: %s\n", $i
      printf "*********************************\n"
    }
    }
}

$ awk -f for2.awk emp.dat
```

The output on execution of the preceding code is as follows:

```
First Name : Jack
Last Name : Singh
Phone number : 9857532312
Email id : jack@gmail.com
*********************************
First Name : Jane
Last Name : Kaur
Phone number : 9837432312
Email id : jane@gmail.com
*********************************
First Name : Eva
Last Name : Chabra
Phone number : 8827232115
Email id : eva@gmail.com
*********************************
First Name : Amit
Last Name : Sharma
Phone number : 9911887766
Email id : amit@yahoo.com
*********************************
First Name    : Julie
Last Name     : Kapur
Phone number     : 8826234556
Email id      : julie@yahoo.com
*********************************
..........
..........
```

In the next example, we will use the marks.txt sample file to do the total of marks obtained by the student in different subjects. For each line, the program has to add the values of field 2 through to the last field. So, we first initialize i=2 before entering the loop and test using conditional-expression if it has reached the last field in the record (i <= NF). NF represents the total number of fields in each record, as follows:

```
$ vi for3.awk

{
```

```
    total=0;
    for ( i=2; i <=NF; i++ )
    {
    total = total + $i;
    }
    print "Student Name : ",$1, "\t", "Total Marks : ", total;
}

$ awk -f for3.awk marks.txt
```

The output on execution of the preceding code is as follows:

```
Student Name :   ram       Total Marks :   375
Student Name :   amit      Total Marks :   323
Student Name :   vijay     Total Marks :   473
Student Name :   satvik    Total Marks :   386
Student Name :   akshat    Total Marks :   353
Student Name :   rishi     Total Marks :   407
Student Name :   tushar    Total Marks :   359
```

For each loop statement

This is a special loop which is used for processing arrays only. Other variables, constants and functions cannot to be used with this type of loop. (Refer Chapter 4, *Working with Arrays in AWK*).

Statements affecting flow control

Till now we have seen different conditional constructs and loop construct such as if...else, while, for, switch and do statements. Now, we will study break, continue and exit statements which are used to alter the normal flow of program. A loop performs a set of repetitive tasks until the conditional-expression becomes false, but sometimes it is desirable to skip some action statements inside the loop or terminate the loop immediately without checking the conditional-expression. In such cases, break and continue statements are used.

Break usage

The break statement is used to terminate the innermost while, do...while, or for loop that encloses it. The break statement is also used to break out of switch statement. It is meaningful if used inside a loop or with a switch statement because, outside the body of a loop or switch, it has no meaning. All loop constructs have their termination conditional-expression, however sometimes it is possible that you achieve your goal before all iterations have been executed. In such cases break statement is used. Use of the break statement with while loop is illustrated in *Figure 7.8*:

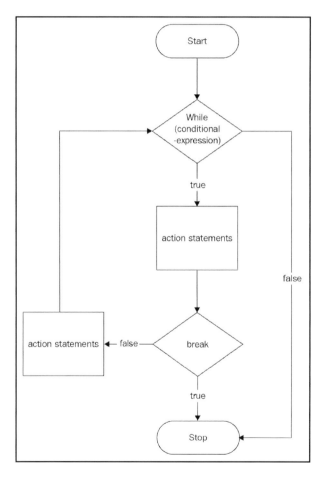

Figure 7.8: A while loop flowchart with break statement

Let's understand the working of the `break` statement with some examples. In the following example, we use car database file `cars.dat` to print records that contains `1995` in any field, using `while` loop and `break` statement. Here loop is set to iterate for each field of current input record. Each time through the loop, the value `1995` is compared with the value of the field referenced as `$i`. If the result is true, we print the record followed by string `OLD MODEL` and then do `break` from the loop. With the use of `break`, we make sure that with the first match of `1995` in the line, we print the comment `OLD MODEL` and don't iterate through the remaining fields:

```
$ vi break1.awk

{
    i=1;
    while ( i <= NF )
    {
        if ( $i == 1995 )
        {
        print $0,"OLD MODEL"
        break;
        }
    i++
    }
}

$ awk -f break1.awk cars.dat
```

The output on execution of the preceding code is as follows:

```
toyota   corolla 1995 95000 2 OLD MODEL
ford     ikon    1995 80000 1 OLD MODEL
```

In the next example, we will create an infinite loop by passing a conditional expression set as 1. To break the loop, we have to press *Ctrl* + *C*:

```
$ vi break2.awk

BEGIN {
  while (1)
  print "infinite loop"
  }

$ awk -f break2.awk
```

The preceding loop prints the `infinite loop` string forever because the conditional-expression is always true. So, we modify the loop to execute exactly 10 times only, using the `break` statement inside the loop. Here, `break` causes the loop to terminate immediately and continue the execution at the line after the loop's code block:

```
$ vi break3.awk

BEGIN    {
    x=1
    while(1)
    {
    print x,"iteration"
        if ( x == 10 )
        {
        break
        }
    x++
    }
    print "This statement is outside while loop..!"
}

$ awk -f break3.awk
```

The output on execution of the preceding code is as follows:

```
1 iteration
2 iteration
3 iteration
4 iteration
5 iteration
6 iteration
7 iteration
8 iteration
9 iteration
10 iteration
This statement is outside while loop..!
```

Usage of continue

Like `break`, the `continue` statement is also used only inside `do`, `while`, and `for` loops. It is used to skip the statements given after the `continue` keyword inside the loop body and execute the next iteration of the loop. It is useful when we want to skip a statement from getting executed but don't want to break the loop. The usage of the `continue` statement with a `while` loop is illustrated in *Figure 7.9*:

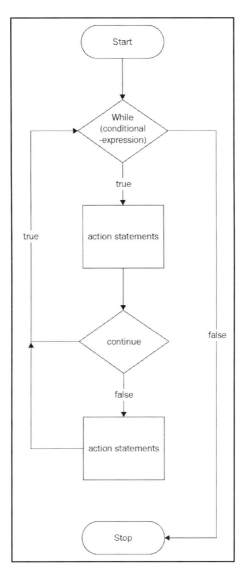

Figure 7.9: A while flowchart with continue statement

The `continue` statement does not have any special meaning with the `switch...case` statement and also no meaning if used outside the loop.

Let's understand the working of the `continue` statement with some examples. In the following example, we print the even numbers between 1 to 20 as follows:

```
$ vi continue1.awk

BEGIN    {
    i=0
    while ( i <= 20 )
    {
    i++
        if ( i%2 == 0 )
            print i
        else
            continue
    }
}

$ awk -f continue1.awk
```

The output on execution of the preceding code is as follows:

```
2
4
6
8
10
12
14
16
18
20
```

In the next example, we will print information of employee database, field by field, for each record in the database `emp.dat`, except the field 2, field 5 or field 6 or field 7. The `if` conditional statement inside loop tests the field number, and if it is 2, 5, 6, or 7, then the `continue` statement is executed and it skips the remaining statement inside the `for` loop and begins the next iteration, as follows:

```
$ vi continue2.awk

{
for ( x=1; x <=NF; x++ )
    {
    if ( x == 2 || x == 5 || x == 6 || x == 7 )
        continue
    printf( "%s\t", $x )
    }
```

```
    printf("\n")
}

$ awk -f continue2.awk emp.dat
```

The output on execution of the preceding code is as follows:

```
Jack      9857532312    jack@gmail.com
Jane      9837432312    jane@gmail.com
Eva       8827232115    eva@gmail.com
Amit      9911887766    amit@yahoo.com
Julie     8826234556    julie@yahoo.com
Ana       9856422312    anak@hotmail.com
Hari      8827255666    hari@yahoo.com
Victor    8826567898    vics@hotmail.com
John      9911556789    john@gmail.com
Billy     9911664321    bily@yahoo.com
Sam       8856345512    sam@hotmail.com
Ginny     9857123466    ginny@yahoo.com
Emily     8826175812    emily@gmail.com
Amy       9857536898    amys@hotmail.com
Vina      8811776612    vina@yahoo.com
```

Exit usage

As the name suggests, the `exit` statement is used to immediately stop the execution of AWK script. On getting the `exit` statement at any place in AWK script, AWK stops executing current rule and current processing of input. Any remaining input if any is ignored. The syntax of the `exit` statement is as follows :

exit [return status]

It accepts an integer value as an argument to set the `exit`/`return` status of the AWK process. Supplying of a *return status* as an argument is optional. If no argument is given to the `exit` statement, it returns the `exit` status as zero.

If an exit statement is executed from the `BEGIN` statement, the program stops processing everything immediately and no input records are read. And if an `END` statement is present, after the execution of the `exit` statement, the `END` statement is executed:

```
$ vi   exit1.awk

BEGIN    {
    x=1
```

```
        while(1)
        {
        print x,"iteration"
            if ( x == 10 )
            {
            exit(5)
            }
        x++
        }
        print "This statement is outside while loop..!"
    }
    END { print "Inside exit statement" }

    $ awk -f exit1.awk
```

The output on execution of the preceding code is as follows:

```
    1 iteration
    2 iteration
    3 iteration
    4 iteration
    5 iteration
    6 iteration
    7 iteration
    8 iteration
    9 iteration
    10 iteration
    Inside exit statement
```

To view the exit status (return status) of the AWK program, execute the following command:

```
    $ echo $?
```

The output on execution of the preceding code is as follows:

```
    5
```

In the following program, we use the `exit` statement to exit the AWK program with different exit codes for different conditions. Here, if the length of line in the file is greater then 60 characters, the program exits with exit status 2, and if number of lines in the file is less than 60 characters, it exits with exit status 1, as follows:

```
    $ vi exit2.awk

    {
        if ( length($0) > 60 )
```

```
    {
     exit 2
    }
    else if ( length($0) < 60 )
    {
    exit 1
    }
    print
}

$ awk -f exit2.awk  emp.dat

$ echo $?
```

The output on execution of the preceding code is as follows:

```
2
```

Next usage

The `next` command is also used to change the flow of an AWK program. It causes the AWK to stop processing the current input record or pattern space and go on to next record. The program reads the next line and starts executing the commands again with the newline.

If we consider the analogy of AWK program execution with a loop that reads an input record and then performs the pattern matching against it, then the `next` statement is equivalent to the `continue` statement. It skips to the end of the body of the loop and begins the next iteration. Similarly, on getting `next` statement execution, the remaining AWK commands are not processed for current input record. The next input record is read and the execution of the AWK command in the given script begins from start.

In the following program, AWK processes the input record one by one and prints each field separated by tab. On getting the field match to the string `akshat`, it skips the subsequent `printf` commands and reads the next input record for processing, as follows:

```
$ vi next.awk

{
    for ( i = 1; i <= NF; i++ )
    {
    if ( $i == "akshat" )
    {
    next
    }
```

```
    printf ( "%s\t", $i )
}
    printf ("\n")
}

$ awk -f next.awk marks.txt
```

The output on execution of the preceding code is as follows:

```
ram       80    78    60    85    72
amit      64    67    69    61    62
vijay     90    98    92    96    97
satvik    81    74    72    79    80
rishi     85    80    82    76    84
tushar    70    82    68    79    60
```

Following is a summary of control flow statement:

Construct	Explanation
{ statements }	Grouping of statements
If (conditional-expression) action statement	If the expression is true, execute the action statements
If (conditional-expression) action1 else action2	If the expression is true, execute *action1*, else *action2*
Switch (expr) case1 (match) action1 case2(match) action2..	If *case1* matches *expr*, execute *action1*; if *case2* matches *expr*, execute *action2*, and so on
While (conditional-expression) action	If the expression is true, execute the action statements
Do actions while (conditional-expression)	Execute the action statement, if the expression is true, repeat
For (exp1 ; exp2; exp3) action statement	First initialize with *exp1*, then if *exp2* is true, execute action statements, then execute *exp3*
For (var in array) action statement	Execute statement with *var* set to each subscript in array in each turn
Break	Immediately exit innermost loop (`while`, `do` and `for`)
Continue	Start next iteration of innermost loop (`while`, `do` and `for`)

| *Next* | Start next iteration of main input loop |
| *Exit return status* | Exit AWK script, setting return status |

Summary

In this chapter, we learned about the different types of control structures that are used in the AWK programming language. We learned types of conditional statements such as `if`, `if...else`, `if...else...if`, and `switch...case`. Then we learned about different looping constructs like `while`, `do...while`, and `for` loops. Finally, we saw the usage of different flow control statements such as `break`, `continue`, `exit`, and `next`.

In next chapter, we will learn about the different types of built-in and user-defined functions available in AWK.

8
AWK Functions

A function, also known as a named procedure, is a set of instructions that is used by programming languages to return a single result or a set of results. The statement that requests the function is called a function call. The functions extend the usefulness and functionality of AWK. This chapter covers the different types of built-in functions that are available in AWK. The built-in functions of AWK arc generally divided into three categories, namely numeric, string, and I/O. Apart from these, we will cover the additional functions provided by GAWK to represent time, to provide type information, and to enable bit manipulation. Then, we will discuss how AWK is used for writing user-defined functions for use in the rest of the program.

In this chapter, we will cover the following topics:

- Arithmetic functions
- String functions
- Input/output functions
- Time functions
- Bit-manipulating functions
- User-defined functions

Built-in functions

Built-in functions are always available to the programmer for use in the program. This section covers the built-in functions in AWK. These functions generally accept arguments as input and return a value. Whitespace is ignored between the built-in function name and the opening parenthesis; however, we should avoid using whitespace in this way as user-defined functions do not permit whitespace.

If an expression is given as an argument to the function, the expression is evaluated before the call is made to the function. For example:

$$p = 5$$
$$q = sqrt(p + +)$$

In the preceding case, p is incremented to the value of 6 before the *sqrt* function is called. It is good practice to evaluate the expression first and then pass the argument to the function.

Arithmetic functions

Arithmetic functions are those built-in functions that deal with numbers. The optional argument is enclosed in square brackets ([]).

The sin (expr) function

The `sin(expr)` function returns the sine of the expression `expr`, where `expr` is expressed in radians. The following code block shows an example of a sine function:

```
$ vi sinefunc.awk

BEGIN   {
    print "sin(90) = ", sin(90);
    print "sin(45) = ", sin(45);
    }

$ awk -f sinefunc.awk
```

The output of the execution of the previous code is as follows:

```
sin(90)  =   0.893997
sin(45)  =   0.850904
```

The cos (expr) function

The `cos (expr)` function returns the cosine of the expression `expr`, where `expr` is expressed in radians. The following code block shows an example of a cosine function:

```
$ vi cosfunc.awk

BEGIN    {
    print "cos(90) = ", cos(90);
```

```
    print "cos(45) = ", cos(45);
    }

$ awk -f cosfunc.awk
```

The output of the execution of the previous code is as follows:

```
cos(90) =  -0.448074
cos(45) =  0.525322
```

The remaining trigonometric functions, such as sec(), cosec(), tan(), and cot(), are measured in radians, and can be obtained with the use of the sin() and cos() functions.

The atan2 (x, y) function

The atan2 (x,y) function returns the arc tangent of *x/y* in radians. It is similar to the arc tangent, except that the signs of both arguments are used to determine the quadrant of the result, which is expressed in radians. The following code block shows an example of the atan2 function:

```
$ awk 'BEGIN { print "atan2(45,30) = ",atan2(45,30)}'
```

The output of the execution of the previous code is as follows:

```
atan2(45,30) =  0.982794
```

The int (expr) function

The int (expr) function returns the truncated numeric value by removing the digits to the right of the decimal point for the given argument that is the lowest integer of the given number that is returned. If a whole number is given as an argument, it is returned as such, whereas if a floating point number is given as an argument, it returns an integer value truncated towards zero. It does not round the argument value up or down. The following code block shows an example of an integer function:

```
$ vi intfunc.awk

BEGIN    {
    print "int(3.5678)  = ", int(3.5678);
    print "int(5.9876)  = ", int(5.9876);
    print "int(4)       = ", int(4);
    print "int(-3.1234) = ", int(-3.1234);
    print "int(-4)      = ", int(-4);
```

```
    }

$ awk -f intfunc.awk
```

The output of the execution of the previous code is as follows :

```
int(3.5678)  =   3
int(5.9876)  =   5
int(4)       =   4
int(-3.1234)=   -3
int(-4)      =  -4
```

The exp (expr) function

The `exp(expr)` function returns the natural exponential (e^x) of an expression given as an argument. It is also known as base-*e* exponentiation. The `exp (expr)` function reports an error if the expression is out of range. The maximum value of the argument supplied to the `exp (expr)` depends on the computer system's floating-point representation. The following code block shows an example of an `exp(expr)` function:

```
$ vi expfunc.awk

BEGIN    {
    print "exp(1)     = ", exp(1);
    print "exp(0)     = ", exp(0);
    print "exp(-12)    = ", exp(-12);
}

$ awk -f expfunc.awk
```

The output of the execution of the previous code is as follows :

```
exp(1)     =   2.71828
exp(0)     =   1
exp(-12)    =   6.14421e-06
```

The log (expr) function

The `log (expr)` function is the inverse of the `exp(expr)` function. The `log (expr)` function returns the natural logarithm of the expression given as an argument. The expression used as an argument must evaluate to a positive number or an error message `NaN` (not a number) will be thrown by the function.

In addition to the error message, it will print a warning message if a negative number is used as an argument to the `log()` function. The following code block shows an example of a `log(expr)` function:

```
$ vi logfunc.awk

BEGIN    {
    print "log(5)     = ",  log(5);
    print "log(0)     = ",  log(0);
    print "log(-1)     = ",  log(-1);
}

$ awk -f logfunc.awk
```

The output of the execution of the previous code is as follows :

```
log(5)     =  1.60944
log(0)     =  -inf
awk: logfunc.awk:4: warning: log: received negative argument -1
log(-1)     =  nan
```

The sqrt (expr) function

The `sqrt(expr)` function returns the positive square root for the given integer evaluated from the `expr` expression. This function also requires a positive number as an argument; otherwise, it returns an error message NaN for a negative number. It also prints a warning message if a negative number is used as an argument. The following code block shows an example of a `sqrt (expr)` function:

```
$ vi sqrtfunc.awk

BEGIN    {
    print "sqrt(5)     = ",  sqrt(5);
    print "sqrt(0)     = ",  sqrt(0);
    print "sqrt(-5)     = ",  sqrt(-5);
    }

$ awk -f sqrtfunc.awk
```

The output of the execution of the previous code is as follows:

```
sqrt(5)     =  2.23607
sqrt(0)     =  0
awk: sqrtfunc.awk:4: warning: sqrt: called with negative argument -5
sqrt(-5)     =  -nan
```

The rand() function

The `rand()` function returns a random number *x*, between 0 and 1, such that *0 <= x <1*. The value returned by the random function could be zero but it is never returned as zero. In AWK, `rand()` starts generating numbers from the same starting number (also known as the seed) on each run. The algorithm used to generate the random numbers is fixed, so the numbers are repeatable. Numbers are random within one AWK run, but they are predictable from run to run. To generate different numbers in each run, you must change the seed value for each run. This is generally done using `srand()`. The following code block shows an example of a `rand(expr)` function:

```
$ vi rand1.awk

BEGIN    {
    print "Random num1 = ",  rand()
    print "Random num2 = ",  rand()
    print "Random num3 = ",  rand()
    }

$ awk -f rand1.awk
```

The output of the execution of the previous code is as follows:

```
Random num1 =   0.237788
Random num2 =   0.291066
Random num3 =   0.845814
```

Upon executing the previous code multiple times, it will generate the same numbers in the output. Often, random numbers are required to be integers. The following example generates 10 random repeatable numbers between 0 and 100 and displays each number generated, as follows:

```
$ vi rand2.awk

BEGIN     {
    i=0;
    while( i <= 10 )
    {
        n=int(rand()*100);
        rand_num[i]=n;
        i++;
    }
    for ( i=0; i<=10; i++ )
    {
        print "Random number is : ", rand_num[i] ;
    }
```

```
}

$ awk -f rand2.awk
```

The output of the execution of the previous code is as follows:

```
Random num1 =    0.237788
Random num2 =    0.291066
Random num3 =    0.845814
```

The srand ([expr]) function

The srand([expr]) function generates the random number with the given argument integer set as the seed value. Whenever the program execution starts, AWK generates its random number from the seed value that is given as the argument. If no argument is given, AWK uses the time of day to generate the seed, and thus, without an argument, it always generates different random numbers.

Generally, the srand ([expr]) function is used to set the seed value for the rand function and then the rand() function is used for random value creation. The following code block shows an example of a srand ([expr]) function:

```
$ vi srand1.awk

BEGIN    {
    print "Random num1 = ",  srand()
    print "Random num2 = ",  srand()
}

$ awk -f srand1.awk
```

The output of the execution of the previous code is as follows:

```
Random num1 =    1
Random num2 =    1517928812
```

Let's generate random numbers using the srand() function. To do this, we initialize and set the seed value to 5, using the srand() function. Then, the rand() function is used to generate a random number that is multiplied with the desired value to generate numbers less than 50. This time, we check whether the generated random number already exists in the array. If the number exists, it increments the index and loop count.

This program will generate five numbers using this process. Finally, it prints the value from the minimum to the maximum value:

```
$ vi srand2.awk

BEGIN     {
    srand(5);
    total_num=5;
    count=0;
    while( count < total_num )
    {
        n=int(rand()*50);
        rand_num[count]=n;
        count++;
    }
    asort(rand_num)
    for ( i in rand_num )
    {
    print rand_num[i]
    }
}

$ awk -f srand2.awk
```

The output of the execution of the previous code is as follows:

```
14
16
23
33
35
```

Different versions of AWK generate different random numbers.

Summary table of built-in arithmetic functions

The following table summarizes the different built-in arithmetic functions available in AWK:

Function	Value returned
sin(x)	Returns the sine of *x*, with *x* in radians
cos(x)	Returns the cosine of *x*, with *x* in radians
atan2(x,y)	Returns the arc tangent of *x/y* in the range of -22/7 to +22/7
int(x)	Returns the integer part of *x*, truncated towards 0
log(x)	Returns the natural (*base-e*) logarithm of *x*
exp(x)	Returns *e* to the power of *x* , *e^x*
sqrt(x)	Returns the square root of *x*
rand()	Generates the random number *x*, where *0 <= x < 1*
srand()	*X* is the new seed value for rand()

String functions

The built-in string functions are much more significant as AWK is primarily designed as a string-processing language. These functions enhance AWK's power and functionality. In this section, we will discuss the following functions in detail:

- index (str, sub)
- length (string)
- split (str, arr, regex)
- substr (str, start, [length])
- sub (regex, replacement, string)
- gsub (regex, replacement, string)
- gensub (regex, replacement, occurrence, [string])
- match (string, regex)
- tolower (string)
- toupper (string)
- sprintf (format, expression)
- strtonum (string)

The index (str, sub) function

The `index (str,sub)` function is used to get the index (location) of the given substring (or character) in an input string. On a success, it returns the position where the substring started; otherwise, it returns 0. The first character of the input `str` string is at position 1. If the substring consists of two or more characters, all of those characters should match in the same order for a nonzero return value. This function is useful for checking proper input conditions. The following is an example of the index `(str, sub)` function:

```
$ vi index.awk

BEGIN    {
     str = "Awk is a powerful utility. Unix is awesome."
       search = "power"
       location = index(str, search)
       printf("Substring \"%s\" found at location : %d\n", search,
location)

     if ( index(str, ",") == 0 )
     {
     print "Comma (,) not found in sentence"
     }
}

$ awk -f index.awk
```

The output of the execution of the previous code is as follows:

```
Substring "power" found at location : 10
Comma (,) not found in sentence
```

The length (string) function

The `length (string)` function is used to calculate the length of a string. If the string is a number, the length of the digits in the string representing the number is returned—for example:

```
$ vi length1.awk

BEGIN    {
     print "Example of length calculation of string"
     print "length(hello..!) : "  length("hello..!")
     print "Example of length calculation of number"
     print "length(10*20) : " length(10*20)
```

```
}

$ awk -f length1.awk
```

The output of the execution of the previous code is as follows:

```
Example of length calculation of string
length(hello..!)  : 8
Example of length calculation of number
length(10*20)  : 3
```

If no argument is given to the length function, then it returns the length of $0. For example, we can use the length function to ignore empty lines by checking the length of each line before processing it. In the next example, we use the `length` function to print all lines shorter than 80 characters in the center of the screen, as follows:

```
$ vi length2.awk

{
    if (length($0) < 80)
    {
        prefix = "";
        for (i = 1; i < (80-length($0)) / 2 ;i++)
        prefix = prefix " ";
        print prefix $0;
    }
    else
    {
        print;
    }
}

$ awk -f length2.awk
```

The output of the execution of the previous code is as follows:

maruti	swift	2007	50000	5
honda	city	2005	60000	3
maruti	dezire	2009	3100	6
chevy	beat	2005	33000	2
honda	city	2010	33000	6
chevy	tavera	1999	10000	4
toyota	corolla	1995	95000	2
maruti	swift	2009	4100	5
maruti	esteem	1997	98000	1

ford	ikon	1995	80000	1
honda	accord	2000	60000	2
fiat	punto	2007	45000	3

The split (str, arr, regex) function

The `split` function splits the `str` string using a field separator specified using `regex` and stores it into the `arr` array. It returns the number of array elements created on splitting the string. If no separator is specified, then the string is split using the current **field separator** (**FS**) value. The following example illustrates the usage of the `split` function:

```
$ vi split1.awk

BEGIN    {
    string = "one-two-three-four"
    regex = "-"
    n = split ( string, arr, regex )
    print "Array contains the following values: "
    for ( i=1; i<=n; i++ )
    {
    printf("arr[%d] : %s\n", i, arr[i])
    }
}

$ awk -f split1.awk
```

The output of the execution of the previous code is as follows:

```
Array contains the following values:
arr[1] : one
arr[2] : two
arr[3] : three
arr[4] : four
```

We can specify multiple separators using a regular expression, as shown in the following example:

```
$ vi split2.awk

BEGIN    {
    string = "one:two+three=four"
    regex = "[:,+,=]"
    n = split ( string, arr, regex )
    print "Array contains the following values: "
    for ( i=1; i<=n; i++ )
    {
```

```
    printf("arr[%d] : %s\n", i, arr[i])
    }
}

$ awk -f split2.awk
```

The output of the execution of the previous code is as follows:

```
Array contains the following values:
arr[1] : one
arr[2] : two
arr[3] : three
arr[4] : four
```

The substr (str, start, [length]) function

The substr (str,start, [length]) function is used to extract a portion of a string. It returns the substring from the str string, starting from the character number's start, and its length is the number of characters to extract. If the length is not given as an argument to the function, then the remaining string from the starting position to the end of the string is extracted. If the starting position is less than 1, then it is treated as if it were one. If the starting position is greater than the number of characters in the string, it returns the null string. If the length is present but less than or equal to zero, it returns the null string. The first character of the string is character number one. The following is an example of the substring function:

```
$ vi substr1.awk

BEGIN    {
    str = "Winter is coming.!"
    print "STRING IS : ", str
    # substr function with start position and length
    printf("substr( str, 5, 5 ) : %s\n", substr( str, 5, 5 ));
    # substr function with start position only
    printf("substr( str, 5 ) : %s\n", substr( str, 5 ));
    # substr function with less than 1 as start position is treated as 1
    printf("substr( str, -1, 5 ) : %s\n", substr( str, -1, 5 ));
    # substr function with start position more than number of char in
string returns null string
    printf("substr( str, 25, 5 ) : %s\n", substr( str, 25, 5 ));
}

$ awk -f substr1.awk
```

The output of the execution of the previous code is as follows:

```
STRING IS : Winter is coming.!
substr( str, 5, 5 ) : er is
substr( str, 5 ) : er is coming.!
substr( str, -1, 5 ) : Winte
substr( str, 25, 5 ) :
```

In the next example, we specify the third field from the employee database file `emp.dat` to print the first five characters from that field, as follows:

```
$ awk '{ print substr($3,1,5)}' emp.dat
```

The output of the execution of the previous code is as follows:

```
98575
98374
88272
99118
88262
98564
88272
88265
99115
99116
88563
98571
88261
98575
88117
```

So we can say that the substring function has two use cases, one with length and one without length in the function argument.

The sub (regex, replacement, string) function

GAWK and NAWK have seed-like string substitution functions, such as `sub`, `gsub`, `match`, and `gensub`. The `sub` function is used to substitute an original substring with a new substring from the given string. The original substring can be a regular expression. If the string in which the substitution is to be performed is not given, then `$0` is assumed to be the searched string.

The `sub()` function only changes the first occurrence of the matched substring with the replacement substring once in a line. If the regular expression is not enclosed in forward slashes in the first argument of the `sub` function, then it is treated as a variable containing a regular expression. If the special character `&` is used as the replacement of the string, it represents the substring that was matched by the regular expression.

The following example illustrates how the `sub` function works:

```
$ vi sub1.awk

BEGIN    {
    str = "Unix is Beautiful"
    original_substring = "Unix"
    replacement_substring = "Awk"
    print "String before replacemnt = " str
    sub( original_substring, replacement_substring, str)
    print "String after replacement = " str
}

$ awk -f sub1.awk
```

The output of the execution of the previous code is as follows:

```
String before replacemnt = Unix is Beautiful
String after replacement = Awk is Beautiful
```

Now, in our next example, we put multiple occurrences of Unix in a single string. With the `sub` function, we can substitute only the first occurrence of a string in a single sentence, as seen in the following code block:

```
$ vi sub2.awk

BEGIN    {
    str = "Linux is derived from Unix. Unix is oldest OS."
    sub("Unix", "YOONIX", str);
    print str;
}

$ awk -f sub2.awk
```

The output of the execution of the previous code is as follows:

```
Linux is derived from YOONIX. Unix is oldest OS.
```

If the third argument is not given, $0 is taken to be the string in the search, as shown in following example:

```
$ awk '{sub("maruti","MARUTI");print $0}' cars.dat
```

The output of the execution of the previous code is as follows:

MARUTI	swift	2007	50000	5
honda	city	2005	60000	3
MARUTI	dezire	2009	3100	6
chevy	beat	2005	33000	2
honda	city	2010	33000	6
chevy	tavera	1999	10000	4
toyota	corolla	1995	95000	2
MARUTI	swift	2009	4100	5
MARUTI	esteem	1997	98000	1
ford	ikon	1995	80000	1
honda	accord	2000	60000	2
fiat	punto	2007	45000	3

The function returns 1 if a substitution occurs successfully and 0 if it does not. The following example illustrates this functionality of the sub function:

```
$ awk '{ if (sub("maruti","MARUTI SUZUKI"))print $0}' cars.dat
```

The output of the execution of the previous code is as follows:

MARUTI SUZUKI	swift	2007	50000	5
MARUTI SUZUKI	dezire	2009	3100	6
MARUTI SUZUKI	swift	2009	4100	5
MARUTI SUZUKI	esteem	1997	98000	1

In the following example, we use the regular expression for substituting the J with j in the employee database if it is the first character on the line:

```
$ awk '{if (sub(/^J/, "j"))print}' emp.dat
```

The output of the execution of the previous code is as follows:

jack	Singh	9857532312	jack@gmail.com	M	hr	2000
jane	Kaur	9837432312	jane@gmail.com	F	hr	1800
julie	Kapur	8826234556	julie@yahoo.com	F	Ops	2500
john	Kapur	9911556789	john@gmail.com	M	hr	2200

In the following example, we illustrate the use of & in a replacement string to represent the string matched in the original string. In this example, we search for the lines that begin with the `maruti` string and replace that string with `& Suzuki`. Here, & represents the original string match, `maruti`, so the new replacement string becomes `maruti Suzuki`, as follows:

```
$ awk '{if (sub(/^maruti/, "& Suzuki"))print}' cars.dat
```

The output of the execution of the previous code is as follows:

```
maruti Suzuki        swift     2007      50000     5
maruti Suzuki        dezire    2009      3100      6
maruti Suzuki        swift     2009      4100      5
maruti Suzuki        esteem    1997      98000     1
```

The gsub (regex, replacement, string) function

gsub stands for global substitution (replace everywhere). It replaces every occurrence of a regular expression (original string) with the replacement string in the given string. The third argument is optional. If it is not specified, then $0 is used.

The gsub() function returns the number of substitutions made. The special character & works the same way as it worked in the sub() function earlier. It is similar to the g option used in sed, for converting all the occurrences apart from the first. So, if a pattern occurs more than once per line or string, the substitution will be performed for each pattern. The following example illustrates how the gsub() function works.

In this example, we have multiple occurrences of Unix in a single string. With the gsub function, we substitute all the occurrences of a string in a single sentence, as opposed to the sub function where we could convert only the first occurrence:

```
$ vi  gsub1.awk

BEGIN    {
    str = "Linux is derived from Unix. Unix is oldest OS."
    gsub("Unix", "YOONIX", str);
    print str;
}

$ awk -f  gsub1.awk
```

The output of the execution of the previous code is as follows:

```
Linux is derived from YOONIX. YOONIX is oldest OS.
```

As it was with the `sub()` function, if the third argument is not given, `$0` is taken to be the string for the search, as shown in the following example:

```
$ awk '{gsub("maruti","MARUTI");print $0}' cars.dat
```

The output of the execution of the previous code is as follows:

```
MARUTI          swift       2007        50000       5
honda           city        2005        60000       3
MARUTI          dezire      2009        3100        6
chevy           beat        2005        33000       2
honda           city        2010        33000       6
chevy           tavera      1999        10000       4
toyota          corolla     1995        95000       2
MARUTI          swift       2009        4100        5
MARUTI          esteem      1997        98000       1
ford            ikon        1995        80000       1
honda           accord      2000        60000       2
fiat            punto       2007        45000       3
```

The `gsub` function can be used with the `if` condition only if there is one substitution of a string in the single line because it returns the number of the string substitution.

The gensub (regex, replacement, occurrence, [string]) function

`gensub` stands for general substitution. It adds more features that are not available in the `sub()` and `gsub()` functions. With `gensub()`, we can specify the number of occurrences of the matched regular expression that is to be replaced. It returns the modified string as the result of executing the function, and the original string is not changed. Its syntax is as follows:

```
gensub ( regex for original-string, replacement-string, occurrence-number,
[string] )
```

- `regex for original-string`: This is the original string that needs to be replaced. This can also be a regular expression.
- `replacement-string`: This is the new string that is to be used for substitution.

- `Occurrence-number`: This is the number of occurrences of the matched `regex` that is to be substituted. If `g` or `G` is used, then it means that all occurrences of the match are to be substituted.
- `String`: This is an input string variable whose contents will get modified upon the execution of the function. This option is optional. If it is not specified, then the current input record (`$0`) is used.

The special character `&` works the same way as it worked in the `sub()` and `gsub()` functions earlier. The following example illustrates how the `gensub()` function works:

```
$ vi gensub1.awk

BEGIN   {
    str = "Linux is derived from Unix. Unix is oldest OS."
    newstr = gensub( /Unix/, "YOONIX", "g", str)
    print "NEW STRING : "newstr;
    print "OLD STRING : "str;
}

$ awk -f gensub1.awk
```

The output of the execution of the previous code is as follows:

```
NEW STRING : Linux is derived from YOONIX. YOONIX is oldest OS.
OLD STRING : Linux is derived from Unix. Unix is oldest OS.
```

In this example, we use the third argument to control the substitution by specifying the number of regular expressions that should be changed. Here we use the same string used in the previous example to change the second occurrence of Unix and not the first, as follows:

```
$ vi gensub2.awk

BEGIN   {
    str = "Linux is derived from Unix. Unix is oldest OS."
    newstr = gensub("Unix", "YOONIX", 2, str);
    print newstr;
}

$ awk -f gensub2.awk
```

The output of the execution of the previous code is as follows:

```
Linux is derived from Unix. YOONIX is oldest OS.
```

The `gensub()` function also provides an additional feature that is not available in `sub()` and `gsub()`. It modifies the specific components of a regular expression in the replacement string (this is also known as backreferencing in regular expressions). This is achieved using `\N` in the replacement string, where the value of `N` varies from 1 to 9. The following example illustrates how it works:

```
$ vi gensub3.awk

BEGIN   {
    str = "hello:world"
    newstr = gensub(/(.+):(.+)/, "\\2:\\1", "g", str)
    print "OLD STRING : ", str
    print "NEW STRING : ", newstr
}

$ awk -f gensub3.awk
```

The output of the execution of the previous code is as follows:

```
OLD STRING :  hello:world
NEW STRING :  world:hello
```

The match (string, regex) function

The `match` function searches for a string/regular expression in the specified string. Here, the string in which the match will search is given as the first argument and the regular expression to be matched is given as the second argument. The `match` function returns the starting position of the substring (the longest match string) that was matched by the regular expression.

This function also sets the following two AWK variables in the following ways:

- `RSTART`: This is set up to contain the starting value returned by the function that is the starting position of the substring. If the pattern does not match, `RSTART` is set to `0`.
- `RLENGTH`: This is set up to contain the length of the search string. It is set to `-1` if a match is not found.

The following example will illustrate how the `match()` function works:

```
$ vi match1.awk

BEGIN    {
    str = "linux is derived from UNIX. UNIX is oldest OS."
    position = match( str, /derived/ )
    print "String : ",str
    print "Starting Position of matched string : ",position
    print "RSTART : ", RSTART
    print "RLENGTH : ", RLENGTH
}

$ awk -f match1.awk
```

The output of the execution of the previous code is as follows:

```
String :  linux is derived from UNIX. UNIX is oldest OS.
Starting Position of matched string :   10
RSTART :   10
RLENGTH :   7
```

We can use the input record read from the file as the string to search for the match. For example, in the next example we have used the `match` function to print those records from the cars database file `cars.dat` that contain the `maruti` string in them, as follows:

```
$ vi match2.awk

{
    if (match( $0, /maruti/ ))
    print
}

$ awk -f match2.awk cars.dat
```

The output of the execution of the previous code is as follows:

```
maruti        swift       2007       50000       5
maruti        dezire      2009       3100        6
maruti        swift       2009       4100        5
maruti        esteem      1997       98000       1
```

The tolower (string) function

AWK has two functions for converting the case of the characters of a string. These functions are called `tolower()` and `toupper()`. The `tolower()` function takes a single string as an argument and returns a copy of that string, with all the uppercase characters converted to lowercase. The nonalphabetic characters are left unchanged. The following example illustrates the usage of the `tolower()` function:

```
$ vi tolower1.awk

BEGIN   {
    str = "Linux is derived from Unix. Unix is oldest OS."
    lower_case_str = tolower(str)
    print "Original String : ", str
    print "Lowercase String : ", lower_case_str
}

$ awk -f tolower1.awk
```

The output of the execution of the previous code is as follows:

```
Original String :  Linux is derived from Unix. Unix is oldest OS.
Lowercase String :  linux is derived from unix. unix is oldest os.
```

Similarly, in our next example, we convert the contents of our `emp.dat` employee database file to lowercase using the `tolower()` function, as follows:

```
$ awk '{ printf("%s\n", tolower($0)) }' emp.dat
```

The output of the execution of the previous code is as follows:

```
jack      singh      9857532312    jack@gmail.com       m    hr     2000
jane      kaur       9837432312    jane@gmail.com       f    hr     1800
eva       chabra     8827232115    eva@gmail.com        f    lgs    2100
amit      sharma     9911887766    amit@yahoo.com       m    lgs    2350
julie     kapur      8826234556    julie@yahoo.com      f    ops    2500
ana       khanna     9856422312    anak@hotmail.com     f    ops    2700
hari      singh      8827255666    hari@yahoo.com       m    ops    2350
victor    sharma     8826567898    vics@hotmail.com     m    ops    2500
john      kapur      9911556789    john@gmail.com       m    hr     2200
billy     chabra     9911664321    bily@yahoo.com       m    lgs    1900
sam       khanna     8856345512    sam@hotmail.com      f    lgs    2300
ginny     singh      9857123466    ginny@yahoo.com      f    hr     2250
emily     kaur       8826175812    emily@gmail.com      f    ops    2100
amy       sharma     9857536898    amys@hotmail.com     f    ops    2500
vina      singh      8811776612    vina@yahoo.com       f    lgs    2300
```

The toupper (string) function

The `toupper()` function takes a single string as an argument and returns a copy of that string, with all the lowercase characters converted to uppercase. The nonalphabetic characters are left unchanged. The following example illustrates the usage of the `toupper()` function:

```
$ vi toupper1.awk

BEGIN    {
    str = "Linux is derived from Unix. Unix is oldest OS."
    upper_case_str = toupper(str)
    print "Original String : ", str
    print "Uppercase String : ", upper_case_str
}

$ awk -f toupper1.awk
```

The output of the execution of the previous code is as follows:

```
Original String :  Linux is derived from Unix. Unix is oldest OS.
Uppercase String :  LINUX IS DERIVED FROM UNIX. UNIX IS OLDEST OS.
```

Similarly, in our next example, we convert the contents of our `emp.dat` employee database file to uppercase using the `toupper()` function, as follows:

```
$ awk '{ printf("%s\n", toupper($0)) }' emp.dat
```

The output of the execution of the previous code is as follows:

```
JACK     SINGH    9857532312    JACK@GMAIL.COM      M    HR     2000
JANE     KAUR     9837432312    JANE@GMAIL.COM      F    HR     1800
EVA      CHABRA   8827232115    EVA@GMAIL.COM       F    LGS    2100
AMIT     SHARMA   9911887766    AMIT@YAHOO.COM      M    LGS    2350
JULIE    KAPUR    8826234556    JULIE@YAHOO.COM     F    OPS    2500
ANA      KHANNA   9856422312    ANAK@HOTMAIL.COM    F    OPS    2700
HARI     SINGH    8827255666    HARI@YAHOO.COM      M    OPS    2350
VICTOR   SHARMA   8826567898    VICS@HOTMAIL.COM    M    OPS    2500
JOHN     KAPUR    9911556789    JOHN@GMAIL.COM      M    HR     2200
BILLY    CHABRA   9911664321    BILY@YAHOO.COM      M    LGS    1900
SAM      KHANNA   8856345512    SAM@HOTMAIL.COM     F    LGS    2300
GINNY    SINGH    9857123466    GINNY@YAHOO.COM     F    HR     2250
EMILY    KAUR     8826175812    EMILY@GMAIL.COM     F    OPS    2100
AMY      SHARMA   9857536898    AMYS@HOTMAIL.COM    F    OPS    2500
VINA     SINGH    8811776612    VINA@YAHOO.COM      F    LGS    2300
```

The sprintf (format, expression) function

The `sprintf()` function is similar to the `printf()` function and uses the same format specifications as `printf()`, with the only difference being that instead of printing the output on the screen, it returns a string that can be assigned to a variable. The following example illustrates the usage of the `sprintf()` function:

```
$ vi sprintf.awk

BEGIN    {
    for (  i = 97; i <= 122; i++ )
    {
    char = sprintf( "%c", i );
    printf("%s ", char )
    }
    print
}

$ awk -f sprintf.awk
```

The output of the execution of the previous code is as follows:

```
a b c d e f g h i j k l m n o p q r s t u v w x y z
```

The strtonum (string) function

This function is used to examine an argument supplied as a string and returns its numeric value. If the string supplied begins with a leading 0, it is treated as an octal number. If the string begins with a leading 0x, it is treated as a hexadecimal number. The following example illustrates the working `strtonum()` function:

```
$ vi strtonum.awk

BEGIN    {
    print "Decimal num strtonum(123)     : ", strtonum(123)
    print "Octal num strtonum(0123)      : ", strtonum(0123)
    print "Hexadecimal num strtonum(0x123)  : ", strtonum(0x123)
}

$ awk -f strtonum.awk
```

The output of the execution of the previous code is as follows:

```
Decimal num strtonum(123)     :   123
Octal num strtonum(0123)      :   83
Hexadecimal num strtonum(0x123) :   291
```

Apart from the preceding function, we have asort (sring,[a]) and asorti(string, [a]), which are available only in GAWK and which we will ;discuss in Chapter 9, *GNU's Implementation of AWK - GAWK (GNU AWK)*.

Summary table of built-in string functions

The following table gives us a short description of the built-in string functions in AWK:

Function	Description
index(str, sub)	Returns the position of the sub substring in the str string . Returns 0 if it is not present.
length(string)	Returns the length of the str string or the length of $0 if no string is supplied.
substr(str, pos)	Returns the substring of the str string, beginning at the pos position and the remaining string.
substr(str, pos, num)	Returns the substring of the str string, beginning at the pos position up to the length of num.
sub(regex, replacement)	Substitutes a replacement string matched with the regex / string in $0 and returns the number of substitutions made.
sub(regex, replacement,str)	Substitutes a replacement string matched with the regex / string in str and returns the number of substitutions made.
gsub(regex, replacement)	Substitutes regex for a replacement string globally in $0 and returns the number of substitutions made.
gsub(regex, replacement, str)	Substitutes regex for a replacement string globally in the str string and returns the number of substitutions made.

`gensub( regex, replacement, occ)`	Returns the substituted `regex` for the replacement string for the number of occurrences `occ` specified in `$0`.
`gensub(regex,replacement, occ, str)`	Returns the substituted `regex` for the replacement string for the number of occurrences `occ` specified in the `str` string.
`match(str, regex)`	Tests whether the `str` string contains the substring matched by `regex` and returns `index` or 0 if it is not found. Also sets `RSTART` and `RLENGTH`.
`split(str, arr)`	Splits the `str` string into the `arr` array based on `fs` and returns the number of elements in the array.
`split(str,arr, fs)`	Splits the `str` string into the `arr` array based on the `fs` field separator and returns the number of elements in the array.
`sprintf(fmt, expression)`	Returns the formatted expression according to the `fmt` format string.
`tolower(str)`	Returns the `str` string converted into lowercase.
`toupper(str)`	Returns the `str` string converted into uppercase.
`strtonum(str)`	Returns the numeric value of the `str` string . Returns an octal number if the string begins with 0 and returns a hexadecimal number if the string begins with `0x`.
`asort(arr)`	Sorts the contents of the `arr` array and the index sequentially, starting with 1.
`assorti(arr)`	Sorts the `arr` array as per the indexes and returns the new array with array elements containing the previous `arr` array's indexes.

Input/output functions

The following functions are used to perform input/output (I/O) tasks. Optional parameters are given in square brackets ([]).

The close (filename [to/from]) function

The `close` function is used to close the file. The argument to close could also be a shell command used for creating coprocesses, or for redirecting to or from a pipe, or it could be a coprocess or pipe that is used to close a file. The second argument to the `close()` function is the GAWK extension. The following example illustrates how the `close()` function works:

```
$ vi close1.awk

BEGIN    {
    cmd = "wc"
    print "Linux is derived from Unix. Unix is oldest OS." |& cmd
    close(cmd, "to")
    cmd |& getline var
    print var
    close(cmd);
}

$ awk -f close1.awk
```

The output of the execution of the previous code is as follows:

```
      1       9      47
```

In the previous example, the `print` command provides the input to the `wc` command. The `|&` indicates two-way communication in the coprocess, and it is also known as the coprocess operator. The `close(cmd, "to")` used here closes the sending end of the coprocess. It is essential to use the `wc` command because otherwise our command will not get the end of the file and so will not give the output. The next command, `cmd|& getline var`, stores the output of the coprocess `wc` in the `var` variable, and then we print the output. Finally, the `close` function is again used to close the command pipe (both to and from) of the `wc` shell command.

The fflush ([filename]) function

The `fflush` function flushes any buffers associated with an open output file or pipe. Many Linux utilities buffer their output (they save information to be written on a disk file or to be output to the screen in their memory until there is enough worthwhile info to share). This buffering saves many I/O operations on disk. If sometimes you need to flush the buffers forcefully, even when the buffer is not full, then you can uses the `fflush()` function. This forcefully empties the buffers and flushes any buffered info. If no argument is given to the `fflush` function, then it flushes all open output files and pipes.

The system (command) function

The `system` function is used to execute any operating system command and then return back to the AWK program. It returns the exit status of the program. If the command is executed successfully, we get the return value of 0. If a nonzero value is returned, this indicates the failure of the command execution. Using the `system` command, we can pass any shell command as an argument, and it will get executed exactly as given on the command line and the output will be returned on screen.

The following example illustrates how the `system` function works:

```
$ awk 'BEGIN { system("pwd")}'
```

The output of the execution of the previous code is as follows:

```
/home/shiwang/Desktop/
```

In the next example, we print the system date with the `system()` function:

```
$ awk 'BEGIN { system("date")}'
```

The output of the execution of the previous code is as follows:

```
Wed Feb  7 20:21:12 IST 2018
```

In the following example, we create an array of system commands to be executed. After each command execution with the `system` function, we store the return status of the system command in a variable as follows:

```
$ vi system.awk

BEGIN    {
    arr[1] = "ls"
    arr[2] = "pwd"
    arr[3] = "uptime"
    for ( v in arr )
    {
    print "Executing the Shell command : " arr[v]
    ret=system(arr[v])
    print "Return status of command : " ret
    print "==============================="
    }
}

$ awk -f system.awk
```

The output of the execution of the previous code is as follows:

```
Executing the Shell command : ls
and.awk         gensub1.awk                 gsub1.awk    or.awk
strftime.awk
cars.dat        gensub2.awk                 index.awk    rand1.awk
strtonum.awk
func1.awk       getline_var.awk             marks.txt    sqrtfunc.awk
tolower1.awk
func2.awk       getline_var_coprocess.awk   match1.awk   srand1.awk
toupper1.awk
func3.awk       getline_var_file.awk        match2.awk   srand2.awk
xor.awk
func4.awk       getline_var_pipe.awk        mktime.awk   strftime1.awk
Return status of command : 0
==============================
Executing the Shell command : pwd
/home/shiwang/Desktop/CHAPTER8
Return status of command : 0
==============================
Executing the Shell command : uptime
 20:22:23 up  1:41,  1 user,  load average: 0.28, 0.28, 0.28
Return status of command : 0
==============================
```

If the AWK program is run with the `--sandbox` option, the `system` function will not work. If this is the case, it is disabled.

The getline command

The default behavior of the AWK program is to automatically get input data for processing from a file or standard input device. To do this, AWK has the `getline` command, which enables the user to control the reading of the input from the current file or from another file. Whenever `getline` is executed, AWK sets the value of the NF, NR, FNR, and $0 built-in variables accordingly.

The `getline` command returns 1 if it finds the record and 0 if it gets to the end of the file without finding the record. If for any reason `getline` is unable to fetch the input record, it returns −1. The different ways in which we can use the `getline` command in AWK programs are discussed in the following sections.

Simple getline

This is the simplest way to use the `getline` command. In this method, we specify the `getline` command without any arguments in the body block to read the next input line from the current input file. It reads the next input record and splits it into fields. The following example illustrates how the simple `getline` command works:

```
$ awk '{getline; print NR,$0;}' cars.dat
```

Here, at the beginning of body block, before executing any statement, AWK reads the first line from the current input file and stores it in `$0`. The `getline` command is the first statement in the body block, and makes AWK read the next line from the current input file and store it in the `$0` variable. Thus, on execution of the `$0` print command, it prints the second line and not the first line. The body block continues in the same manner for the rest of the current input file's lines and prints only even-numbered lines.

The output of the execution of the previous code is as follows:

```
2  honda         city      2005       60000      3
4  chevy         beat      2005       33000      2
6  chevy         tavera    1999       10000      4
8  maruti        swift     2009       4100       5
10 ford          ikon      1995       80000      1
12 fiat          punto     2007       45000      3
```

Getline into a variable

In this method, we fetch the next input line of the current file into a variable instead of storing it in `$0`. Its syntax is `getline var`. The following example illustrates how this method works:

```
$ vi getline_var.awk

{
    print "$0 ->     : ",NR, $0
    getline tmp;
    print "tmp ->     : ",NR, tmp;
}

$ awk -f getline_var.awk cars.dat
```

The output of the execution of the previous code is as follows:

```
$0 ->    :  1 maruti      swift      2007      50000     5
tmp ->   :  2 honda       city       2005      60000     3
$0 ->    :  3 maruti      dezire     2009      3100      6
```

```
tmp ->   :  4 chevy      beat      2005      33000      2
$0 ->    :  5 honda      city      2010      33000      6
tmp ->   :  6 chevy      tavera    1999      10000      4
$0 ->    :  7 toyota     corolla   1995      95000      2
tmp ->   :  8 maruti     swift     2009      4100       5
$0 ->    :  9 maruti     esteem    1997      98000      1
tmp ->   :  10 ford       ikon     1995      80000       1
$0 ->    :  11 honda      accord   2000      60000       2
tmp ->   :  12 fiat       punto    2007      45000       3
```

In the previous example, at the beginning of the body block, before executing any statement, AWK reads the first line from the current input file and stores it in $0. The print statement prints the first line from the current input file. Using the getline command, we force the AWK to read the next line from the current input file and store it in the tmp variable. Then we print the second line stored in the tmp variable. This body block continues to work in the same manner for the rest of the current input file's lines. The $0 will print the odd-numbered line and the tmp variable will print the even-numbered lines of the input file.

Getline from a file

In this method, we use the getline command to read the next line from a file other than the current input file. Here, the filename is called using the < "filename" redirection operator and is enclosed between double quotes. In this case, the values of NR and FNR are not changed. However, the value of NF is changed; its syntax is getline < "filename". The following examples illustrate how this method works:

```
$ vi getline_file.awk

{
    print "cars.dat : ",NR,$0;
    getline < "emp.dat"
    print "emp.dat  : ",NR,$0;
}

$ awk -f getline_file.awk cars.dat
```

The output of the execution of the previous code is as follows:

```
cars.dat :  1 maruti      swift     2007      50000      5
emp.dat  :  1 Jack    Singh   9857532312  jack@gmail.com    M   hr
2000
cars.dat :  2 honda      city      2005      60000      3
emp.dat  :  2 Jane    Kaur    9837432312  jane@gmail.com    F   hr
1800
```

```
cars.dat :  3 maruti           dezire      2009        3100         6
emp.dat  :  3 Eva     Chabra   8827232115  eva@gmail.com       F    lgs
2100
cars.dat :  4 chevy            beat        2005        33000        2
emp.dat  :  4 Amit    Sharma   9911887766  amit@yahoo.com      M    lgs
2350
cars.dat :  5 honda            city        2010        33000        6
emp.dat  :  5 Julie   Kapur    8826234556  julie@yahoo.com     F    Ops
2500
cars.dat :  6 chevy            tavera      1999        10000        4
emp.dat  :  6 Ana     Khanna   9856422312  anak@hotmail.com    F    Ops
2700
cars.dat :  7 toyota           corolla     1995        95000        2
emp.dat  :  7 Hari    Singh    8827255666  hari@yahoo.com      M    Ops
2350
cars.dat :  8 maruti           swift       2009        4100         5
emp.dat  :  8 Victor  Sharma   8826567898  vics@hotmail.com    M    Ops
2500
cars.dat :  9 maruti           esteem      1997        98000        1
emp.dat  :  9 John    Kapur    9911556789  john@gmail.com      M    hr
2200
cars.dat : 10 ford             ikon        1995        80000        1
emp.dat  : 10 Billy   Chabra   9911664321  bily@yahoo.com      M    lgs
1900
cars.dat : 11 honda            accord      2000        60000        2
emp.dat  : 11 Sam     khanna   8856345512  sam@hotmail.com     F    lgs
2300
cars.dat : 12 fiat             punto       2007        45000        3
emp.dat  : 12 Ginny   Singh    9857123466  ginny@yahoo.com     F    hr
2250
```

In the previous example, at the beginning of the body block, before executing any statement, AWK reads the first line from the current input file and stores it in $0. The print statement prints the first line from the current input file. Using the getline command, we force AWK to read the next line from the emp.dat input file and store it in $0. Then we print the first line from emp.dat, stored in the $0 variable. This body block continues to work in the same manner for the rest of the current input file's lines and the employee database emp.dat.

The getline command can also be used to read the input from the standard input, in place of a file, by using a special minus symbol –. It represents the standard input file here.

The following example illustrates how the standard input and `getline` command work:

```
$ vi getline_user.awk

BEGIN    {
    printf "Enter your name : "
    getline < "-"
    print "Welcome to awk programming : ",$0
}

$ awk -f getline_user.awk
```

The output of the execution of the previous code is as follows:

```
Enter your name : jack
Welcome to awk programming :   jack
```

This simple program prompts the user to `Enter your name  :` and then calls the `getline` command to store the user response in the `$0` variable. The print statement outputs the user message stored in `$0`.

Using getline to get a variable from a file

Instead of reading both files' current input lines into `$0`, we can use the `getline var` format to read lines from a different file into a variable. In this method, none of the predefined variables are changed except the `var` variable. Its syntax is `getline var < "filename"`. The following examples illustrate how this method works:

```
$ vi getline_var_file.awk

{
    print "cars.dat($0)     : ",NR,$0;
    getline tmp < "emp.dat"
    print "emp.dat(tmp)     : ",NR,tmp;
}

$ awk -f getline_var_file.awk
```

The output of the execution of the previous code is as follows:

```
cars.dat($0)   :  1 maruti          swift       2007        50000       5
emp.dat(tmp)   :  1 Jack     Singh   9857532312  jack@gmail.com    M   hr
2000
cars.dat($0)   :  2 honda           city        2005        60000       3
emp.dat(tmp)   :  2 Jane     Kaur    9837432312  jane@gmail.com    F   hr
1800
```

cars.dat($0)	:	3	maruti		dezire	2009	3100		6
emp.dat(tmp)	:	3	Eva	Chabra	8827232115	eva@gmail.com		F	lgs 2100
cars.dat($0)	:	4	chevy		beat	2005	33000		2
emp.dat(tmp)	:	4	Amit	Sharma	9911887766	amit@yahoo.com		M	lgs 2350
cars.dat($0)	:	5	honda		city	2010	33000		6
emp.dat(tmp)	:	5	Julie	Kapur	8826234556	julie@yahoo.com		F	Ops 2500
cars.dat($0)	:	6	chevy		tavera	1999	10000		4
emp.dat(tmp)	:	6	Ana	Khanna	9856422312	anak@hotmail.com		F	Ops 2700
cars.dat($0)	:	7	toyota		corolla	1995	95000		2
emp.dat(tmp)	:	7	Hari	Singh	8827255666	hari@yahoo.com		M	Ops 2350
cars.dat($0)	:	8	maruti		swift	2009	4100		5
emp.dat(tmp)	:	8	Victor	Sharma	8826567898	vics@hotmail.com		M	Ops 2500
cars.dat($0)	:	9	maruti		esteem	1997	98000		1
emp.dat(tmp)	:	9	John	Kapur	9911556789	john@gmail.com		M	hr 2200
cars.dat($0)	:	10	ford		ikon	1995	80000		1
emp.dat(tmp)	:	10	Billy	Chabra	9911664321	bily@yahoo.com		M	lgs 1900
cars.dat($0)	:	11	honda		accord	2000	60000		2
emp.dat(tmp)	:	11	Sam	khanna	8856345512	sam@hotmail.com		F	lgs 2300
cars.dat($0)	:	12	fiat		punto	2007	45000		3
emp.dat(tmp)	:	12	Ginny	Singh	9857123466	ginny@yahoo.com		F	hr 2250

In the previous example at the beginning of the body block, before executing any statement, AWK reads the first line from the current input file and stores it in $0. The print statement prints the first line from current input file. Using the getline command, we force the AWK to read the next line from the emp.dat input file and store it in the tmp variable this time. Then we print the first line from emp.dat, stored in the tmp variable. This body block continues to work in the same manner for the rest of the lines of the current input file and the employee database emp.dat.

In our next example, we use the `getline` command to read the input from the standard input into a variable instead of the file by using the special minus symbol –. This simple program prompts the user to `Enter your name :` and then calls the `getline` command to store the user response in the `uname` variable. The `print` statement outputs the user message stored in the `uname` variable as follows:

```
$ vi getline_user_var.awk


BEGIN    {
    printf "Enter your name : "
    getline uname < "-"
    print "Welcome to awk programming : ", uname
}

$ awk -f getline_user_var.awk
```

The output of the execution of the previous code is as follows:

```
Enter your name : jack
Welcome to awk programming :   jack
```

Using getline to output into a pipe

In this method, the output of a shell command can be piped into the `getline` using `"command" | getline`, which can be further used to generate output. The following examples illustrate how this method works:

```
$ vi getline_pipe.awk

BEGIN    {

        "date" | getline
        print "Date is : ", $0
        close("date")
        print "====================="
        print "DISK FREE SPACE INFO"
        print "====================="

        # using loop to print multiple lines
        while (("df -h" | getline) > 0 )
                print "Disk info : ", $0
        close("df -h")
}

$ awk -f getline_pipe.awk
```

The output of the execution of the preceding code is as follows:

```
Date is : Wed Mar 7 00:13:17 IST 2018
=====================
DISK FREE SPACE INFO
=====================
Disk info : Filesystem Size Used Avail Use% Mounted on
Disk info : udev 5.9G 0 5.9G 0% /dev
Disk info : tmpfs 1.2G 18M 1.2G 2% /run
Disk info : /dev/sda3 100G 65G 30G 69% /
Disk info : tmpfs 5.9G 12M 5.9G 1% /dev/shm
Disk info : tmpfs 5.0M 4.0K 5.0M 1% /run/lock
Disk info : tmpfs 5.9G 0 5.9G 0% /sys/fs/cgroup
Disk info : /dev/sda1 453M 36M 390M 9% /boot
Disk info : tmpfs 1.2G 16K 1.2G 1% /run/user/118
Disk info : tmpfs 1.2G 48K 1.2G 1% /run/user/1000
Disk info : /dev/sda6 550G 494G 29G 95% /mnt/WIP
```

In the previous example output, the date command is given as input to the awk command getline, which stores it in $0. Then we use the print command to print the output stored in $0. After, we used the close() function to close the command. We use the while loop if the output of the shell command is given as input to the getline command and is more than one line. The getline command reads one record at a time from the pipe. Once all the lines are output, we use the close() function to close the command.

If the expression is used instead of the command to give the input to getline using a pipe, then the expression is enclosed in parentheses, as shown in the following example:

```
$ vi getline_pipe2.awk

BEGIN    {

         ("echo " "Hello World..!") | getline
         print "Msg : ", $0
         close("echo " "Hello World..!")
}

$ awk -f getline_pipe2.awk
```

The output of the execution of the previous code is as follows:

```
Msg :  Hello World..!
```

Using getline to change the output into a variable from a pipe

In this method, we store the output of a command sent through a pipe to `getline` as a variable instead of storing it in `$0`. Its syntax is `command | getline var`. The following example shows how this method works:

```
$ vi getline_var_pipe.awk

BEGIN   {

        "date" | getline current_time
        print "Date is : ", current_time
        close("current_time")
}

$ awk -f getline_var_pipe.awk
```

The output of the execution of the previous code is as follows:

```
Date is :   Wed Feb  7 23:31:01 IST 2018
```

Using getline to change the output into a variable from a coprocess

Reading input into the `getline` command through a pipe is one-way communication. The command output is only sent to the AWK program through the pipe in one direction. If we need to send and receive the data from a program in AWK, then we have to use two-way communication using the `|&` operator. The data from the process is received generally with the help of `getline` using this process. The following example illustrates how this method works:

```
$ vi getline_var_coprocess.awk

BEGIN    {
    cmd = "tr [a-z] [A-Z]"
    print "Linux is derived from Unix. Unix is oldest OS" |& cmd
    close(cmd, "to")
    cmd |& getline
    print $0
    close(cmd)
}

$ awk -f getline_var_coprocess.awk
```

The output of the execution of the previous code is as follows:

```
LINUX IS DERIVED FROM UNIX. UNIX IS OLDEST OS
```

If we use a variable name in front of the `getline` command in the previous case, the output of the shell command will be stored in the variable name in place of `$0`. We can use that variable to print the output or perform any other task.

The nextfile() function

The `nextfile()` function is similar to the `next` statement function in the sense that it instructs AWK to stop processing the current input file. Upon execution of the `nextfile` statement, the `filename` built-in variable is updated and `FNR` is reset. The processing restarts with the first rule in the program, except in the case of `nextfile` being invoked in `END` rule.

This is useful when we have multiple files to process, but you don't have to process each record of every file. Without the `nextfile` statement to move from one file to another, a program would have to go through all the records of the current input file. The following example illustrates how the `nextfile` statement works:

```
$ awk '{ if ($1 ~/Eva/) nextfile; print $0}' emp.dat cars.dat
```

The output of the execution of the previous code is as follows:

Jack	Singh	9857532312	jack@gmail.com		M	hr	2000
Jane	Kaur	9837432312	jane@gmail.com		F	hr	1800
maruti		swift	2007	50000	5		
honda		city	2005	60000	3		
maruti		dezire	2009	3100	6		
chevy		beat	2005	33000	2		
honda		city	2010	33000	6		
chevy		tavera	1999	10000	4		
toyota		corolla	1995	95000	2		
maruti		swift	2009	4100	5		
maruti		esteem	1997	98000	1		
ford		ikon	1995	80000	1		
honda		accord	2000	60000	2		
fiat		punto	2007	45000	3		

The time function

This section discusses the built-in time functions available in AWK. There are three functions that come under the category of `time` function, named `systime()`, `mktime(datespec)`, and `strftime(format,timestamp)`. With the help of these AWK functions, we can produce useful reports with timestamps. On POSIX-compliant Unix/Linux systems, the `time()` system call is generally used, which returns the number of seconds since the epoch (1970-01-01 00:00:00 UTC).

The systime() function

The `systime()` function returns the current time of day as the number of seconds elapsed since midnight, January 1 1970, not counting leap seconds. This allows you to create a log file containing a timestamp using a `seconds since the epoch` format. This function can also be used to compare the timestamp with a file with the current time of day and for measuring how long a GAWK program takes to execute. The following example shows how the `systime()` function works:

```
$ vi systime.awk

BEGIN    {
    print "Timestamp of program run : ", systime()
    LOOPS=10000000;
    start=systime();
    print start;
    for (i=0;i<LOOPS;i++) {
    }
    end = systime();
    print end;
    totaltime = ( end -start )
    print ("totaltime : ", totaltime)
}

$ awk -f systime.awk
```

The output of the execution of the previous code is as follows:

```
Timestamp of program run :   1518026994
1518026994
1518026994
totaltime :   0
```

The mktime (datespec) function

The `mktime` function converts the `datespec` string into a timestamp of the same format as returned by the `systime()` function, the number of seconds elapsed since the epoch. The `datespec` is a string of the `YYYY MM DD HH MM SS` format :

```
$ vi mktime.awk

BEGIN    {
    print "Number of seconds since the Epoch"
    print "mktime(\"2018 01 15 20 20 10\") : " mktime("2014 12 14 30 20
10")}

$ awk -f mktime.awk
```

The output of the execution of the previous code is as follows:

```
Number of seconds since the Epoch
mktime("2018 01 15 20 20 10") : 1418604610
```

The strftime (format, timestamp) function

The `strftime()` function is used to create a human-readable time string based on the current time. It is quite similar to the shell command `date`. It returns the current date in seconds by default; however, we can use this to create a string based on the time. The first argument to the `strftime` function takes a string to specify the format of the output date. The second argument is a timestamp in the same format as the value returned by the `systime` function. If the second argument is not specified, then GAWK uses the current time of day as the timestamp. The following example shows how the `strftime()` function works:

```
$ vi strftime.awk

BEGIN    {
    format = "Todays date is : %d-%m-%Y %H:%M:%S"

    print strftime( format, systime())
}

$ awk -f strftime.awk
```

The output of the execution of the previous code is as follows:

```
Todays date is : 08-02-2018 08:17:44
```

In our next example, we use the `strftime()` function to calculate a future time by providing a timestamp in place of the current system time as the second argument, as follows:

```
$ vi strftime1.awk

BEGIN    {
    current_time = systime();
    timestamp = (7*24*60*60) + current_time
    format = "%d-%m-%Y %H:%M:%S"
    present_time = strftime ( format, current_time )
    new_time = strftime( format, timestamp )
    print "Current  Time     : ", present_time
    print "Next Week     : ", new_time
    }

$ awk -f strftime1.awk
```

The output of the execution of the previous code is as follows:

```
Current   Time      :   08-02-2018 08:18:17
Next Week           :   15-02-2018 08:18:17
```

The following table lists the `strftime` format specifications, beginning with `%`:

Format	Description
%a	The locale's abbreviated weekday name
%A	The locale's full weekday name
%b	The locale's abbreviated month name
%B	The locale's full month name
%c	The locale's appropriate date and time representation
%C	The century, as a number between 00 and 99
%d	The day of the month as a decimal number (0-31)
%D	Equivalent to specifying `%m/%d/%y`
%e	The day of the month, padded with a blank if it is only one digit
%h	Equivalent to `%b`, as previously defined
%H	The hour (24 hr clock) as a decimal number (00-23)

`%I`	The hour (12 hr clock) as a decimal number (01-12)
`%j`	The day of the year as a decimal number (001-366)
`%k`	The hour as a decimal number (0-23)
`%l`	The hour (12-hour clock) as a decimal number (1-12)
`%m`	The month as a decimal number (01–12)
`%M`	The minute as a decimal number (00–59)
`%n`	A newline character
`%p`	The locale's equivalent of AM/PM
`%r`	Equivalent to specifying `%I:%M:%S %p`
`%R`	Equivalent to specifying `%H:%M`
`%S`	The second as a decimal number (00–61)
`%t`	A tab character
`%T`	Equivalent to specifying `%H:%M:%S`
`%u`	Replaced by the weekday as a decimal number `[Monday == 1]`
`%U`	The week number of the year (Sunday is the first day of the week)
`%v`	The date in VMS format (for example, 20-JUN-1991)
`%V`	Replaced by the week number of the year (using ISO 8601)
`%w`	The weekday as a decimal number (0–6). Sunday is day 0
`%W`	The week number of the year (Monday is the first day of the week)
`%x`	The locale's appropriate date representation
`%X`	The locale's appropriate time representation
`%y`	The year (not including the century) as a decimal number (00-99)
`%Y`	The year (including the century) as a decimal number
`%Z`	The time zone name or abbreviation
`%%`	A `literal%`

Bit-manipulating functions

AWK has C-like bit-manipulating functions. Although they are not used much in day-to-day AWK programming, as it is primarily used for text manipulation and extraction, this a feature can nevertheless be handy for someone dealing with statistics or numbers.

The following table shows a list of single-digit decimal numbers and their binary equivalent:

Decimal	Binary
2	10
3	11
4	100
5	101
6	110
7	111
8	1000
9	1001

The and (num1, num2) function

This function returns the result of a bitwise AND operation on arguments. There must be at least two arguments. Its syntax is as follows:

```
and(num1, num2 [, ...])
```

In the and operation, for the output to be 1, both the bits that are given as input should be 1 and not 0. The following truth table summarizes how the and operation works when processing two bits:

0 and 0 = 0

0 and 1 = 0

1 and 0 = 0

1 and 1 = 1

The following shows how the and operation works when processing the decimal 5, and 6 illustrates the working of and() function:

5 = 101

6 = 110

5 and 6 = 100 which is decimal 4

The following example shows how the and(num1, num2) functions work:

```
$ vi and.awk

BEGIN    {
    num1 = 5
    num2 = 6
    result = and(num1,num2)
    printf "(%d AND %d) = %d\n", num1, num2, result
}

$ awk -f and.awk
```

The output of the execution of the previous code is as follows:

```
(5 AND 6) = 4
```

The or (num1, num2) function

This function return the result of a bitwise OR operation on arguments. There must be at least two arguments. Its syntax is as follows:

```
or ( num1, num2 [, ...])
```

With the or operation, for the output to be 1, either of the bits given as input should be 1. The following truth table summarizes the or operation's working when processing two bits:

0 or 0 = 0

0 or 1 = 1

1 or 0 = 1

1 or 1 = 1

The following `or` operation on the decimal 5 and 6 illustrate the working of `or()` function:

5 = 101

6 = 110

5 or 6 = 111 which is decimal 7

The following example shows how the `or()` functions work:

```
$ vi or.awk

BEGIN    {
    num1 = 5
    num2 = 6
    result = or(num1,num2)
    printf "(%d OR %d) = %d\n", num1, num2, result
}

$ awk -f or.awk
```

The output of the execution of the previous code is as follows:

```
(5 OR 6) = 7
```

The xor (num1, num2) function

This function returns the result of a bitwise XOR operation on arguments. There must be at least two arguments. Its syntax is as follows:

```
xor(num1, num2, [, ...])
```

In the XOR operation, for the output to be 1, both of the input bits should be different—that is, one of the bits should be 1. When both bits are the same, XOR returns 0. The following truth table summarizes how the XOR operation works when processing two bits:

0 xor 0 = 0

0 xor 1 = 1

1 xor 0 = 1

1 xor 1 = 0

The following XOR operation on decimal 5 and 6 illustrates the working of the xor() function.

5 = 101

6 = 110

5 and 6 = 011 which is decimal 3

The following example shows how the xor() functions work:

```
$ vi xor.awk

BEGIN    {
    num1 = 5
    num2 = 6
    result = xor(num1,num2)
    printf "(%d XOR %d) = %d\n", num1, num2, result
}

$ awk -f xor.awk
```

The output of the execution of the previous code is as follows:

```
(5 XOR 6) = 3
```

The lshift (val, count) function

The lshift function returns the value of val, shifted to the left side by the count number of bits specified in the argument. 0s are shifted in from the right side. For example, let us left shift, or lshift, the decimal 5 once to illustrate how the lshift() function works:

5 = 101

lshift *once = 1010, which is decimal 10*

The following example shows how the lshift() functions work:

```
$ vi lshift.awk

BEGIN    {
    num1 = 5
    count =1
    result = lshift(num1,count)
    printf "lshift(%d,%d) = %d\n", num1, count, result
```

```
}
$ awk -f lshift.awk
```

The output of the execution of the previous code is as follows:

```
lshift(5,1) = 10
```

The rshift (val, count) function

This function returns the value of `val`, shifted to the right side by the `count` number of bits specified in the argument. 0s are shifted in from the left side. For example, let us right shift the decimal 5 once time to show how the `rshift()` function works:

5 = 101

rshift once = 010 which is decimal 2

The following example shows how the `rshift()` functions work:

```
$ vi rshift.awk

BEGIN   {
    num1 = 5
    count =1
    result = rshift(num1,count)
    printf "rshift(%d,%d) = %d\n", num1, count, result
}

$ awk -f rshift.awk
```

The output of the execution of the previous code is as follows:

```
rshift(5,1) = 2
```

The compl (num) function

The `compl` function returns the bitwise complement of numbers specified as an argument. In the `complement` operation, it converts 0 to 1 and 1 to 0:

0 complement = 1

1 complement = 0

The following `complement` operation on decimal `5` shows how the `compl()` function works:

5 = 101

5's complement = 010 which is decimal 2

 The usage of a negative argument in any bit-manipulating function is not allowed.

User-defined functions

AWK allows us to define user-defined functions. A large complex can be divided into functions where each function performs a specific task. These functions can be written and tested independently. This functionality means that we can reuse code.

Function definition and syntax

The definition of functions can be given anywhere between the rules of an AWK program. It is not mandatory in AWK to define a function before calling it because AWK first reads the entire program before it starts to execute it. The general syntax for defining a user-defined function is as follows:

```
function function_name(argument1, argument2, ...local variable.) {
                                       body-of-function
}
```

- `function_name`: This is the name of the function to be defined. A valid function name could consist of letters, digits, and underscores, but doesn't start with a digit and could be 52 letters in length. In a single AWK program, a variable name, array, or function should be unique. AWK keywords cannot be used as function names.
- `argument`: An argument is an optional list consisting of arguments or local variable names separated by commas. A function cannot have argument names that are the same as a function name.

- `body-of-function`: The `body-of-function` consists of AWK statements. It is the main part of function definition. The body of the function can consist of local variables, arguments, calls to another function or the same function (a recursive call), and other AWK statements.

Like built-in functions, user-defined functions can also return a value to their caller function using the `return` statement.

The following is an example of function definition. In this AWK program, we create a total of four functions, three of which are used for performing mathematical calculations on the supplied function arguments and the fourth of which reads the input from the user and passes that input as the function argument to the other three functions while making the function call:

```
$ vi   func1.awk

function find_add(num1, num2){
    result = num1 + num2
    printf ("Addition of %d + %d : %d\n", num1,num2,result)
}

function find_sub(num1, num2){
    result = num1 - num2
    printf ("Subtraction of %d - %d : %d\n", num1,num2,result)
}

function find_mul(num1, num2){
    result = num1 * num2
    printf ("Multiplication of %d * %d : %d\n", num1,num2,result)
}

# Main function
function main(){
    printf "Enter first number : "
    getline num1 < "-"
    printf "Enter second number : "
    getline num2 < "-"
    find_add(num1,num2)
    find_sub(num1,num2)
    find_mul(num1,num2)
}


BEGIN {

main()
```

```
}

$ awk -f func1.awk
```

The output of the execution of the previous code is as follows:

```
Enter first number : 10
Enter second number : 5
Addition of 10 + 5 : 15
Subtraction of 10 - 5 : 5
Multiplication of 10 * 5 : 50
```

Calling user-defined functions

A function call consists of the function name followed by the arguments of the function in parentheses. Whitespace characters (spaces and tabs) are not allowed between the function name and opening parenthesis of the argument list.

In the previous function example, the `func1.awk` main function is called inside the `BEGIN` block by simply putting `main()`. The main function, in turn, has other function calls with their arguments, such as `fund_add(num1, num2)`, `find_sub(num1, num2)`, and `find_mul(num1, num2)`.

Controlling variable scope

All variables in AWK are global, except when we make variables local to function. To make a variable local to a function, we simply declare the variable as an argument after the other function arguments.

The following example explains the scope of a variable. Here, q is a global variable declared in the `BEGIN` block and p is local variable of the `one()` function, where and is passed to the function as a parameter list:

```
$ vi func2.awk

function one(p)
{
    result = p + q
    print "p + q : ", result
    print "local variable \"p\" : ", p
    print "global variable \"q\" : ", q
}
```

```
BEGIN    {
    q = 10
    one(5)
    print "value of p : ", p
    print "value of q : ", q
}

$ awk -f func2.awk
```

The output of the execution of the previous code is as follows:

```
p + q :  15
local variable "p" :   5
global variable "q" :   10
value of p :
value of q :   10
```

Return statement

The body of the user-defined function can also contain a `return` statement, similar to return statements found in other programming languages. The statement returns control to the calling part of the AWK program. Its syntax is as follows:

```
return [ expression ]
```

In the following example, the `func_add()`, `func_sub()`, and `func_mul()` functions return the addition, subtraction, and multiplication of the numbers passed as arguments to them:

```
$ vi func3.awk

function find_add(num1, num2){
    result = num1 + num2
    return result
}

function find_sub(num1, num2){
    result = num1 - num2
    return result
}

function find_mul(num1, num2){
    result = num1 * num2
    return result
}

# Main function
```

```
function main(){
    printf "Enter first number : "
    getline num1 < "-"
    printf "Enter second number : "
    getline num2 < "-"
    add = find_add(num1,num2)
    print "Addition of above num : ", add
    subtraction = find_sub(num1,num2)
    print "Subtraction of above num : ", subtraction
    mult = find_mul(num1,num2)
    print "Multiplication of above num : ", mult
}


BEGIN {

main()
}

$ awk -f func3.awk
```

The output of the execution of the previous code is as follows:

```
Enter first number : 20
Enter second number : 10
Addition of above num :   30
Subtraction of above num :   10
Multiplication of above num :   200
```

Making indirect function calls

Using indirect function calls, we can specify the name of the function to be called as a string to a variable and then call the function with the new variable. In indirect function calls, we tell GAWK to use the value of the variable as the name of the function to be called. The indirect function is called by prefixing the @ character with the variable name that has been assigned the function as a string. The following example shows how indirect function calls work:

```
$ vi func4.awk

function demo(){
    abc = "Welcome to awk"
    return abc
}
```

```
BEGIN {
    myfunc = "demo"
    print @myfunc()
}

$ awk -f func4.awk
```

The output of the execution of the previous code is as follows:

```
Welcome to awk
```

In the previous example, we assign the demo() function as a string to the myfunc variable. Now, to call the demo() function, we can prefix @ with the myfunc variable to make an indirect call to the demo() function.

Summary

In this chapter, we learned about different types of built-in and user-defined functions that accept zero or more arguments and return a value. Function arguments can be made up of expressions that are evaluated before calling a function. We began by looking at built-in functions such as arithmetic functions, which are used for numeric processing. We followed this up by looking at string functions that are used for string manipulations and for matching the occurrences of a pattern in a string. Then, we looked at various input/output functions, such as the close() function for closing files and pipes. After this, we looked at the time functions, which can be quite useful when it comes to timestamping or creating log files. We followed this by bit-manipulation functions, which perform bitwise operations on two or more integers. Finally, we looked at how to define and call user-defined functions for solving complex problems using our own functions.

In our next chapter, we will learn about the features that are exclusively available in GAWK and not in AWK.

9
GNU's Implementation of AWK – GAWK (GNU AWK)

This chapter covers the features of **GNU AWK** (**GAWK**) that are not available in primitive AWK. These features are not connected to each other, but are quite useful when used in the appropriate scenarios. Features such as reading non-decimal input, arbitrary precision arithmetic, array sorting, and some advance features such as network communication, debugging, and inter-process communication, are explained in this chapter using simple example programs. Some of these features are quite advanced, in the sense that their explanation requires a separate chapter devoted to them. However, we will discuss the main details of these features, so that we are able to use them when the situation arises. These features enhance the power of AWK and make it more productive.

In this chapter, we will cover the following :

- Reading non-decimal input
- Using the GAWK built-in command line debugger
- Sorting arrays
- Two-way interprocess communication
- Network programming using AWK
- Profiling using AWK

Things you don't know about GAWK

All features which are there in AWK are available as default in GAWK. In addition to these features, there are some other features of GAWK that essentially require a mention—they are covered in this section. These are not interrelated, so moving from one feature to another will be like picking up a random tool from a box filled with essential utilities.

Reading non-decimal input

The non-decimal values are like octal numbers or hexadecimal numbers. We cannot use these values to print their decimal equivalent with AWK; GAWK provides the option, `--non-decimal-data`, to print non-decimal values in the output. Octal values need to be prefixed with `0` and hexadecimal values need to be prefixed with `0x` for reading in GAWK. For example, the following `gawk` command can be used to convert hexadecimal input to the corresponding decimal output, as follows:

```
$ echo 088 | gawk --non-decimal-data '{ printf "Decimal equivalent of octal
%s is : %d \n", $1, $1 }'
```

The output of the previous code is as follows:

```
Decimal equivalent of octal 088 is : 88
```

Simply using `print` will treat the expression as a string. Although we have input a number, it gets converted to a string automatically, as follows:

```
$ echo 0123| gawk --non-decimal-data '{ print "Decimal value of argument is
:" $1 }'
```

The output of the previous code is as follows:

```
Decimal value of argument is :0123
```

We need to add a zero to a field to force it to be treated as numeric and not a string, as follows:

```
$ echo 0123| gawk --non-decimal-data '{ print "Decimal value of argument is
:" $1+0 }'
```

The output of the previous code is as follows:

```
Decimal value of argument is :83
```

In the next example, we will use a file, num.txt, that contains the octal and hexadecimal numbers from 50 to 1 in descending order. The first column contains the decimal number, the second column contains the hexadecimal number prefixed with 0x, and the third column contains the octal number prefixed with 0:

```
Contents of file num.txt are :
50 0x32 062
49 0x31 061
48 0x30 060
47 0x2F 057
46 0x2E 056
45 0x2D 055
44 0x2C 054
43 0x2B 053
....... ................. .
```

We use the --non-decimal-data command line option of GAWK to convert the numbers in a given file to decimal, as follows:

```
$ vi nondecimal.awk

BEGIN    {
    printf "deci\thex\toct\n"
    }
    {
    printf "%d\t%d\t%d\t\n", $1,$2,$3
    }

$ gawk --non-decimal-data -f nondecimal.awk num.txt
```

The output of the previous code is as follows:

```
deci    hex    oct
50      50     50
49      49     49
48      48     48
47      47     47
46      46     46
45      45     45
44      44     44
43      43     43
42      42     42
41      41     41
40      40     40
39      39     39
39      39     39
38      38     38
```

```
37    37    37
36    36    36
35    35    35
34    34    34
33    33    33
32    32    32
31    31    31
30    30    30
29    29    29
28    28    28
27    27    27
26    26    26
25    25    25
24    24    24
23    23    23
22    22    22
. . . . . . . . . . . . .
. . . . . . . . . . . . .

3     3     3
2     2     2
1     1     1
0     0     0
```

The print statement always treats its expression as a string, irrespective of the value stored in the field. Sometimes, we need to treat the value stored in the field as a numeric and not a string. If we want to use the `print` statement instead of `printf` for printing the number, then we have to add zero to the field variable so it is treated as a number, not a string.

The following example illustrates the treatment of the field value as a numeric instead of as a string in `print` statement:

```
$ echo 0123 | gawk --non-decimal-data '{ print $1 ; print $1 + 0 }'
```

The GAWK user guide and manual do not recommend use of this option as it can break old programs very badly; use the `strtonum( )` function to convert your data instead.

GAWK's built-in command line debugger

Debugging is the process of finding and resolving errors or abnormalities in the program that prevent its correct operation. Like most programming languages, GAWK has a built-in interactive debugger that is modeled after **GNU Debugger** (GDB).

What is debugging?

Debugging is the art of removing the bugs or errors from a program, with the help of debugging tools, so that the program functions as intended. Debugging enables the programmer to watch a program execute its instructions one by one, thus giving the programmer enough time to understand what is happening when the code is being executed.

It also gives the programmer the opportunity to control and change the path of execution of a program without making changes to its source file.

Debugging enables the programmer to see the values stored in variables and arguments, at any point in the execution of a program, and also gives them the ability to change those values at runtime, if required.

All these features enable a programmer to discover what went wrong in a program, using his/her own skills.

Debugger concepts

The following terms are used while discussing debugging and they are standard across all debuggers:

- **Breakpoint**: This is one of the most important and coolest feature of debuggers. Breakpoint is an intentional stopping place in a program, inserted via the debugger for debugging purposes. Generally, during this interruption, the programmer inspects the various environment variables, arguments, functions, files, logs, memory, and so on, to find out if the program is working as expected. It is the point up to which a program runs directly and then, from here on, it continues its execution one statement (instruction) at a time. So, a breakpoint is where the execution of a program stops and the debugger takes control of it's execution. We can add and remove one or more breakpoints in a program, as per our requirements.
- **Watchpoint**: Functionality wise, a watchpoint is similar to a breakpoint. The difference between a breakpoint and a watchpoint lies in the fact that breakpoints are code oriented, which means that they stop when a certain point in the code is reached. Watchpoints are centered around data, which means that they specify that program execution should stop when a data value is changed. They are helpful in tracking down if the program has received an incorrect value, which is difficult to find out by looking at the code.

- **Stackframe**: A program generally contains one or more functions that are called when a program executes. One function can call another, and that function can call itself or another function, and so on. This stack of executing functions is called a **call stack** and can be viewed during runtime with the help of a debugger. The data area reserved by the system that contains the functions parameter, local variables, and return values for each function on the call stack is known as the **stack frame**.

Using GAWK as a debugger

In this section, we will illustrate the use of GAWK as a debugger with the help of a sample program which contains certain functions and variables. The program used for the implementation is called `calc.awk` because it performs certain basic mathematical operations. Let's create the program first, as follows:

```
$ vi calc.awk

function find_add(num1, num2){
    result = num1 + num2
    printf ("Addition of %d + %d : %d\n", num1,num2,result)
}

function find_sub(num1, num2){
    result = num1 - num2
    printf ("Subtraction of %d - %d : %d\n", num1,num2,result)
}

function find_mul(num1, num2){
    result = num1 * num2
    printf ("Multiplication of %d * %d : %d\n", num1,num2,result)
}

# Main function
function calc(){
    find_add(30,10)
    find_sub(40,10)
    find_mul(5,6)
}


BEGIN {
```

```
calc()
}

$ gawk -f calc.awk
```

The output of the previous code is as follows :

```
Addition of 30 + 10 : 40
Subtraction of 40 - 10 : 30
Multiplication of 5 * 6 : 30
```

Starting the debugger

We have to pass the option `--debug` or `-D`, in addition to the `-f` option used to supply the AWK script on the command line. We cannot use GAWK debug for command line programs. It is essential to run `awk` commands from files with the `-f` option to launch the GAWK debugger as follows:

```
$ gawk  -D  -f  calc.awk
```

Now, instead of immediately executing the program from `calc.awk` and returning the output on screen, this time GAWK loads the program source files, compiles them and gives us a prompt, as follows:

```
gawk>
```

From this prompt, we can issue commands to the debugger. At this point, no code has been executed.

Set breakpoint

The first thing we should do while running a debugger to investigate a problem, is to put in a breakpoint otherwise the program will run as if it was not under the debugger. The `break` command or its shortcut, `b` is used to set the breakpoint with any of the following arguments:

- **break function_ name**: Sets the breakpoint at the entry to the first instruction of the function
- **break line-number (n)**: Sets the breakpoint at the line number n in the current source file
- **break filename:n**: Sets the breakpoint at the line number n in the specified source filename

Each breakpoint is designated a number that can be used to delete it from the breakpoint list, using the `delete` command.

In our example, the file `calc.awk` has four functions. We set a breakpoint on these three functions, `find_add()`, `find_sub()`, and `find_mul()`, which are invoked from the main function, `calc()`, as shown:

```
gawk> break find_add
Breakpoint 1 set at file `calc.awk', line 2
gawk>

gawk> break find_sub
Breakpoint 2 set at file `calc.awk', line 7
gawk>

gawk> b find_mul
Breakpoint 3 set at file `calc.awk', line 12
gawk>
```

The debugger tells the filename and line number of the breakpoint.

Removing the breakpoint

The `clear` and `delete` command are used to delete the breakpoints. The `clear` command accepts the following arguments to delete the breakpoint:

- **clear function_name**: Deletes the breakpoint set at the entry of the function
- **clear line-number (n)**: Deletes the breakpoint set at the line number n in the current source file
- **clear filename**: Deletes the breakpoint set at the line number n in the specified source filename

Now, we remove the breakpoint using the `clear` command as follows:

```
gawk> clear find_add
Deleted breakpoint 1
gawk> clear 12
Deleted breakpoint 3
gawk>
```

Deleting the breakpoint using a line number is done as follows:

```
gawk> clear calc.awk:7
Deleted breakpoint 2
```

The `Delete` command requires the breakpoint number as an argument to delete the breakpoint, as shown in this example which deletes breakpoint number 2:

```
gawk> delete 2
```

Running the program

The `run` or `r` command is used to start/restart the execution of the program. If the `run` command is used to restart the program execution, the debugger retains the current breakpoints, watchpoints, command history, and debugger options.

Now, we run the program after again putting in the earlier set three breakpoints. To run, type `r` or `run` and the program runs until it hits the first breakpoint:

```
gawk> run
Starting program:
Stopping in BEGIN ...
Breakpoint 1, find_add(num1, num2) at `calc.awk':2
2 result = num1 + num2
gawk>
```

Looking inside the program

When we run a program that contains a function call, GAWK maintains a stack of all function calls to lead you up to where you are executing. We can see how we got there, where we are and also move inside the stack with the help of the `backtrace` command or `bt` or the alias `where`. Any of these three commands can be used to print the backtrace of function calls (stack frames).

Here, frame 0 is the currently executing innermost frame (function call). Frame 1 is the frame that called the innermost frame 0 and the highest-numbered frame represents the main program:

```
gawk> backtrace
#0 find_add(num1, num2) at `calc.awk':2
#1 in calc() at `calc.awk':18
#2 in main() at `calc.awk':26
gawk>
```

The output contains the frame number, function and argument names, source file, and the source line. This tells us the `find_add()` function was called by the `calc()` function at line number 18.

You can switch between different frames using the `up` command to go to the outer frame and the `down` command to come to the inner frame. You can selectively print a stack frame by using the command `frame n`, where n is the frame number to be printed.

Displaying some variables and data

Now, we will look at the values stored in variables or fields using the `print` command. Its syntax is very simple, `print var1, var2, ....` Here, `var1` and `var2` are the variable or field names. A variable can also be an array element. To print the contents of an array, prefix the name of the array with the `@` symbol, as follows:

- `print $3`: Prints the value stored in field $3
- `print @arrayname`: Prints the contents of array `arrayname`
- `print n1, n2, n3`: Prints the value stored in variable n1, n2, and n3

Let's print the value of variables `num1`, `num2` and `result` in our running program, as follows:

```
gawk> print num1, num2, result
num1 = 30
num2 = 10
result = untyped variable
```

Here, the result is still not assigned any value, so it is an untyped variable.

Setting watch and unwatch

We can add a watchpoint for a variable or a field so that whenever its value changes, the debugger stops. Each watch item is assigned a number that can be used to delete it from the watch list, using the `unwatch` command:

- `watch var`: Sets watchpoint for variable `var`
- `unwatch [n]`: Unsets the watchpoint specified with number n

Let's set the watchpoint for the variable `result` in our program `calc.awk`, which is being debugged, as follows:

```
gawk> watch result
Watchpoint 4: result
```

Here, we have set the watchpoint for the variable result, so during execution, whenever its value changes, the debugger will give a notification and stop there.

Controlling the execution

To execute the program further, we have to step through the lines. For controlling execution, we have different commands. We will discuss some essential and basic ones in this section:

- `next` [count]: This is used to continue execution to the next source line, stepping over function calls. The count argument controls how many times it repeats this action.
- `return` [value]: This cancels the execution of the current function call (frame). If any current function contains any inner frames, they are discarded as well. If the value (string or number) is specified, it is used as a function return value.
- `finish`: Execute until the selected stack frame returns and print the returned value.
- `Continue`: Resume the program execution till next breakpoint.
- `stepi` or `si` [count]: Execute one (or count) instructions, stepping inside function calls.

Let's execute the next instruction using the `next` command in our running program, `calc.awk`, as follows:

```
gawk> next
Watchpoint 4: result
Old value: untyped variable
New value: 40
find_add(num1, num2) at `calc.awk':3
3 printf ("Addition of %d + %d : %d\n", num1,num2,result)
```

On execution of the `next` command, watchpoint 4, which was set earlier—is reached, that is, the value stored in the result variable is modified. So it outputs both the old value and the new value, and the next command displays the next instruction execution.

If we again select the `next` command, we step through one more instruction, as follows:

```
gawk> next
Addition of 30 + 10 : 40
calc() at `calc.awk':19
19 find_sub(40,10)
```

Viewing environment information

The `info` command or `i`, can be used to view the state of our program and the debugging environment itself. It is used with one of the following argument options to view corresponding information. Its usage syntax is as follows :

```
info <argument name>
```

Or we can also use the following abbreviated form:

```
i <argument name>
```

The following is list of argument options which can be used with the `info` command to display different information while debugging:

- **info break**: List all currently set breakpoints
- **info display**: List all items in an automatic display list
- **info frame**: Give a description of the selected stack frame
- **info args**: List arguments of the selected frame
- **info functions**: List all functions' definitions, including source filenames and line numbers of functions
- **info locals**: List the local variables of the selected frame
- **info source**: List the name of the current source filename
- **info sources**: List all program sources
- **list variables**: List all global variables
- **list watch**: List all items in the watch list

Now, we display certain debugging environment information using the `info` command with different arguments for our running program, `calc.awk`, as follows:

- This is an example to display set breakpoints:

  ```
  gawk> info break
  Number Disp Enabled Location
  1 keep yes file calc.awk, line #2
  ```

---
[316]

```
no of hits = 1
2 keep yes file calc.awk, line #7
3 keep yes file calc.awk, line #12
gawk>
```

- This example prints a description of the selected frame:

```
gawk> info frame
Current frame: #0 calc() at `calc.awk':19
Called by frame: #1 in main() at `calc.awk':26
gawk>
```

- This example displays the arguments set for the selected frame after stepping through once, using the `next` command:

```
gawk> info args
num1 = 40
num2 = 10
```

- The following example displays a list of global variables set in our program:

```
gawk> info variables
All defined variables:
ARGC: 1
ARGIND: 0
ARGV: array, 1 elements
BINMODE: 0
CONVFMT: "%.6g"
ENVIRON: array, 48 elements
ERRNO: ""
FIELDWIDTHS: ""
FILENAME: ""
FNR: 0
FPAT: "[^[:space:]]+"
FS: " "
FUNCTAB: array, 45 elements
IGNORECASE: 0
LINT: 0
NF: 0
NR: 0
OFMT: "%.6g"
OFS: " "
ORS: "\n"
PREC: 53
PROCINFO: array, 30 elements
RLENGTH: 0
ROUNDMODE: "N"
```

```
RS: "\n"
RSTART: 0
RT: ""
SUBSEP: "\034"
SYMTAB: array, 29 elements
TEXTDOMAIN: "messages"
result: 40
gawk>
```

- This example displays a list of defined functions in our program:

```
gawk> info functions
All defined functions:

calc() in file `calc.awk', line 17
find_add(num1, num2) in file `calc.awk', line 1
find_mul(num1, num2) in file `calc.awk', line 11
find_sub(num1, num2) in file `calc.awk', line 6
gawk>
```

- This example displays watchpoints set using a variable:

```
gawk> info watch
Watch variables:

4: result
```

- This example displays a list of source program filenames:

```
gawk> info source
Current source file: calc.awk
Number of lines: 27
gawk> info sources
Source file (lines): calc.awk (27)
gawk>
```

Saving the commands in file

We can save the commands from the current session to the specified filename, to replay them again in future using source commands:

- **save filename**: It saves the current session commands in the specified filename as shown in the following example :

```
gawk> save debug_commands.txt
```

The preceding command will save the commands of current session in the file `debug_commands.txt` for future reference or to replay them again using `source` command.

Exiting the debugger

We can exit from the debugger anytime by typing the `exit` or `quit` or q command. The debugger will give the warning that you are running a program and to press y if you really want to quit. The following is the list of options used for exiting from the debugger:

- `exit`
- `quit`
- `q`

Let's quit from our running debugger session of the `calc.awk` program using the `exit` command as follows:

```
gawk> quit
The program is running. Exit anyway (y/n)? y
```

We can print a list of all of the GAWK debugger commands with a brief description of their usage using the `help` or h command.

Array sorting

GAWK enables us to control the order in which a `for` (index in array) loop traverses an array. GAWK provides two built-in functions, `asort()` and `asorti()`, to sort arrays based on the array values and indexes, respectively. Using these two functions, we can control the criteria used to order the array elements during sorting.

Sort array by values using asort( )

GAWK provides a built-in function, `asort( )`, to sort the array on values. Numeric values come before string values in the sorting order. The following is the syntax for sorting the array:

```
Gn = asort(arr)
```

In the following example, we will use the `asort()` function to sort the array elements, as per the values assigned to them. The only side effect of using the `asort()` function with default parameters is that the array's original indexes will be lost and the new array is assigned an index from 1 to *n* as follows:

```
$ vi asort_arr.awk

BEGIN    {
    arr[30] = "volvo"
    arr[10] = "bmw"
    arr[20] = "audi"
    arr[50] = "toyota"
    arr["car"] = "ferrari"
    arr[70]     = "renault"
    arr[110] = 20
    arr[40]     = "ford"
    arr["num"] = 10
    arr[80] = "porsche"
    arr[60] = "jeep"

    n = asort(arr)
    for ( v in arr )
        print v, arr[v]
}

$ awk -f asort_arr.awk
```

The output of the previous code is as follows:

```
1 10
2 20
3 audi
4 bmw
5 ferrari
6 ford
7 jeep
8 porsche
9 renault
10 toyota
11 volvo
```

To preserve the original array with its indexes, we can pass another argument to the asort() function which is the new array to be used for sorting. In this case, GAWK copies the source array into the destination and then sorts the destination array, allotting it new indexes. However, the source array or original array remains unaffected, as shown here:

```
n = asort ( source, destination )
```

In the next example, we will pass two arguments to the asort function: first the original source array, arr, and second, the new destination array, newarr, to preserve the original array as such. In this case, GAWK copies the source array, arr, into the destination array newarr. The original source array's index and values are not affected:

```
$ vi asort_newarr.awk

BEGIN     {
    arr[30] = "volvo"
    arr[10] = "bmw"
    arr[20] = "audi"
    arr[50] = "toyota"
    arr["car"] = "ferrari"
    arr[70]    = "renault"
    arr[110] = 20
    arr[40]    = "ford"
    arr["num"] = 10
    arr[80] = "porsche"
    arr[60] = "jeep"

    n = asort(arr, newarr)
    print "==========================================="
    print "SORTED ARRAY STORED IN NEW ARRAY VARIABLE..."
    print "==========================================="
    for ( x in newarr )
        print "Index : ", x, "\tValue :", newarr[x]

    print "==========================================="
    print "ORIGINAL ARRAY...."
    print "==========================================="
    for ( v in arr )
        print "Index : ", v, "\tValue :", arr[v]
}

$ awk -f asort_newarr.awk
```

The output of the previous code is as follows:

```
===========================================
SORTED ARRAY STORED IN NEW ARRAY VARIABLE...
===========================================
Index :  1        Value : 10
Index :  2        Value : 20
Index :  3        Value : audi
Index :  4        Value : bmw
Index :  5        Value : ferrari
Index :  6        Value : ford
Index :  7        Value : jeep
Index :  8        Value : porsche
Index :  9        Value : renault
Index :  10       Value : toyota
Index :  11       Value : volvo
===========================================
ORIGINAL ARRAY....
===========================================
Index :  car      Value : ferrari
Index :  num      Value : 10
Index :  10       Value : bmw
Index :  20       Value : audi
Index :  30       Value : volvo
Index :  40       Value : ford
Index :  50       Value : toyota
Index :  60       Value : jeep
Index :  70       Value : renault
Index :  80       Value : porsche
Index :  110      Value : 20
```

Sort array indexes using asorti()

The asorti() function takes all the array indexes, sorts them and stores them in a new array, as array values for the new array with an index starting from 1 to n. Numeric values come before string values in the sorting order. The following is the syntax for sorting the array index using the asorti() function:

```
n = asorti (arr)
```

Let's understand the working of the `asorti()` function using examples. In the following example, we will use the `asorti()` function to sort the array indexes as per their values. The only side effect of using the `asorti()` function with default parameters is that the array's original index will be lost and the new array is assigned indexes from 1 to *n*, and now the new array elements will be the previous array's indexes:

```
$ vi asorti_1.awk

BEGIN    {
    arr[30] = "volvo"
    arr[10] = "bmw"
    arr[20] = "audi"
    arr[50] = "toyota"
    arr["car"] = "ferrari"
    arr[70]    = "renault"
    arr[110] = 20
    arr[40]    = "ford"
    arr["num"] = 10
    arr[80] = "porsche"
    arr[60] = "jeep"

    n = asorti(arr)
    for ( v in arr )
        print v, arr[v]
}

$ awk -f asorti_1.awk
```

The output of the previous code is as follows:

```
1  10
2  110
3  20
4  30
5  40
6  50
7  60
8  70
9  80
10 car
11 num
```

To preserve the original array with its indexes, we can pass another argument to the `asorti()` function, which is the new array to be used for sorting the indexes this time. In this case, GAWK copies the source array indexes into the destination array as values and then sorts the destination array, allotting it new indexes. However, the source array or original array remains unaffected, as shown in the following code:

```
n = asorti ( source, destination )
```

In this example, we will pass two arguments to the `asorti()` function: first, the original source array, `arr`, and second, the new destination array `newarr`, to preserve the original array, as such. In this case, GAWK copies the indexes of the source array, `arr`, into the values of the destination array, `newarr` . The original source arrary's index and values are not affected:

```
$ vi asorti_2.awk

BEGIN    {
    arr[30] = "volvo"
    arr[10] = "bmw"
    arr[20] = "audi"
    arr[50] = "toyota"
    arr["car"] = "ferrari"
    arr[70]    = "renault"
    arr[110] = 20
    arr[40]    = "ford"
    arr["num"] = 10
    arr[80] = "porsche"
    arr[60] = "jeep"

    n = asorti(arr, newarr)
    print "============================================="
    print "SORTED ARRAY INDEXES STORED AS ELEMENTS ..."
    print "============================================="
    for ( x in newarr )
        print "Index : ", x, "\tValue :", newarr[x]

    print "============================================="
    print "ORIGINAL ARRAY...."
    print "============================================="
    for ( v in arr )
        print "Index : ", v, "\tValue :", arr[v]
}

$ awk -f asorti_2.awk
```

The output of the previous code is as follows:

```
================================================
SORTED ARRAY INDEXES STORED AS ELEMENTS ...
================================================
Index :  1        Value : 10
Index :  2        Value : 110
Index :  3        Value : 20
Index :  4        Value : 30
Index :  5        Value : 40
Index :  6        Value : 50
Index :  7        Value : 60
Index :  8        Value : 70
Index :  9        Value : 80
Index :  10       Value : car
Index :  11       Value : num
================================================
ORIGINAL ARRAY....
================================================
Index :  car      Value : ferrari
Index :  num      Value : 10
Index :  10       Value : bmw
Index :  20       Value : audi
Index :  30       Value : volvo
Index :  40       Value : ford
Index :  50       Value : toyota
Index :  60       Value : jeep
Index :  70       Value : renault
Index :  80       Value : porsche
Index :  110      Value : 20
```

Two-way inter-process communication

In Chapter 5, *Printing Output in Awk,* we have seen how redirection can be used to store output to a file in AWK. We also saw how a pipe is used for redirecting the output of one command to another command in AWK. Pipes use one-way communication only; they receive the output from one process and give it as input to another.

However, with GAWK, we can have two-way communication with another process. The second process here is known as a coprocess and it runs parallel to the GAWK process. The two-way communication is created using the `|&` operator (this operator is a borrowed feature from Korn shell (`ksh`)). The following is the process for creating a two-way I/O operation between processes:

```
{    print "data to be shared with coprocess" |& "subprogram"
     "subprogram" |& getline result
     close ( "subprogram", "to")
     print result
     close ( "subprogram" )     }
```

The following is a description of the various action statements used in the previous program:

- `subprogram`: This is the second shell program or command to be used for communication with GAWK, known here as a coprocess.
- `|&`: The I/O operation when executed using the `|&` operator the first time, GAWK creates the two-way pipeline to the child process that runs the other program (subprogram).
- `print`: The `print` or `printf` command is used to give standard input to the subprogram.
- `getline`: The standard output from the subprogram is read using a `getline` statement
- `close (command )`: The `close()` function is used to close the pipeline opened by the exact command used earlier in the subprogram with `|&` for the opening of the pipeline.
- `close (subprogram, to)`: It is possible to close just one end of the two-way pipe to a coprocess, by supplying a second argument to the `close()` function, as either `to` or `from`. The `to` string tells GAWK to close the sending end of the pipe and the `from` string tells GAWK to close the receiving end of pipe.

It is essential when using shell commands, such as `sort`, `wc`, or `tr` and other filter utilities, as a coprocess (subprogram) to use the `to` argument with the `close()` function. For a `sort` or `tr` -like program requires all of its input data be read before it can produce any output. The `sort` or `tr` program does not receive an end of file indication until GAWK closes the write end of the pipe by using the `to` argument with the `close()` function.

In the following example, we will use `tr` as a coprocess for translating a lowercase string, `hello world`, given as input with the `print` command, into capital letters. Once we finish sending/writing data to the `tr` utility, we can close the `to` end of the pipe and then start reading the translated string via the `getline` statement as follows:

```
$ vi 2wayio.awk

BEGIN {
    cmd = "tr [a-z] [A-Z]"
    print "hello, world !!!" |& cmd
    close(cmd,"to")
    cmd |& getline
    print $0
    close(cmd);
}

$ awk -f 2wayio.awk
```

The output of the previous code is as follows:

```
HELLO, WORLD !!!
```

In the next example, we convert the contents of `emp.dat` from lowercase to capital letters as follows:

```
$ vi small2capital.awk

{
    cmd = "tr [a-z] [A-Z]"
    print $0 |& cmd
    close(cmd,"to")
    cmd |& getline
    print $0
    close(cmd);
}

$ awk -f small2capital.awk  cars.dat
```

The output of the previous code is as follows:

```
MARUTI          SWIFT         2007         50000        5
HONDA           CITY          2005         60000        3
MARUTI          DEZIRE        2009         3100         6
CHEVY           BEAT          2005         33000        2
HONDA           CITY          2010         33000        6
CHEVY           TAVERA        1999         10000        4
TOYOTA          COROLLA       1995         95000        2
```

MARUTI	SWIFT	2009	4100	5
MARUTI	ESTEEM	1997	98000	1
FORD	IKON	1995	80000	1
HONDA	ACCORD	2000	60000	2
FIAT	PUNTO	2007	45000	3

Using GAWK for network programming

The networking feature in GAWK was added from version 3.1 onwards after the addition of a two-way pipeline to a coprocess on the same system. Networking is more of a two-way connection to a process on another system, using TCP/IP connections. Before we move ahead in networking with GAWK, we must understand the fundamental construct of network communication. In a network communication model, one system acts as a client and another as a server.

The server is the system that provides the service, such as a web server or email server. It is the system to which the connection is made. The server keeps waiting in a listening state to receive requests for connections.

The client is the system which makes a request for service. It is the system which initiates the connection request. In the TCP/IP model, each connection consists of an IP address and port pair. Until the connection is in place, the ports used at each end are unique and cannot be used by other processes on the same system at the same time.

The AWK programming language was developed as a pattern-matching language for text manipulation; however, GAWK has advanced features, such as file-like handling of network connections. We can perform simple TCP/IP connection handling in GAWK with the help of special filenames. GAWK extends the two-way I/O mechanism used with the |& operator to simple networking using these special filenames that hide the complex details of socket programming to the programmer.

The special filename for network communication is made up of multiple fields, all of which are mandatory. The following is the syntax of creating a filename for network communication:

```
/net-type/protocol/local-port/remote-host/remote-port
```

Each field is separated from another with a forward slash. Specifying all of the fields is mandatory. If any of the field is not valid for any protocol or you want the system to pick a default value for that field, it is set as 0. The following list illustrates the meaning of different fields used in creating the file for network communication:

- `net-type`: Its value is inet4 for IPv4, inet6 for IPv6, or inet to use the system default (which is generally IPv4).
- `protocol`: It is either `tcp` or `udp` for a TCP or UDP IP connection. It is advised you use the TCP protocol for networking. UDP is used when low overhead is a priority.
- `local-port`: Its value decides which port on the local machine is used for communication with the remote system. On the client side, its value is generally set to 0 to indicate any free port to be picked up by the system itself. On the server side, its value is other than 0 because the service is provided to a specific publicly known port number or service name, such as `http`, `smtp`, and so on.
- `remote-host`: It is the remote hostname which is to be at the other end of the connection. For the server side, its value is set to 0 to indicate the server is open for all other hosts for connection. For the client side, its value is fixed to one remote host and hence, it is always different from 0. This name can either be represented through symbols, such as `www.google.com`, or numbers, `123.45.67.89`.

- `remote-port`: It is the port on which the remote machine will communicate across the network. For clients, its value is other than 0, to indicate to which port they are connecting to the remote machine. For servers, its value is the port on which they want connection from the client to be established. We can use a service name here such as `ftp`, `http`, or a port number such as `80`, `21`, and so on.

TCP client and server (/inet/tcp)

TCP gaurantees that data is received at the other end and in the same order as it was transmitted, so always use TCP.

In the following example, we will create a tcp-server (sender) to send the current date time of the server to the client. The server uses the `strftime()` function with the coprocess operator to send to the GAWK server, listening on the `8080` port. The remote host and remote port could be any client, so its value is kept as 0.

The server connection is closed by passing the special filename to the `close()` function for closing the file as follows:

```
$ vi tcpserver.awk

#TCP-Server
BEGIN   {
    print strftime() |& "/inet/tcp/8080/0/0"
    close("/inet/tcp/8080/0/0")
    }
```

Now, open one Terminal and run this program before running the client program as follows:

```
$ awk -f  tcpserver.awk
```

Next, we create the `tcpclient` (receiver) to receive the data sent by the `tcpserver`. Here, we first create the client connection and pass the received data to the `getline()` using the coprocess operator. Here the local-port value is set to 0 to be automatically chosen by the system, the remote-host is set to the localhost, and the remote-port is set to the tcp-server port, `8080`. After that, the received message is printed, using the `print $0` command, and finally, the client connection is closed using the `close` command, as follows:

```
$ vi tcpclient.awk

#TCP-client
BEGIN   {
    "/inet/tcp/0/localhost/8080" |& getline
    print $0
    close("/inet/tcp/0/localhost/8080")
    }
```

Now, execute the `tcpclient` program in another Terminal as follows :

```
$ awk -f  tcpclient.awk
```

The output of the previous code is as follows :

```
Fri Feb  9 09:42:22 IST 2018
```

UDP client and server (/inet/udp)

The server and client program that use the UDP protocol for communication are almost identical to their TCP counterparts, with the only difference being that the protocol is changed to udp from tcp. So, the UDP-server and UDP-client program can be written as follows:

```
$ vi udpserver.awk

#UDP-Server
BEGIN    {
    print strftime() |& "/inet/udp/8080/0/0"
    "/inet/udp/8080/0/0" |& getline
    print $0
    close("/inet/udp/8080/0/0")
    }

$ awk -f udpserver.awk
```

Here, only one addition has been made to the client program. In the client, we send the message hello from client ! to the server. So when we execute this program on the receiving Terminal, where the udpclient.awk program is run, we get the remote system date time. And on the Terminal where the udpserver.awk program is run, we get the hello message from the client:

```
$ vi udpclient.awk

#UDP-client
BEGIN    {
    print "hello from client!" |& "/inet/udp/0/localhost/8080"
    "/inet/udp/0/localhost/8080" |& getline
    print $0
    close("/inet/udp/0/localhost/8080")
    }

$ awk -f udpclient.awk
```

GAWK can be used to open direct sockets only. Currently, there is no way to access services available over an SSL connection such as https, smtps, pop3s, imaps, and so on.

Reading a web page using HttpService

To read a web page, we use the **Hypertext Transfer Protocol (HTTP)** service which runs on port number 80. First, we redefine the record separators RS and ORS because HTTP requires CR-LF to separate lines. The program requests to the IP address 35.164.82.168 (www.grymoire.com) of a static website which, in turn, makes a GET request to the web page: http://35.164.82.168/Unix/donate.html . HTTP calls the GET request, a method which tells the web server to transmit the web page donate.html. The output is stored in the getline function using the co-process operator and printed on the screen, line by line, using the while loop. Finally, we close the http service connection. The following is the program to retrieve the web page:

```
$ vi  view_webpage.awk

BEGIN {
RS=ORS="\r\n"
http =  "/inet/tcp/0/35.164.82.168/80"
print "GET http://35.164.82.168/Unix/donate.html" |& http
while ((http |& getline) > 0)
  print $0
close(http)
}

$ awk -f view_webpage.awk
```

Upon executing the program, it fills the screen with the source code of the page on the screen as follows:

```
<!DOCTYPE HTML PUBLIC "-//W3C//DTD HTML 4.0 Transitional//EN">

<HTML lang="en-US">
<HEAD>
    <TITLE> Welcome to The UNIX Grymoire!</TITLE>
<meta name="keywords" content="grymoire, donate, unix, tutorials, sed,
awk">
<META NAME="Description" CONTENT="Please donate to the Unix Grymoire"  >
<meta http-equiv="Content-Type" content="text/html; charset=utf-8">
<link href="myCSS.css" rel="stylesheet" type="text/css">
<!-- Place this tag in your head or just before your close body tag -->
<script type="text/javascript"
src="https://apis.google.com/js/plusone.js"></script>
<link rel="canonical" href="http://www.grymoire.com/Unix/donate.html">
<link href="myCSS.css" rel="stylesheet" type="text/css">
........
........
```

Profiling

Profiling of code is done for code optimization. In GAWK, we can do profiling by supplying a profile option to GAWK while running the GAWK program. On execution of the GAWK program with that option, it creates a file with the name `awkprof.out`. Since GAWK is performing profiling of the code, the program execution is up to 45% slower than the speed at which GAWK normally executes.

Let's understand profiling by looking at some examples. In the following example, we create a program that has four functions; two arithmetic functions, one function prints an array, and one function calls all of them. Our program also contains two `BEGIN` and two `END` statements. First, the `BEGIN` and `END` statement and then it contains a pattern action rule, then the second `BEGIN` and `END` statement, as follows:

```
$ vi codeprof.awk

func z_array(){

    arr[30] = "volvo"
    arr[10] = "bmw"
    arr[20] = "audi"
    arr[50] = "toyota"
    arr["car"] = "ferrari"

    n = asort(arr)
    print "Array begins...!"
    print "====================="
    for ( v in arr )
        print v, arr[v]
    print "Array Ends...!"
    print "====================="
}

function mul(num1, num2){
    result = num1 * num2
    printf ("Multiplication of %d * %d : %d\n", num1,num2,result)
}

function all(){
    add(30,10)
    mul(5,6)
    z_array()
}


BEGIN    { print "First BEGIN statement"
```

```
        print "===================="
    }
END     { print "First END statement "
        print "===================="
    }

/maruti/{print $0 }


BEGIN     {
    print "Second BEGIN statement"
    print "===================="
    all()
}
END     { print "Second END statement"
        print "===================="
    }

function add(num1, num2){
    result = num1 + num2
    printf ("Addition of %d + %d : %d\n", num1,num2,result)
}

$ awk  -- prof -f codeprof.awk cars.dat
```

The output of the previous code is as follows:

```
First BEGIN statement
====================
Second BEGIN statement
====================
Addition of 30 + 10 : 40
Multiplication of 5 * 6 : 30
Array begins...!
====================
1 audi
2 bmw
3 ferrari
4 toyota
5 volvo
Array Ends...!
====================
maruti          swift         2007          50000          5
maruti          dezire        2009          3100           6
maruti          swift         2009          4100           5
maruti          esteem        1997          98000          1
First END statement
====================
```

```
Second END statement
=====================
```

Execution of the previous program also creates a file with the name awkprof.out. If we want to create this profile file with a custom name, then we can specify the filename as an argument to the --profile option as follows:

```
$ awk   --prof=codeprof.prof  -f  codeprof.awk cars.dat
```

Now, upon execution of the preceding code we get a new file with the name codeprof.prof. Let's try to understand the contents of the file codeprof.prof created by the profiles as follows:

```
# gawk profile, created Fri Feb  9 11:01:41 2018

# BEGIN rule(s)

BEGIN {
 1      print "First BEGIN statement"
 1      print "====================="
}

BEGIN {
 1      print "Second BEGIN statement"
 1      print "====================="
 1      all()
}

# Rule(s)

12  /maruti/ { # 4
 4      print $0
}

# END rule(s)

END {
 1      print "First END statement "
 1      print "====================="
}

END {
 1      print "Second END statement"
 1      print "====================="
}
```

```
# Functions, listed alphabetically

  1   function add(num1, num2)
  {
  1        result = num1 + num2
  1        printf "Addition of %d + %d : %d\n", num1, num2, result
  }

  1   function all()
  {
  1        add(30, 10)
  1        mul(5, 6)
  1        z_array()
  }

  1   function mul(num1, num2)
  {
  1        result = num1 * num2
  1        printf "Multiplication of %d * %d : %d\n", num1, num2, result
  }

  1   function z_array()
  {
  1        arr[30] = "volvo"
  1        arr[10] = "bmw"
  1        arr[20] = "audi"
  1        arr[50] = "toyota"
  1        arr["car"] = "ferrari"
  1        n = asort(arr)
  1        print "Array begins...!"
  1        print "===================="
  5        for (v in arr) {
  5            print v, arr[v]
       }
  1        print "Array Ends...!"
  1        print "===================="
  }
```

This profiling example explains the various basic features of profiling in GAWK. They are as follows:

- The first look at the file from top to bottom explains the order of the program in which various rules are executed. First, the BEGIN rules are listed followed by the BEGINFILE rule, if any. Then pattern-action rules are listed. Thereafter, ENDFILE rules and END rules are printed. Finally, functions are listed in alphabetical order. Multiple BEGIN and END rules retain their places as separate identities. The same is also true for the BEGINFILE and ENDFILE rules.

- The pattern-action rules have two counts. The first number, to the left of the rule, tells how many times the rule's pattern was tested for the input file/record. The second number, to the right of the rule's opening left brace, with a comment, shows how many times the rule's action was executed when the rule evaluated to true. The difference between the two indicates how many times the rules pattern evaluated to false.

- If there is an if-else statement then the number shows how many times the condition was tested. At the right of the opening left brace for its body is a count showing how many times the condition was true. The count for the else statement tells how many times the test failed.

- The count at the beginning of a loop header (for or while loop) shows how many times the loop conditional-expression was executed.

- In user-defined functions, the count before the function keyword tells how many times the function was called. The counts next to the statements in the body show how many times those statements were executed.

- The layout of each block uses C-style tabs for code alignment. Braces are used to mark the opening and closing of a code block, similar to C-style.

- Parentheses are used as per the precedence rule and the structure of the program, but only when needed.

- Printf or print statement arguments are enclosed in parentheses, only if the statement is followed by redirection.

- GAWK also gives leading comments before rules, such as before BEGIN and END rules, BEGINFILE and ENDFILE rules, and pattern-action rules and before functions.

GAWK provides standard representation in a profiled version of the program. GAWK also accepts another option, `--pretty-print`. The following is an example of a pretty-printing AWK program:

```
$ awk  --pretty-print  -f  codeprof.awk cars.dat
```

When GAWK is called with `pretty-print`, the program generates `awkprof.out`, but this time without any execution counts in the output. Pretty-print output also preserves any original comments if they are given in a program while the profile option omits the original program's comments. The file created on execution of the program with `--pretty-print` option is as follows:

```
# gawk profile, created Fri Feb  9 11:04:19 2018

# BEGIN rule(s)

BEGIN {
    print "First BEGIN statement"
    print "===================="
}

BEGIN {
    print "Second BEGIN statement"
    print "===================="
    all()
}

# Rule(s)

/maruti/ {
    print $0
}

# END rule(s)

END {
    print "First END statement "
    print "===================="
}

END {
    print "Second END statement"
    print "===================="
}
```

```
# Functions, listed alphabetically

function add(num1, num2)
{
    result = num1 + num2
    printf "Addition of %d + %d : %d\n", num1, num2, result
}

function all()
{
    add(30, 10)
    mul(5, 6)
    z_array()
}

function mul(num1, num2)
{
    result = num1 * num2
    printf "Multiplication of %d * %d : %d\n", num1, num2, result
}

function z_array()
{
    arr[30] = "volvo"
    arr[10] = "bmw"
    arr[20] = "audi"
    arr[50] = "toyota"
    arr["car"] = "ferrari"
    n = asort(arr)
    print "Array begins...!"
    print "===================="
    for (v in arr) {
        print v, arr[v]
    }
    print "Array Ends...!"
    print "===================="
}
```

Summary

In this chapter, we learned about the features which are available in GAWK but not in AWK. We began with features such as handling non-decimal input, two-way inter-process communication, sorting of arrays, network programming and the GAWK built-in command line debugger. Finally, we learned about profiling using GAWK, for optimizing GAWK programs.

In our next chapter, we will cover some use case examples of text-processing using AWK for system administrators and programmers.

10
Practical Implementation of AWK

This chapter covers different use case examples of text processing and pattern matching with AWK. These examples include some quick one-liner collections for system administrators, that can be directly used inside shell scripts, while performing automation. Some examples are written from the programmers' and data scientists' perspective for dealing with raw data cleaning and reformatting. These sample programs and one-liners are aimed at saving time while carrying out automation, and making AWK programs, clean and more productive.

In this chapter, we will cover the following:

- One-liner collections for text processing and pattern matching with AWK
- Use case examples of pattern matching using AWK

Working with one-liners for text processing and pattern matching with AWK

AWK is the best tool for breaking data into smaller chunks to make it suitable for input to other applications, or for manipulation. We can write complex scripts using AWK that can run into 100s or even 1,000s of lines, but for system administrators, most of the time, use of AWK is limited to relatively short scripts, and one-liners are best suited to the command line to give the desired output.

A one-liner is an AWK program consisting of a sequence of pattern-action statements in a single line. They are very useful in performing day-to-day file processing. They help in breaking down large files into chunks of information. These one-liners are often combined with a bash shell script for automation of sysadmin tasks.

Selective printing of lines with AWK

In this section, we look at various one liners used for printing lines of a file selectively with AWK:

- **Printing the top 10 lines of a file (similar to the head 10 shell command)**: In this example, we use a built-in AWK variable called NR with an input of record number/line number. After reading each line, AWK increments this variable value by one. An AWK action statement gets executed for each pattern match. In this example, we do not specify any action statements. In the absence of any action statement, the default operation is print. So, it will print the line, if the line number is less than 11, as follows:

    ```
    $ awk 'NR < 11' cars.dat
    ```

    The previous command processes all the lines in a file, although in the output it prints only the first 10 files:

    ```
    $ awk '{print};NR == 10{ exit }' cars.dat
    ```

    Or this can be written as:

    ```
    $ awk '1;NR == 10{ exit }' cars.dat
    ```

- **Print the first line of a file only (similar to the head 1 shell command)**: In this example, we again use the built-in variable NR. Here, we give the condition to first check if the input record number is greater than one. If it is true, then exit; otherwise, execute the next action statement of print. Hence, it prints the first line only when NR is equal to 1:

    ```
    $ awk 'NR > 1{ exit }; { print }' cars.dat
    ```

- **Print last line of a file only (similar to the tail 1 shell command):** In this example, AWK processes the whole file but prints only the last line, as we have used the `print` statement in the END block as follows:

  ```
  $ awk 'END { print }' cars.dat
  ```

Or this can be written as:

  ```
  $ awk '{ line=$0 }END { print line }' cars.dat
  ```

  This way of printing the last line using AWK is more CPU intensive than the tail -1 command.

- **Print last two lines of a file (similar to tail -2 shell command):** In this example, we store the two lines in one variable (here, variable is y). Both lines are separated by a linefeed character \n. The first line is stored in variable x and the second in $0. Later, both x and $0 are assigned to y. So, if we have N no of lines, then x stores line number N-1 and $0 will store line number N, as follows:

  ```
  $ awk '{ y=x "\n" $0; x=$0 }; END { print y }' cars.dat
  ```

- **Print those lines that match a regular expression /regex/ (similar to the grep shell command):** In this example, we specify the pattern as a regular expression, /regex/. If the current line matches the regex, AWK prints the whole line; otherwise, it prints nothing:

  ```
  $ awk '/regex/' <FILENAME>
  ```

Or this can be written as:

  ```
  $ awk '{ if( $0 ~ /ikon/) print $0}' cars.dat
  ```

Or:

  ```
  $ awk '$0 ~/ikon/{print $0}' cars.dat
  ```

Or:

  ```
  $ awk '/ikon/{print $0}' cars.dat
  ```

Or:

  ```
  $ awk '/ikon/{print}' cars.dat
  ```

Or:

```
$ awk '/ikon/' cars.dat
```

- **Print those lines that do not match the given regular expression /regex/ (similar to the grep -v shell command):** In this example, we negate the specified regular expression /regex/. If the current line does not match the regex, AWK prints the whole line; otherwise, it prints nothing:

```
$ awk '!/regex/' <FILENAME>
```

Or:

```
$ awk '!/ikon/' cars.dat
```

- **Print those lines that match a regular expression /regex/ and ignore case (similar to the grep -i shell command):** In this example, we set the AWK built-in variable IGNORECASE to true inside the BEGIN block and specify as a regular expression /regex/. If the current line matches the regex, AWK prints the whole line; otherwise, it prints nothing:

```
$ awk 'BEGIN { IGNORECASE=1 };/regex/' <FILENAME>
```

Or:

```
$ awk 'BEGIN { IGNORECASE=1 };{ if( $0 ~ /IKON/) print $0}'
cars.dat
```

Or:

```
$ awk 'BEGIN { IGNORECASE=1 };$0 ~/IKON/{print $0}' cars.dat
```

Or:

```
$ awk 'BEGIN { IGNORECASE=1 };/IKON/{print $0}' cars.dat
```

Or:

```
$ awk 'BEGIN { IGNORECASE=1 };/IKON/{print}' cars.dat
```

Or:

```
$ awk 'BEGIN { IGNORECASE=1 };/Ikon/' cars.dat
```

- **Printing a line immediately before a line that matches /regex/ (but not the line with the regex itself)**: In this example, we store the current line in a variable (here the x variable is used). When the next line is read, the previous line is still available in variable x, and if the current line matches /regex/, the variable x is printed containing the previous line, as follows:

```
$ awk '/regex/{ print x }; { x=$0 }' <FILENAME>
```

Or:

```
$ awk '/ford/{ print x }; { x=$0 }' cars.dat
```

If regex is found on the first line, then it prints an empty line; so to make it more meaningful, we can modify the preceding one-liner as follows:

```
$ awk '/regex/{ print ( x == "" ? "match found on line 1" : x ) };
{ x=$0 }'
```

- **Printing the line immediately after the line that matches /regex/ (but not the line that has the regex itself)**: In this example, we use the getline function in the action statement. If a regex match is found on a line, the getline function is used to fetch the next line in $0 and then prints it with the print statement:

```
$ awk '/regex/{ getline; print }' <FILENAME>
```

Or:

```
$ awk '/ford/{ getline; print }' cars.dat
```

- **Print the lines that match one of three given regular expressions, AAA or BBB or CCC**: In this example, we use an extended regular expression alternation meta-character |. It separates each regex and prints the lines matching them separately on each line. The ones containing one or more matches get printed as follows:

```
$ awk '/AAA|BBB|CCC/' <FILENAME>
```

Or:

```
$ awk '/AAA|BBB|CCC/' cars.dat
```

Or:

```
$ awk '/ford|punto|1999/' cars.dat
```

- **Print lines that contain multiple regular expressions AAA and BBB and CCC in a given order in a line**: In this example, we use the regular expression meta-char dot (.) and asterisk (*). We build a `regex` as `AAA.*BBB.*CCC` to match the lines containing AAA followed by any text, followed by BBB, followed by any text, followed by CCC in that order and print it if a match is found, as follows:

  ```
  $ awk '/AAA.*BBB.*CCC/' <FILENAME>
  ```

  Or:

  ```
  $ awk '/maruti.*swift.*2007/' cars.dat
  ```

- **Print the length of characters in a line followed by the line itself**: In this example, we use the built-in length function (`length [ str ]`), to prefix the line with the number of characters in each line, as follows:

  ```
  $ awk '{print length " : " $0}' <FILENAME>
  ```

  Or:

  ```
  $ awk '{print length " : " $0}' label.dat
  ```

- **Print only the lines that are a specified number of characters in length or more**: In this example, we use the length function again to print only those lines that contain at least a specific numbers of characters each line, as follows:

  ```
  $ awk 'length >= 10' <FILENAME>
  ```

  Or:

  ```
  $ awk 'length >= 10' label.dat
  ```

- **Print only the lines that have a specified number of characters or less**: In this example, we use the length function with the relational operators less than and equal to, for printing the lines, as follows:

  ```
  $ awk 'length <= 10' <FILENAME>
  ```

  Or:

  ```
  $ awk 'length <= 10' label.dat
  ```

- **Print a range of lines (section of file) from regular expression to end of file:** In this example, we specify the first range pattern in the format `/pattern1/`, `/pattern2/`. If in place of `pattern2`, we put `0`, then it will print all the lines up to the end of file. `0` represents false, so all lines starting from `pattern1` to the end of the file:

    ```
    $ awk '/regex/,0' cars.dat
    ```

  Or:

    ```
    $ awk '/beat/,0' cars.dat
    ```

- **Print a range of lines (section of file) specified between two patterns:** In this example, we print a range of lines by specifying two patterns, `/pattern1/`, `/pattern2/`, as follows:

    ```
    $ awk '/regex/,/regex/' cars.dat
    ```

  Or:

    ```
    $awk '/beat/,/ikon/' cars.dat
    ```

- **Print a range of lines specified by line number (4 to 8 in our example scenario):** In this example, we use `NR`, input a record number and specify the range of lines to be printed as `pattern1`, `pattern2`. Here, `pattern1` is `NR==4` and `pattern2` is `NR==8` as follows:

    ```
    $ awk 'NR==4,NR==8' <FILENAME>
    ```

  Or:

    ```
    $ awk 'NR==4,NR==8' cars.dat
    ```

- **Print a specified line number:** In this example, we use `NR` to print a specified line number. If say `NR==4` is specified, so when an input record number is equal to `4`, AWK prints the line as follows:

    ```
    $ awk 'NR==4' <FILENAME>
    ```

  Or:

    ```
    $ awk 'NR==4' cars.dat
    ```

A more appropriate way of printing a specified line number would be to stop processing after printing the matching line, as follows:

```
$ awk 'NR==4 { print; exit }' cars.dat
```

- **Print all lines where a particular field is equal to a specified string**: In this example, we use the relational operator equal to (==) to match the value contained in a field with the string specified. Here, we will match the second field with a string, swift, and print the lines, as follows:

```
$ awk '<field number> == <string>' <FILENAME>
```

Or:

```
$ awk '$2 == "swift"' cars.dat
```

Or:

```
$ awk '$2 == "swift"{ print }' cars.dat
```

Or:

```
$ awk '{ if ( $2 == "swift" ) { print $0 } }' cars.dat
```

- **Print any line but the one containing a specified string in a specified field**: In this example, we use the negation relational operator to print those lines which do not contain the specified string in the specified field of a file. Here, we print those lines that do not contain the string swift in the second field, as follows:

```
$ awk '<FIELD NUMBER> != <STRING>' <FILENAME>
```

Or:

```
$ awk '$2 != "swift"' cars.dat
```

Or:

```
$ awk '$2 != "swift"{ print }' cars.dat
```

Or:

```
$ awk '{ if ( $2 != "swift" ) { print $0 } }' cars.dat
```

- **Print those lines whose specified field matches a given regular expression**: In this example, we use the match operator ~ to test if a field matches a specified regular expression. Here, we will print all those lines whose second field matches a regular expression [^a-j]. This regular expression means all those lines whose second field begins with a lowercase letter a, b, c, d, e, f, g, h, i, or j will be printed:

  ```
  $ awk '<FIELNAME> ~ /<REGEX>/' <FILENAME>
  ```

  Or:

  ```
  $ awk '$2 ~ /^[a-j]/' cars.dat
  ```

- **Print those lines whose specified field does not match a given regular expression**: In this example, we use the not match operator ! ~ to test if a field does not match a specified regular expression.

  Here, we will print all those lines whose second field does not match a regular expression [^a-j]. This regular expression means all those lines whose second field begins with a lowercase letter a, b, c, d, e, f, g, h, i, or j will be printed:

  ```
  $ awk '<FIELNAME> ~ /<REGEX>/' <FILENAME>
  ```

  Or:

  ```
  $ awk '$2 !~ /^[a-j]/' cars.dat
  ```

- **Print each line with specified field deleted**: In the following example, we set the specified field value to null for each line and then print it as follows:

  ```
  $ awk '{ <FIELD> =""; print }' <FILENAME>
  ```

  Or:

  ```
  $ awk '{ $2 =""; print }' cars.dat
  ```

- **Print all lines of a file (similar to "cat filename" shell command)**: In the following example, we print all the input records of files processed by AWK. In this, we use a universal true condition such as 1 and string a as an argument to AWK. Since the pattern specified is always true, AWK will print the current input line being processed, as follows:

```
$ awk 1 <FILENAME>
```

Or:

```
$ awk ' "a" ' <FILENAME>
```

Or:

```
$ awk '{print}' <FILENAME>
```

Or:

```
$ awk '/.*/' <FILENAME>
```

Or:

```
$ awk '$0' <FILENAME>
```

The previous syntax, `awk 1 <filename>`, is generally used in combination with other AWK statements. For example, we operate on some input records but we also want to print all records, whether they were affected by the other operation or not, as given in the following example:

```
$ awk '{sub(/maruti/,"XYZ")}1' cars.dat
```

Or:

```
$ awk '{sub(/maruti/,"XYZ")}{print}' cars.dat
```

- **Print the fields of every line in reverse order**: In this example, we use NF, the number of fields built-in variable. Here, we begin printing with the last field in each line until the first field in the line is printed. Then, we give the linefeed before printing the next line, as follows:

```
$ awk '{ for( i=NF; i>0; i-- ) printf("%s\t", $i); printf("\n")
}' cars.dat
```

- **Joining the two lines if first line ends with matching string**: In the following example, we use a ternary operator. The string that ends the line to be joined with the next line is specified as a conditional expression; if the string match is found at the end of line, the ORS value is set to FS (space); otherwise, ORS is set as RS (newline), as follows:

```
$ awk 'ORS=/regex$/ ? FS : RS' <FILENAME>
```

Or:

```
$ awk 'ORS=/Jack$/ ? FS : RS' label.dat
```

Modifying line spacing in a file with AWK

In this section, we look at various one-liners used for modifying the spacing between lines in a file, using AWK.

- **Double-space a file**: In the following example, we first use the print statement with $0 to hold an entire line, followed by the second print statement to print nothing. In this, each print statement is followed by ORS, which prints a newline. Thus, each line gets double-spaced, as follows:

```
$ awk '{print $0 }{print ""}' label.dat
```

Or:

```
$ awk '{print}{print ""}' label.dat
```

Or:

```
$ awk '1{print}{print ""}' label.dat
```

Or:

```
$ awk '1;{print ""}' label.dat
```

Or:

```
$ awk '{print $0 "\n"}' label.dat
```

We can also double-space a file by setting the ORS variable value to 2 newlines instead of the default value of 1, as follows:

```
$ awk 'BEGIN{ORS="\n\n"};{print}' label.dat
```

Or:

```
$ awk 'BEGIN{ORS="\n\n"};1' label.dat
```

- **Double-space a file so that only one empty line appears between lines of text**: In this case, we use NF, the number of fields built-in variable of AWK, as the pattern. If a line is empty, the value of NF is 0 for that and it will skip the action part for those lines where NF is set as 0; otherwise, it will execute the action part of the AWK statement, as follows:

```
$ awk 'NF{print $0 "\n"}' label.dat
```

Or:

```
$ awk 'BEGIN{ORS="\n\n"} NF{print $0}' label.dat
```

- **Triple-spacing a file**: In this case, instead of a two-line feed, we specify a three-line feed in the AWK program, used earlier for double-spacing, as follows:

```
$ awk '1;{print "\n"}' label.dat
```

Or:

```
$ awk '{print ; print "\n"}' label.dat
```

Or:

```
$ awk '{print $0 "\n\n"}' label.dat
```

Or:

```
$ awk 'BEGIN{ORS="\n\n\n"}{print $0}' label.dat
```

Numbering and calculations with AWK

In this section, we look at the working of one-liners for the numbering of lines in a file, and performing calculations on fields and line numbers:

- **Numbering lines in multiple files separately**: The following example uses FNR – the file line number AWK built-in variable before each line to print the current line number for each file, separately. If we use this one-liner with 2 files, named cars.dat containing 12 lines and the second file, label.dat containing 7 lines, it will print the first line number from 1 to 12, and then 1 to 7 for 2 files, respectively. The FNR value is reset for each file:

```
$ awk '{ print FNR "\t" $0 }' cars.dat label.dat
```

- **Numbering all lines for multiple files together**: In this example, we use NR – the line number built-in variable to print the line number. The NR variable value does not get reset from file to file. It counts the input line for each input record. Hence, if we replace FNR with NR in the previous example, we will get line numbers from 1 to 19:

```
$ awk '{ print NR "\t" $0 }' cars.dat label.dat
```

Or:

```
$ awk '$0 = NR " " $0' cars.dat label.dat
```

- **Using printf to prefix line number in a fancy manner**: In this example, we use the printf() function to number lines in a custom format, to print numbers right aligned followed by a space and a colon and the current input line:

```
$ awk '{ printf("%3d : %s\n", NR, $0) }' cars.dat label.dat
```

- **Number and print only non-blank lines in a file**: In the following example, we use variable a to store the line number. Its value is incremented each time when the line is non-empty, and then we append the colon symbol followed by the current input line. This whole new string value is assigned to $0 for printing, as follows:

```
$ awk 'NF { print $0=++a " : " $0 }' label.dat
```

- **Number only non-blank lines but print all lines in a file**: In the following example, we use variable a to store the line number. Its value is incremented each time when the line is non-empty, and then we append the colon symbol followed by the current input line. This whole new string value is assigned to $0. Then, we use the print statement for printing whatever is stored in the $0 variable for each input line, as follows :

```
$ awk 'NF{ $0=++a " : " $0};{print}' label.dat
```

Or:

```
$ awk 'NF{ $0=++a " : " $0};1' label.dat
```

Or:

```
$ awk '/^..*$/{ $0=++a " : " $0};1' label.dat
```

The example of using a ternary operator to print lines having NF not equal to 0:

```
$ awk '{print (NF ? ++a " : " : "" ) $0}' label.dat
```

- **Counting number of lines in a file (similar to wc -l)**: In this example, we use NR – the line number built-in variable and END input block to print the total number of input lines:

```
$ awk 'END{print "Total lines in file : ",NR}' label.dat
```

- **Print the sum of the fields of every line**: In this example, we use the for loop, similar to the C-language for loop construct. This one-liner loops over all the fields in the current input line (NF represents the number of fields in line) and adds the result to the variable sum. Then, it prints the total of fields stored in the variable sum before processing the next line, as follows:

```
$ awk '{ sum=0; for ( i=1; i<=NF; i++) sum=sum+$i; print sum}'
marks.txt
```

- **Print the sum of all fields in all lines**: In this example, the variable sum is not initialized to 0 for each line, hence the value for all fields for each line gets stored in it. Then, we use the END block to print the last value stored in the sum variable, as follows:

```
$ awk '{ for ( i=1; i<=NF; i++) sum=sum+$i}END {print "SUM OF
ALL FIELDS : " sum+0 }' marks.txt
```

- **Replace every field with its absolute value**: In this example, we use the for loop over the field for each input line followed by the if conditional statement to check whether the value of the field is less than 0. If any of the fields have a value less than 0, then its value is negated to make it positive:

```
$ echo -2 | awk '{ for (i=1; i<=NF; i++) if ( $i< 0 ) $i= -$i;
print}'
```

Or:

```
$ echo -2 | awk '{for (i=1; i<=NF; i++) $i = ( $i < 0 ) ? -$i :
$i ; print }'
```

- **Count and print total number of fields (words) in a file**: In this example, we keep adding the number of fields in each line in a variable total. Once all the lines of the file are processed, the output is printed in the END block. We have also added 0 in the string variable total in the case of the file being empty, that is the number of fields is 0:

```
$ awk '{ total = total + NF }; END { print "Total Words : "
total+0 }'
```

- **Printing total number of lines containing a regular expression**: In this example, we specify the pattern between two forwardslashes and then store the count of the number of lines containing the pattern in a variable. Finally, we print the value stored in the variable in the END block:

```
$ awk '/maruti/{ n++ };END{ print n+0 }' cars.dat
```

- **Prefix each line by number of fields in it**: In this example, we use NF- the number of fields built-in variable followed by a colon and the line itself, as follows:

```
$ awk '{ print NF ":" $0 }' label.dat
```

- **Print last field of last line**: In this example, we store the value of the last field in a variable, `var`. Once it has processed all the lines, the last field value is stored in the variable `var` and then we use the END block to print the value stored in it, as follows:

```
$ awk '{ var=$NF }END{ print var }' label.dat
```

Or:

```
$ awk 'END{ print $NF }' label.dat
```

- **Print lines having more than four fields**: In this example, we use NF – the number of fields to print lines with more than four fields, giving the action part is not essential here:

```
$ awk 'NF > 4' cars.dat
```

- **Print lines having value of last field greater than 4**: In this example, we use $NF – value stored in fields, to print the lines having a value greater than 4, as follows:

```
$ awk '$NF > 4' cars.dat
```

Selective deletion of certain lines in a file with AWK

In this section, we look at the working of one-liners for the selective deletion of lines and fields in a file:

- **Delete all blank lines from a file (similar to grep)**: In this example, we use NF– the number of fields built-in variable in each line. For empty lines, NF evaluates to 0, that is, false. Since it is a false statement, the does not get printed; we get only non-empty lines in our output, as follows:

```
$ awk NF <FILENAME>
```

Or:

```
$ awk '/./' label.dat
```

Or:

```
$ awk '!/^$/' label.dat
```

Or:

```
$ awk NF label.dat
```

- **Deleting consecutive duplicate lines from a file**: In this example, we use a variable (here a) to store the current input line. The value stored in variable a is matched using the string match operator (~) with the value in the current input line next input line processed as follows:

```
$ awk 'a !~ $0 ; {a=$0}' <FILENAME>
```

- **Deleting non-consecutive duplicate lines from a file**: In this example, we use an array variable (here a) to store the current input line. Then, we check if the current input line is stored in the array element. If it is not stored in the array element, then it is added in array a and printed as follows:

```
$ awk '!($0 in a){ a[$0] ; print}' <FILENAME>
```

Or:

```
$ awk '!($0 in a){ a[$0] ; print}' cars.dat
```

String operation on selected lines with AWK

In this section, we understand the workings of one-liners for various string operations on lines of a file with AWK:

- **Append the text in the matching line**: In this example, we match the specified regular expression in the current input line. If a match is found, we append the desired text in the $0 variable and print; otherwise, we print the current input line only. On finding a match after printing a line with appended text, we use the next statement to start processing the next input line and skip the subsequent statement, as follows:

```
$ awk '/regex/{print $0 " **ADDITIONAL TEXT **";next}{print}'
<FILENAME>
```

Or:

```
$ awk '/maruti/{print $0 " **ADDITIONAL TEXT **";next}{print}'
cars.dat
```

- **Insert a new line after the matching line**: In this example, we first match the specified regular expression pattern in the current input line. If a match is found, then we print the specified text in a new line, and it is followed by the `next` statement, otherwise we print the current input line, as follows:

```
$ awk '/regex/{print $0; print " **ADDITIONAL LINE
**";next}{print}' <FILENAME>
```

Or:

```
$ awk '/maruti/{print $0; print " **ADDITIONAL LINE
**";next}{print}' cars.dat
```

- **Create a string of a specific length (generate a string of xs of length 50)**: In this example, we use the `BEGIN{}` block to create the string. In this block, a `while` loop is used to append a character to the variable `str` 50 times. On completion of the loop, the value stored inside that variable is printed as follows:

```
$ awk 'BEGIN { while ( a++<50 ) str=str "x" ; print str }'
```

- **Insert a string at a certain character position**: In this example, we use the subfunction to insert a string in each line after a specified character position. We declare the string in the `BEGIN` block and then use it in the body block of AWK, as follows:

```
$ awk 'BEGIN{ str="**NEWSTRING**"};{sub(/^....../,"&" str)};1'
label.dat
```

Array creation with AWK one-liner

In this section, we understand the workings of one-liners in creating arrays with AWK:

- **Creating an array from string**: In this example, we use split functions to create an array. A `split` function accepts three arguments, the first argument is a string which we want to split into an array. The second argument is the array name, and the third argument is the regular expression which is to be used for creating the splitting of the string into fields to create the array elements, as follows:

    ```
    $ awk 'BEGIN{ split("orange red green", trafficlight, " ")}'
    ```

    If we want to print the array, after creating it we can proceed as follows :

    ```
    $ awk 'BEGIN{ split("orange red green", arr, " "); for( v in
    arr ) print arr[v]}'
    ```

Text conversion and substitution in files with AWK

In this section, we look at the working of one-liners in text conversion and substitution in files with AWK.

- Let's create a sample file for practicing substitutions and conversions:

    ```
    $ vi sample.txt

        foo baz ruby
    baz foo foo foo
    foo gold\
    silver foo
    silver foo
    baz foo foo foo
        foo baz ruby
    ```

- **Convert Windows/DOS newlines (CRLF) to Unix newlines (LF) using AWK**: In this example, we use the `sub(regex, replacement, [string])` function. Here, we replace the `\r` (CR) character at the end of the line with nothing; we erase CR at the end. The `print` statement prints out the line and appends the ORS variable, which is `\n` by default. So, a line that ends with CRLF is converted into a line that ends with LF:

      $ awk '{ sub(/\r$/ , ""); print}' <FILENAME>

  Or:

      $ awk '{ sub(/\r$/ , "")};1' <FILENAME>

- **Convert Unix newlines (LF) to Windows/DOS newlines (CRLF) using AWK**: In this example, we again use the `sub()` function. This time, it replaces the end of the line (`$`) with a `\r` (CR). This adds the carriage return at the end of the line. After that, AWK prints the line and appends ORS, making the line terminate with CRLF:

      $ awk '{ sub(/$/ , "\r"); print}' <FILENAME>

      $ awk '{ sub(/$/ , "\r")};1' <FILENAME>

- **Deleting leading whitespace (spaces and tabs) at the beginning of each line**: In this example, we use the `sub()` function to delete the whitespaces. The regular expression for whitespace is `^[ \t]+`. Here, `^` means at the beginning of the line, `\t` means tab, and `' '` means space, and the plus `+` symbol here represents one or more match:

      $ awk '{ sub (/^[\t]+/, ""); print }' <FILENAME>

  Or:

      $ awk '{ sub (/^[\t]+/, "")};1' <FILENAME>

  Or:

      $ awk '{ sub (/^[\t]+/, ""); print }' sample.txt

- **Deleting trailing whitespace (spaces and tabs) at the end of a line**: In this example, we again use the same `sub()` function to delete trailing whitespaces. The regular expression used here is very similar to the previous one, except the anchor used here is `$` to match the whitespace `[ \t]+$` at the end of line, as follows:

```
$ awk '{ sub( /[ \t]+$/ , "" ); print}' <FILENAME>
```

Or:

```
$ awk '{ sub( /[ \t]+$/ , "" )};1' <FILENAME>
```

Or:

```
$ awk '{ sub( /[ \t]+$/ , "" ); print}' sample.txt
```

- **Deleting both leading and trailing whitespaces from a line**: In this example, we use the `gsub()` function. The `Gsub()` function is similar to the `sub()` function, except it performs the multiple substitutions in the same line. `Gsub()` stands for global substitution. Here, we combine both the regular expressions, to delete the leading whitespace `^[ \t]+` and the trailing whitespace `[ \t]+$`, to substitute with nothing, as follows:

```
$ awk '{ gsub( /^[ \t]+|[ \t]+$/ , "" ); print}' <FILENAME>
```

Or:

```
$ awk '{ gsub( /^[ \t]+|[ \t]+$/ , "" )};1' <FILENAME>
```

Or:

```
$ awk '{ gsub( /^[ \t]+|[ \t]+$/ , "" ); print}' sample.txt
```

We can remove multiple whitespaces between fields, using the following:

```
$ awk '{ $1=$1;print}' <FILENAME>
```

Or:

```
$ awk '{ $1=$1};1' cars.dat
```

- **Add some characters/tab/spaces at the beginning of each line:** In this example, we use the sub() function with the regular expression anchor (^) to insert at the beginning of each line. In the replacement part of the sub() function, we can put the desired string, tab, or spaces we want to be at the beginning of each line, as follows :

```
$ awk '{ sub( /^/, "***" ); print }' <FILENAME>
```

Or:

```
$ awk '{ sub( /^/, "***"); print }' cars.dat
```

Or:

```
$ awk '{ sub( /^/, "\t"); print }' cars.dat
```

Or:

```
$ awk '{ sub( /^/, " "); print }' cars.dat
```

- **Add some characters/tab/spaces at the end of each line:** In this example, we use the sub() function with the regular expression anchor ($) to insert at the end of each line. In the replacement part of the sub() function, we can put the desired string, tab, or spaces which we want to be at the end of each line, as follows:

```
$ awk '{ sub( /$/, "***" ); print }' <FILENAME>
```

Or:

```
$ awk '{ sub( /$/, "***"); print }' cars.dat
```

Or:

```
$ awk '{ sub( /$/, "\t"); print }' cars.dat
```

Or:

```
$ awk '{ sub( /^/, " "); print }' cars.dat
```

- **Centrally align all lines of a file to the specified width**: In this example, we use the `length` function to calculate the length of each line. Then, the number of whitespaces to be padded at the beginning of the line is stored in a variable, say `s`. In the end, we use pretty printing with `printf()` to print the exact number of whitespaces followed by the line, as follows:

```
$ awk '{ l=length(); s=int((80/2)); printf( "%"(s+l)"s\n",$0)}'
<FILENAME>
```

Or:

```
$ awk '{ l=length(); s=int((80/2)); printf( "%"(s+l)"s\n",$0)}'
cars.dat
```

- **Substitute (find and replace) a given string with a replacement string on each line**: In this example, we use the `sub()`, `gsub()`, and `gensub()` functions for performing the substitution of `pattern1` with `pattern2` in each line. In this one-liner, we use the `sub()` function to replace `foo` with `bar`. The `sub()` function substitutes only the first match in each line, as follows:

```
$ awk '{ sub(/foo/,"bar"); print }' sample.txt
```

In our next example, we use the `gsub()` function to globally substitute the match of the `foo` string with `bar`. It substitutes the multiple occurrences of `foo` with `bar`, as follows:

```
$ awk '{ gsub(/foo/,"bar"); print }' sample.txt
```

In our next example, we use the `gensub()` function to globally substitute the match, a particular numbered occurrence can also be replaced. It has one difference from the `sub()` and `gsub()` function in that it returns the modified string, as compared to the `sub()` and `gsub()` function which modify the string in place:

```
$ awk '{ $0 = gensub(/foo/,"bar",2 ); print }' sample.txt
```

- **Substitute the text with a replacement string only if the given line contains the specified string**: In the following example, we use the `gsub()` function prefixed with a specified pattern to perform substitution in matching lines only, as follows:

```
$ awk '/baz/{ gsub(/foo/,"bar" ); print }' sample.txt
```

- **Substitute the text with a replacement string only if the given line do not contain the specified string**: In the following example, we use the `gsub()` function prefixed with a specified pattern to perform substitution in lines that do not match, as follows:

    ```
    $ awk '!/baz/{ gsub(/foo/,"bar" ); print }' sample.txt
    ```

- **Substitute the text with replacement string only if the given line contains any of the multiple strings specified**: In the following example, we use the `gsub()` function with the extended regular expression alternation operator | (pipe), as follows:

    ```
    $ awk '{ gsub(/gold|silver|ruby/, "DIAMOND"); print}'
    sample.txt
    ```

- **Substitute text if a match is found and print each line**: In the following example, we use the `gsub()` function to perform a substitution on the current input line, if a match is found. If a match is not found, then print the current input line without substitution, as follows:

    ```
    $ awk '/regex/{execute A; next}{execute B}' <FILENAME>
    ```

    Or:

    ```
    $ awk '/maruti/{gsub(/swift/,"SWIFT");print; next}' cars.dat
    ```

- **Print lines of a file in reverse order (bottom to top, similar to the tac shell command)**: In this example, we first store all the lines of the file in an array, a. Then, we use the `for` loop inside the END block to print the lines in reverse order, as follows:

    ```
    $ awk '{ a[i++] = $0 } END { for ( j=i-1; j>=0; ) print a[j--]
    }' <FILENAME>
    ```

    Or:

    ```
    $ awk '{ a[i++] = $0 } END { for (j=i-1; j>=0;) print a[j--] }'
    label.dat
    ```

- **Join a line that ends with a backslash to the next line in the file:** In the example, we use the `sub()` function to search for lines ending with a backslash, using a regular expression. Then, we substitute the backslash in a matching line with `**newline**` and use the `getline` method to fetch the subsequent line in a variable. Then, both the current line and next line stored in a variable using the `getline` method is printed on the screen, as follows:

```
$ awk '/\\$/ { sub(/\\$/,"**newline**"); getline t; print $0 t;
next }; 1' sample.txt
```

- **Printing the first two fields in reverse order on each line:** In this example, we reverse the order of fields, `$1` and `$2`, as follows:

```
awk '{ print $2, $1 }' cars.dat
```

- **Printing fields by changing the delimiter:** In this example, we specify a single delimiter using the command line option `-F` to change the value of the delimiter. Here, we change the default delimiter from the space or tab to pipe, using the `-F` option, as follows:

```
$ echo "a|b|c|d" | awk -F"|" '{print $3}'
```

> Or:

```
$ echo "a|b|c|d" | awk -F'|' '{print $3}'
```

> Or:

```
$ echo "a|b|c|d" | awk -F\| '{print $3}'
```

> Or:

```
$ echo "a|b|c|d" | awk 'BEGIN{FS="|"}{print $3}'
```

- **Printing fields by setting multiple values for the delimiter:** In this example, we again change the default value of the field delimiter and specify multiple values for the delimiter, using a regular expression as follows:

```
$ echo "a:b=c|d" | awk 'BEGIN{FS="[|=:]"}{print $3}'
```

> Or:

```
$ echo "a:b=c|d" | awk -F'[:=|]' '{print $3}'
```

One-liners for system administrators

In this section, we look at the workings of various one-liners used for the automation of system administration tasks in shell scripts and day-to-day admin tasks.

- Print and sort the login name of all users on Linux OS:

```
$ awk -F ":" '{ print $1 | "sort" }' /etc/passwd
```

- List all filenames whose size is greater than zero:

```
$ ls -al | awk '$5 > 0{ print $9} '
```

- Print all lines of a file prefixed with a line number:

```
$ awk '{print NR, $0}' <FILENAME>
```

- Calculate and print the total size of a directory in Mb:

```
$ ls -al | awk '{total +=$5};END {print "Total size: "
total/1024/1024 " Mb"}'
```

- Calculate and print the total size of a directory, including sub directories, in Mb:

```
$ ls -lR |awk '{total +=$5};END {print "Total size: "
total/1024/1024 " Mb"}'
```

- Find the largest file and its size in a directory, including subdirectories:

```
$ ls -lR |awk '{print $5 "\t" $9}' |sort -n |tail -1
```

- Print the number of hits to a website from a unique host IP address from an Apache access log file (the first field stores the IP address of the client making the request):

```
$ awk '{print $1}' | sort | uniq -c | sort -rn
/var/www/html/access_log
```

- Print all lines from the Apache log file, if the HTTP error code is `500` (the ninth field stores the status error code for each HTTP request):

    ```
    $ awk ' $9 == 500 {print $0 }' /var/log/httpd/access_log
    ```

    Or:

    ```
    $ awk ' $9 == 500 {print }' /var/log/httpd/access_log
    ```

    Or:

    ```
    $ awk ' $9 == 500 ' /var/log/httpd/access_log
    ```

- Print the lines with specific usernames:

    ```
    $ awk '/sanjay/rahul/jack ' /etc/passwd
    ```

- Print the first line from a file:

    ```
    $ awk 'NR==1{print;exit}' /etc/resolv.conf
    ```

- List your top 10 favorite commands using AWK:

    ```
    $ history | awk '{print $2}' | sort | uniq -c | sort -rn | awk "NR<11"
    ```

- Print the total number of active TCP connections and their state, using AWK:

    ```
    $ netstat -tn | awk '/tcp/{print $6}' | sort | uniq -c
    ```

- List your assigned IP addresses in your system:

    ```
    $ ifconfig | awk '/inet / {print $2}'
    ```

- Back up all shell script files with a `.sh` extension with `.bak` extension:

    ```
    $ ls *.sh | awk '{print "cp "$0" "$0".bak"}' | bash
    ```

Use case examples of pattern matching using AWK

In this section, we illustrate the workings of AWK using some practical examples such as the parsing of web server log files, transposing the contents of files, and processing multiple files.

Parsing web server (Apache/Nginx) log files

In this section, we will see how AWK can be used for generating reports from log files. Using AWK, we can segregate the different portions of log files to find the bottleneck of different issues that are creating extensive memory usage, CPU usage, or I/O on servers.

We will use a sample log file named `apache_logs.txt` for performing the practice here.

Understanding the Apache combined log format

Before analyzing the log file of web servers, let's look at the log file format. A standard log file entry contains the following information:

```
%h %l %u %t "%r" %>s %b "%{Referer}i" "%{User-agent}i
```

Here is a description of the different fields used in the combined log format:

- `%h`: IP address of the client (remote host) making the request to our site.
- `%l`: RFC 1413 identity of the client (hyphen – here indicates the requested piece of information is not available).
- `%u`: User ID of the person requesting the document.
- `%t`: Time when server finished processing the request. Its format is `[day/month/year:hour:minute:second zone]`.
- `%r`: Request line for the client in double quotes.

- `%>s`: Status Code that the server sends back to the client. Various status codes are used:
  - A successful response begins with - 2
  - A redirection begins with - 3
  - An error caused by a client begins with - 4
  - An error in a server begins with - 5
- `%b`: Size of object returned to the client.
- `%{Referer}i`: It is an HTTP request header, the URL which linked the user to your site.
- `%{User-agent}i`: It is a user-agent HTTP request header used by the client browser for making the request.

The following is a sample log entry:

```
83.149.9.216 - - [17/Feb/2018:10:05:03 +0000] "GET
/presentations/images/search.png HTTP/1.1" 200 203023
"http://semicomplete.com/presentations/2013/" "Mozilla/5.0 (Macintosh;
Intel Mac OS X 10_9_1) AppleWebKit/537.36 (KHTML, like Gecko)
Chrome/32.0.1700.77 Safari/537.36"
```

Description of fields:

- **Field 1 (%h)**: `83.149.9.216`
- **Field 2 (%l)**: Indicates information not available
- **Field 3 (%u)**: Indicates information not available
- **Field 4 (%t)**: `[17/Feb/2018:10:05:03]` (date/time)
- **Field 5 (%t)**: `+0000` (GMT offset)
- **Field 6 (%r)**: `GET /presentations/images/search.png HTTP/1.1`
- **Field 7 (%>s)**: `200`
- **Field 8 (%b)**: `203023`
- **Field 9 (%{Referer})**: `http://semicomplete.com/presentations/2013/`
- **Field 10(%{User-agent})**: Mozilla/5.0 (Macintosh; Intel macOS) AppleWebKit/537.36 (KHTML, like Gecko) Chrome/32.0.1700.77 Safari/537.36

Using AWK for processing different log fields

AWK is used here to split the lines of the log file into fields or columns, using a default separator. Since each line in an Apache log file follows a standard format, we can process it easily with AWK. We will be using a default separator (spaces or tabs) to parse the log file sample line used previously, as follows:

```
$ vi sample.txt

83.149.9.216 - - [17/Feb/2018:10:05:03 +0000] "GET
/presentations/images/search.png HTTP/1.1" 200 203023
"http://semicomplete.com/presentations/2013/" "Mozilla/5.0 (Macintosh;
Intel Mac OS X 10_9_1) AppleWebKit/537.36 (KHTML, like Gecko)
Chrome/32.0.1700.77 Safari/537.36"
```

- Print IP address (%h):

  ```
  $ awk '{print $1}' sample.txt
  ```

- Print RFC 1413 identity (%l):

  ```
  $ awk '{print $2}' sample.txt
  ```

- Print user ID (%u):

  ```
  $ awk '{print $3}' sample.txt
  ```

- Print date/time (%t):

  ```
  $ awk '{print $4,$5}' sample.txt
  ```

- Print status code (%>s):

  ```
  $ awk '{print $9}' sample.txt
  ```

- Print size (%b):

  ```
  $ awk '{print $10}' sample.txt
  ```

For printing the request line (%r), referer, and user agent, we have to change the field separator to double quotes (") as follows:

- Print request line (%r):

  ```
  $ awk -F\" '{print $2}' sample.txt
  ```

- Print referer:

  ```
  $ awk -F\" '{print $4}' sample.txt
  ```

- Print user agent:

  ```
  $ awk -F\" '{print $6}' sample.txt
  ```

These are the fundamental examples for breaking down the Apache combined log format and processing information from it. Now, we will further process the logs using AWK to produce more meaningful information, as follows:

- **List all user agents ordered by the number of times they appear in the log file in ascending order:** In this example, we first extract the user-agent field from the log file and then pipe it through some commands to get the desired result. The first sort command is used for making the unique to count the unique user-agents properly. The last `sort -g` is used to arrange the result in a general numeric number sorted standard in ascending order, as follows:

  ```
  $ awk -F\" '{print $6}' apache_logs.txt | sort | uniq -c |sort -g
  ```

  Or we can print the top 10 user-agent requests in descending order as follows:

  ```
  $ awk -F\" '{freq[$6]++} END {for (x in freq) {print freq[x], x}}'
  apache_logs.txt | sort -rn | head
  ```

- **Identify and print the pages Google has been requesting from your site**: In this example, we narrow down our search and print the request line (stored in field 2) for those user-agents whose value is set as `Googlebot` (field 6), as follows:

  ```
      $ awk -F\" '($6 ~ /Googlebot/){print $2}' apache_logs.txt | sort
  | uniq -c
      |sort -nr
  ```

  Or:

  ```
  $ awk -F\" '($6 ~ /Googlebot/){freq[$2]++} END {for (x in freq)
  {print freq[x], x}}' apache_logs.txt | sort -nr
  ```

- Next, we print the user-agent information, which requests the gnome-2.png file, as follows:

```
$ awk -F\" '($2 ~ /gnome-2.png/){print $6}' apache_logs.txt
```

Or:

```
$ awk -F\" '($2 ~ /gnome-2.png/){freq[$6]++}END{for(x in freq)
{print freq[x], x}}' apache_logs.txt
```

Identifying problems with the running website

Now, we use AWK to identify the problems with our website, by finding out the different server responses and requests that caused them. The following is a list of the most common HTTP server status codes, helpful in identifying problems:

Status code	Meaning
200	OK
206	Partial content
301	Moved permanently
302	Found
304	Not modified
401	Unauthorized (password required)
403	Forbidden
404	Not found
503	Server is currently unavailable (down due to maintenance or overloaded)

A lot of 301 or 302 code means that the request has been redirected.

A lot of 304 code means the file didn't have to be delivered because the server already had a cached version.

A lot of 404 means you might be having the problem of a broken link or someone has linked that page, but it no longer exists on our website.

- **Count and print the different types of status code returned by the server:** In this example, we first extract the status code of the request from field 9 and then pipe it through some commands to get the desired result, as follows:

```
$ awk '{print $9}' apache_logs.txt | sort | uniq -c |sort -nr
```

Or:

```
$ awk '{freq[$9]++} END {for (x in freq) {print freq[x],"\t",
x}}'
apache_logs.txt |sort -nr
```

- List all 404 requests:

```
$ awk '($9 ~ /404/)' apache_logs.txt
```

- Summarize 404 requests:

```
$ awk '($9 ~ /404/)' apache_logs.txt | awk '{print $9,$7}'
| sort | uniq -c | sort -g
```

Or:

```
$ awk '($9 ~ /404/)' apache_logs.txt | awk '{freq[$9" "$7]++}
END
{for (x in freq) {print freq[x], x}}' | sort -nr
```

- **Printing the user-agent and referer for requests generating the most** 404 **status codes:** In this example, first we use the previous command to summarize 404 requests to find out the link that is generating most of the 404 errors. Then we print fields 4 and 6 to identify the referer and user-agent of the request:

```
$ awk -F\" '($2 ~ "/files/logstash/logstash-1.3.2-
monolithic.jar") {print $6}' apache_logs.txt
```

In the previous example, either we should use the Apache mod_rewrite module to resolve the issue of broken links or redirect them to the correct page on our site.

- **Printing requests that didn't return 200 (OK):** In this example, we used no match operator of strings to summarize the requests that did not return status code 200:

```
$ awk '($9 !~ /200/)' apache_logs.txt | awk '{print $9,$7}' |
sort | uniq -c | sort -nr
```

Or:

```
$ awk '($9 !~ /200/)' apache_logs.txt | awk '{freq[$9" "$7]++}
END {for (x in freq) {print freq[x], x}}' | sort -nr
```

- **Identifying the blank user agents and list their IP addresses**: In our next example, we identify the blank user-agents request. A blank user-agent is an indication that the request is from an automated script or someone hiding their user-agent to increase their privacy. The following command gives us a list of those IP addresses which have blank user-agents and we can take our decision to block them or not:

```
$ awk -F\" '($6 ~ /^-?$/)' apache_logs.txt | awk '{print $1}'|
sort |uniq
```

Or:

```
$ awk -F\" '($6 ~ /^-?$/)' apache_logs.txt | awk '{freq[$1]++}
END {for (x in freq) {print x}}'
```

Here, we look for the hyphen symbol (–) in the field number 6 when the field separator is set as double quotes.

- **Printing requests which are generated within a particular time range:** In this example, we specify the start and end range to ignore other lines and print only those lines that lie between the first pattern and the second pattern, as follows:

```
$ awk '/10:05:/,/12:05:/' apache_logs.txt
```

Now, we further narrow down our processing by specifying the pattern to print only those lines that were generated within a particular time range with a matching pattern, as follows:

```
$ awk '/10:05:/,/12:05:/{ if (/POST/) print}' apache_logs.txt
```

This matching may not give us a result if we have a low-traffic site that is not getting hits regularly. In that case, we have to modify our pattern accordingly to match and generate the report.

- **Sort access logs by response size in increasing order**: In this example, we use the field 10 value and prefix it in each line and then pipe the output to the sort command to display the output in a general numeric sort format as follows:

```
$ awk '$10 > 0 {print $10, $0 }' apache_logs.txt | sort -g
```

- **Printing the top 10 IP addresses that made requests to our website**: In this example, we print field 1, which contains the IP address information and then pipe the output to the shell commands `sort` and `uniq`, followed by the `head` command to print the top 10 lines of our output, as follows:

```
$ awk '{ print $1}' apache_logs.txt | sort| uniq -c | sort -rn
| head
```

Or:

```
$ awk '{freq[$1]++} END {for (x in freq) {print freq[x], x}}'
apache_logs.txt | sort -rn | head
```

Printing the top 10 request IP addresses with their GeoIP information

In this example, we first find the top 10 IP addresses which made requests to our website based on their request count, as shown in previous example. Then, we further use the system command to run the GeoIP package to print the geographical information of requesting IP address. The GeoIP package is freely available in the debian repository and the EPEL repository for rpm-based operating systems:

```
$ awk '{ print $1}' apache_logs.txt | sort| uniq -c | sort -rn | head | awk
'{ print $2 };{print "================"};system("geoiplookup " $2);{print
"================"}'
```

Or:

```
$ awk '{freq[$1]++} END {for (x in freq) {print freq[x], x}}'
apache_logs.txt | sort -rn | head | awk '{ print $2 };{print
"================"};system("geoiplookup " $2);{print "================"}'
```

Counting and printing unique visits to a website

- **Print the total number or unique visitors**: In this example, we again fetch the IP address information from field 1 and then pipe it to the shell commands to fetch the total number of unique visitors to our website as follows:

  ```
  $ awk '{ print $1 }' apache_logs.txt | sort | uniq -c| wc -l
  ```

  Or:

  ```
  $ cat apache_logs.txt | awk '{ print $1 }' apache_logs.txt | sort |
  uniq -c| wc -l
  ```

  Or:

  ```
  $ awk '{ freq[$1]++} END {for (x in freq) {print freq[x], x} }'
  apache_logs.txt | wc -l
  ```

- Print the total number of unique visitors today:

  ```
  $ cat apache_logs.txt | grep `date '+%e/%b/%G'`| awk '{ print $1
  }'| sort | uniq -c| wc -l
  ```

  Or:

  ```
  $ cat apache_logs.txt | grep `date '+%e/%b/%G'`| awk '{ freq[$1]++}
  END {for (x in freq) {print freq[x], x} }' | wc -l
  ```

- Print the total number of unique visitors this month:

  ```
  $ cat apache_logs.txt | grep `date '+%b/%G'`| awk '{ print $1 }'|
  sort | uniq -c| wc -l
  ```

  Or:

  ```
  $ cat apache_logs.txt | grep `date '+%b/%G'`| awk '{ freq[$1]++}
  END {for (x in freq) {print freq[x], x} }' | wc -l
  ```

- Print the total number of unique visitors on a specified date:

  ```
  $ cat apache_logs.txt | grep 19/Feb/2018 | awk '{ print $1 }'| sort
  | uniq -c| wc -l
  ```

Or:

```
$ cat apache_logs.txt | grep 19/Feb/2018 | awk '{ freq[$1]++} END
{for (x in freq) {print freq[x], x} }' | wc -1
```

Or:

```
$ cat apache_logs.txt | grep Feb/2018 | awk '{ print $1 }'| sort |
uniq -c| wc -1
```

Or:

```
$ cat apache_logs.txt | grep Feb/2018 | awk '{ freq[$1]++} END {for
(x in freq) {print freq[x], x} }' | wc -1
```

- **Ranking of different status codes/response codes:** In this example, we fetch the different status codes returned by the server in field number 9, and then pass the result to the pipe command for printing them in descending order of their occurrence, as follows:

```
$ awk '{ print $9 }' apache_logs.txt | sort | uniq -c | sort -rn
```

Or:

```
$ awk '{ freq[$9]++} END {for (x in freq) {print freq[x],"\t", x}
}' apache_logs.txt | sort -rn
```

- **Print top 10 most popular URLs of website:** This helps in analytics and summarizing the popularity of different pages on our website, and identifying the most popular URLs as follows:

```
$ awk -F\" '{ print $2 }' apache_logs.txt | sort | uniq -c | sort -
rn | head
```

Or:

```
$ awk -F\" '{ freq[$2]++} END {for (x in freq) {print freq[x], x}
}' apache_logs.txt | sort -rn | head
```

- **Print the amount of data, in MB, transferred in the last 2,000 requests:** This also helps in analyzing the data bandwidth consumption on the website:

```
$ tail -2000 apache_logs.txt | awk '{sum+=$10} END { print
sum/1048576 " MB" }'
```

Real-time IP address lookup for requests

In the following example, we make use of tail -f to keep reading the new entries of log files and pass them to the AWK command for processing. Here also, we use the geoiplookup command to fetch the IP address information and print it on screen, as follows:

```
$ tail -f apache_logs.txt |awk '{print "IPADDRESS : " $1};{
system("geoiplookup " $1)};{print "REQUEST LINE :"$6,$7,"\n""STATUS CODE :
"$9}'
```

We can also print other information such as the user agent in a desired format in output by setting the field separator to double quotes (") and splitting the first and third field into an array to fetch the information, as follows:

```
$tail -f apache_logs.txt | awk -F"\"" 'split($1,a," "){print "IPADDRESS : "
a[1]};{ system("geoiplookup " a[1])};split($3,b," "){print "REQUEST LINE
:"$2 "\n""STATUS CODE : "b[1]"\n" "USERAGENT : " $6,"\n=============="}'
```

Now, we can use various fields of the log file to create an AWK script for processing the web server logs and displaying the report, as follows:

```
$ vi http_report.awk

#Web server log file analysis & filtering

BEGIN{
    FS="\""
}

{
split($1, a, " ")
ip=a[1]
if($2!="")
{
    datetime=a[4]" "a[5]
    request=$2
    referer=$4
    useragent=$6
    split($3, c, " ")
    code=c[1]
    size=c[2]
}
else
{
    split($3, b, " ")
    datetime=b[2]" "b[3]
    request=$4
```

```
        referer=$6
        useragent=$8
        split($5, c, " ")
        code=c[1]
        size=c[2]
    }
    total=NR
    if(match(code, /^[0-9]+$/)==0)
    {
        code="UNKNOWN"
    }
    statuses[code]++

    # Analyze the request
    n=split(request, detail, " ")
    method=detail[1]
    if(match(method, /^[A-Z]+$/)==0)
    {
        method="UNKNOWN"
    }
    methods[method]++

    url=""
    for(i=2; i<n; i++)
    {
        url=(url" "detail[i])
    }
    url=substr(url, 2)

}

END{
    print ("****************************************")
    printf "\t%d \tRequests Filtered\n", total
    print ("****************************************")
    printf "%-8s\t%11s\t%8s\n","STATUS", "OCCURENCES", "% OUTPUT"
    print ("****************************************")
    for(code in statuses)
    {
    printf "%-8d\t%11d\t%6.2f\n",code, statuses[code],
(100*statuses[code]/total)
    }
    print ("****************************************")
    printf "%-8s\t%11s\t%8s\n","METHOD", "OCCURENCES", "% OUTPUT"
    print ("****************************************")
    for(method in methods)
    {
    printf "%-8s\t%11d\t%6.2f\n",method, methods[method],
```

```
(100*methods[method]/total)
    }
    printf "\n"
}

$ awk -f http_report.awk apache_logs.txt
```

The output on execution of the previous command is as follows :

```
****************************************
    10000      Requests Filtered
****************************************
STATUS        OCCURENCES    % OUTPUT
****************************************
200               9126       91.26
206                 45        0.45
301                164        1.64
304                445        4.45
403                  2        0.02
404                213        2.13
416                  2        0.02
500                  3        0.03
****************************************
METHOD        OCCURENCES    % OUTPUT
****************************************
GET               9952       99.52
OPTIONS              1        0.01
POST                 5        0.05
HEAD                42        0.42
```

Converting text to HTML table

In this example, we use FS – the field separator to set it to the desired delimiter for splitting the line of files into fields. Then, we create the heading of the HTML table in the BEGIN block by fetching the elements of the first record, by checking whether NR==1. Then, the body of the table is created using NR >1, until the last line of the file is read. The following is a sample file named table.txt used here to illustrate the text-to-HTML table conversion, as follows:

```
$ vi table.txt

NAME:ENGLISH:MATHS:SOCIAL SCIENCE:MUSIC
Sanjay:70:80:65:95
Hitesh:55:72:82:64
Rahul:80:83:65:70
```

```
Dhirendra:81:82:83:84

$ vi array2html.awk

BEGIN {
    FS =":";
    printf  "%s%s%s",
        "<TABLE cellpadding=\"1pt\" BORDER=\"2pt\" ",
        "CELLSPACING=\"0pt\" bgcolor=\"\#ffffff\" ",
        "bordercolor=\"\#000000\">\n";

}

(NR==1){
    printf "    <TR bgcolor=\"\#dfdfdf\">\n"
    for( i=1; i<=NF; i++ )
    {
        printf "        <TD><center>%s</center></TD>\n", $i;
    }
    printf "    </TR>\n"
}

(NF>0 && NR>1){

    printf "    <TR>\n"
    for( i=1; i<=NF; i++ )
    {
        if ( i==1 ) {
            printf "        <TD align=left>%s</TD>\n", $i;
        } else {
            printf "        <TD align=right>%s</TD>\n", $i;
        }
    }
    printf "    </TR>\n"
}

END {
    printf "</TABLE>\n";
}

$ awk -f array2html.awk table.txt > output.html
```

On execution of the previous code, a file named output.html will be created in the current directory. Open that file in the browser to view the HTML file content.

Converting decimal to binary

In the following example, we give a list of decimal numbers as input to the AWK program, which returns the binary equivalent output on screen. This program reads the decimal number then finds the remainder of that number on division by 2, using the modulus operator. The remainder is stored in a string until the division of the number by 2, returns the 0 as follows:

```
$ vi list.txt
10
20
15
40

$ vi dec2bin.awk

BEGIN    {
    Print "\tDisplay Binary equivalent of Decimal number "
    }

func getnumber(decimal,temp, binary)
{
    binary = "";
    temp=decimal;
    while( temp )
        {
        if ( temp%2==0 )
        {
            binary = "0" binary;
                }
        else
        {
            binary = "1" binary;
                }
        temp = int(temp/2);
    }
        return binary;
}
{
    binval=getnumber( $1 );
    print $1, " --> ", binval
}

$ awk -f dec2bin.awk list.txt
```

The output on execution of the previous AWK program is as follows :

```
10   -->   1010
20   -->   10100
15   -->   1111
40   -->   101000
```

Renaming files in a directory with AWK

We can use AWK to create and execute shell commands, such as the mv command for renaming, by piping them to shell sh for executing them. We should always check a command by printing the output before piping it to sh to avoid any typo errors, as follows :

First, we will just use the print statement to display the command result and not execute it on the command prompt, as follows :

```
$ ls | awk '{ printf("mv \"%s\" \"%s\"\n", $0, toupper($0)) }'
```

If we confirm the command line built using AWK, then we can execute it by piping the AWK output to the sh command, as follows:

```
$ ls | awk '{ printf("mv \"%s\" \"%s\"\n", $0, toupper($0)) }' | sh
```

In out next rename examples, we substitute the occurrence of spaces in the filename with the min minus symbol – as follows:

```
$ ls | awk '{ printf("mv \"%s\" \"%s\"\n", $0, gensub(/ +/,"-","g")) }'
```

And to execute the command line built using AWK, we pipe the AWK output to sh as follows:

```
$ ls | awk '{ printf("mv \"%s\" \"%s\"\n", $0, gensub(/ +/,"-","g")) }' |
sh
```

Printing a generated sequence of numbers in a specified columnate format

In this example, first we generate a sequence of numbers with the shell command `seq <start_number> <end_number>` (here 1 to 50). Then we use `ORS`, the output record separator, `FS` – the field separator and `RS` – the record separator AWK built-in variables with a ternary operator. The `ORS`, as the name suggests, contains the separator to append to the line. By default, `ORS` is set as `\n`. Here, we explicitly set the value of `ORS` depending on the outcome of the ternary operator. If `NR%5` is zero, that is, we are at line 5, 10, 15, 20 and so on, is true then `ORS` gets the value of `RS` which by default is `\n`, otherwise `ORS` gets the value of `FS` (default value of `FS` is space):

```
$ seq 1 50 | awk 'ORS = NR%5 ? FS : RS'
```

The output on execution of the previous code is as follows:

```
1 2 3 4 5
6 7 8 9 10
11 12 13 14 15
16 17 18 19 20
21 22 23 24 25
26 27 28 29 30
31 32 33 34 35
36 37 38 39 40
41 42 43 44 45
46 47 48 49 50
```

We can set the value of `ORS` to space and `\n` in the ternary operator to get the same result, as follows:

```
$ seq 1 50 | awk 'ORS = NR%5 ? " " : "\n"'
```

The output on execution of the previous code is the same as it was in the previous one.

Transposing a matrix

Transposing a matrix is basically interchanging its rows with columns. In this example, we build a string using a separator. Here, we use the fact that AWK variables are dynamic. We use a variable `sep`, which is empty initially on first execution, and then it is set to a semicolon. It will have that value from the second time the code executes onwards. The result is that at the end of the string, we will have a clean list of values with a semicolon at the desired place:

```
$ vi matrix.txt

a1;a2;a3;a4
b1;b2;b3;b4
c1;c2;c3;c4
d1;d2;d3;d4

$ vi transpose_matrix.awk

BEGIN    {
    FS = ";"
    }
{
    for( i=1;  i<=NF;  i++ )
    r[i]=r[i] sep $i
    sep=FS
}

END   {
    for( i=1;  i<=NF;  i++ )
    {
        print r[i]
    }
}

$ awk -f transpose_matrix.awk matrix.txt
```

The output on execution of the previous code is as follows :

```
a1;b1;c1;d1
a2;b2;c2;d2
a3;b3;c3;d3
a4;b4;c4;d4
```

We can use one more method for transposing the elements of the matrix, as follows:

```
$ vi transpose2.awk

BEGIN {
    FS = ";";
    max_x =0;
    max_y =0;
}

{
    max_y++;
    for( i=1; i<=NF; i++ )
    {
        if (i>max_x) max_x=i;
        A[i,max_y] = $i;
    }
}

END {
    for ( x=1; x<=max_x; x++ )
    {
        for ( y=1; y<=max_y; y++ )
        {
            if ( (x,y) in A ) printf "%s",A[x,y];
            if ( y!=max_y ) printf ";";
        }
        printf "\n";
    }
}

$ awk -f transpose2.awk matrix.txt
```

The output on execution of the previous code, is as follows :

```
a1;b1;c1;d1
a2;b2;c2;d2
a3;b3;c3;d3
a4;b4;c4;d4
```

Processing multiple files using AWK

In this example, we use the NR, FNR built-in variables and the next statement for processing multiple files. The following is a construct used for two file processing using AWK:

```
$ awk 'NR == FNR { # file1 actions; next} # file1 condition {# file2
actions}' file1.txt file2.txt
```

The previous construct is used for processing two files. When processing more than one file, AWK reads each file sequentially in the order they are specified on the command line. The built-in variable NR stores the total number of input records processed till now, regardless of the number of files read. The value of NR starts at 1 and always increases until the program finishes. Another built-in variable FNR, stores the number of records read from the current file being processed. The value of FNR starts at 1 and increases until the end of the current file is reached. It is again set to 1, as soon as the first line of the next file is read, and so on.

Hence, the condition NR == FNR will be true only when AWK is reading the first file. Thus, in the preceding AWK program, the actions indicated by #file1 actions are executed only when AWK is reading the first file. The actions indicated by #file2 actions are executed when processing the second file, if the #file1 condition is met. The next statement at the end of the first action block is used to prevent the condition in #file1 condition from being evaluated and #file2 actions from being executed, while processing first file.

The following example illustrates the usage of this AWK construct. The following example is used to print those lines that are both in file1.txt and file2.txt, as follows:

```
$ awk    'NR == FNR{a[$0];next} $0 in a'    file1.txt    file2.txt

$ vi emp2.dat

Jack     Singh     9857532312    jack@gmail.com       M    hr     2000
Eva      Chabra    8827232115    eva@gmail.com        F    lgs    2100
new line one
Amit     Sharma    9911887766    amit@yahoo.com       M    lgs    2350
Victor   Sharma    8826567898    vics@hotmail.com     M    Ops    2500
new line two
Billy    Chabra    9911664321    bily@yahoo.com       M    lgs    1900
Ginny    Singh     9857123466    ginny@yahoo.com      F    hr     2250
Amy      Sharma    9857536898    amys@hotmail.com     F    Ops    2500

$ awk 'NR == FNR{a[$0];next} $0 in a' emp.dat emp2.dat
```

The output on execution of the previous code, is as follows :

```
Jack      Singh     9857532312   jack@gmail.com        M    hr    2000
Eva       Chabra    8827232115   eva@gmail.com         F    lgs   2100
Amit      Sharma    9911887766   amit@yahoo.com        M    lgs   2350
Victor    Sharma    8826567898   vics@hotmail.com      M    Ops   2500
Billy     Chabra    9911664321   bily@yahoo.com        M    lgs   1900
Ginny     Singh     9857123466   ginny@yahoo.com       F    hr    2250
Amy       Sharma    9857536898   amys@hotmail.com      F    Ops   2500
```

In the previous example, all the lines in the first file `emp.dat` are stored in array `a[]`. When the system starts processing the second file, it checks if the current line being read is stored in array `a` (`$0 in a`). If the condition evaluates to true, the current input line from `emp2.dat` is printed; otherwise, AWK starts processing the second line.

In our next example, we print only those lines which are there in `file2.txt` and not in `file1.txt`:

```
$ awk 'NR == FNR{a[$0];next} ! ( $0 in a )' file1.txt file2.txt
```

Or:

```
$ awk 'NR == FNR{a[$0];next} ! ( $0 in a )' emp.dat emp2.dat
```

To print the lines that are only in `emp.dat` and not in `emp2.dat,` we just have to reverse the order of the arguments.

> All AWK programs that use two input files will work correctly if the first file is not empty. If the first input file is empty, then AWK will execute the statement meant for `file1` on `file2`.

To make it work in that case, we can check that `FILENAME` matches `ARGV[1]` while processing `file1`.

Summary

In this chapter, we learned about the workings and usefulness of AWK in one-liners. We looked at various one-liners from a data scientist and system administrator perspective. Finally, we covered some use case examples of the AWK-like parsing of web server logs, using AWK. This chapter is ready reference of various AWK examples for practical implementation in day-to-day life.

With this, our journey into learning AWK programming comes to an end. I hope you enjoyed reading and working with the examples of AWK programming covered in this book. If you have any questions or comments that would help me make this book better, I'd love to hear from you.

My email address is shiwangkalkhanda@outlook.com

Further reading

In this book, we have covered AWK programming concepts in a user friendly and practical way. Once you have read this book, here are few extra resources where you can find more about AWK and related topics :

- For updated documentation of the GNU implementation of AWK refer to the following URL:
  `https://www.gnu.org/software/gawk/manual/gawk.html`
- For Regular expression reference, you can refer to following URL:
  `https://www.regular-expressions.info/reference.html`
- The AWK programming language, written by its creators Aho, Weinberger and Kernighan is really a must read.

Index

Made in the USA
Middletown, DE
20 July 2019